Reviews

"I came to the end of this interesting and inspiring story wanting more! The Andersons' pioneer work in the Chin Hills may be one of the last stories of what it meant to be part of the "early mission work" in the Seventh-day Adventist denomination. They were truly the "entering wedge" as certainly as J.N. Andrews's mission to Europe, or the Robinsons to Africa, the Westphals to Peru, or Anna Knight to India. This story should certainly be recommended reading for young people interested in their own "pioneering adventure."
The Andersons' adaptability to deprivation, the challenges of "making do" or doing without, and their willingness to engage with a culture so different than their own, in order to share the good news of Jesus, is a story that must be told."

—*Ted Mackett, MK (missionary kid) to India, and David's classmate at Vincent Hill School in Mussoorie, India*

"I was impressed with the positive and loving Anderson family. Each member was happy and excited about being missionaries. Every new experience was a great adventure.
It was amazing to read how people in the remote villages of the Chin Hills learned about the Sabbath from reading the Bible and made the decision to keep the day holy even though they might be the only one doing so. They wanted to know what God said in His Word.
I found inspiring stories of God's leading throughout the book."

—*Virginia Siemens, Donna Faye's roommate in college and student missionary soulmate in Palau, accompanied husband as a missionary to Lebanon, Cyprus, Ethiopia, and Kenya*

"I was amazed at the minute details that were gathered after so many years since the stories happened. Much credit goes to the parents who wrote journals and diaries and verbally kept the experiences alive.
I especially enjoyed the chapters when the family reached the Chin Hills. The Andersons have a tremendous history in the Lord's work."

—*Dan Bentzinger, pastor/evangelist*

"This is a beautiful story of a family who loved Jesus. Gene and Lois were true pioneers to the people of the Chin Hills. Their trust in God is an inspiration to all of us."

—*Barbara Morrison, former missionary to Hong Kong*

"Donna Faye Anderson chronicles the life of her father-in-law, Gene Anderson, and his family with emphasis on both the challenges and the deep satisfaction of establishing a Seventh-day Adventist presence in the Chin Hills, which was known for its many adherents to animism.
After establishing a mission center in the community of Tedim, the Andersons' stay in the Chin Hills was cut short when government officials instituted a policy requiring local leadership for religious institutions. Nonetheless, the Seventh-day Adventist work in the region flourished and continues to this day with many Sabbath-keeping Christians populating the area of the Chin Hills.
The book brings to life with descriptive word pictures of mission experiences, including many stories of answered prayers. Readers discover the means God used to introduce the villagers to the biblical doctrine of the seventh-day Sabbath. It is also fascinating to see how the Lord used Pastor Anderson, who was experienced in pastoral work and teaching, to provide much needed medical attention to the native people.
Donna Faye adds delight to her account of the mission work with many anecdotes of the Anderson family life, including Gene's wife, Lois, and their boys, David, Leslie, and Daniel. While this book focuses on Pastor Anderson's role, it is even more an account of God's marvelous leading and His use of a faithful missionary family to bring the everlasting gospel to the precious people of northern Burma."

—*Paul Hawks, retired pastor of the Ukiah Seventh-day Adventist church*

"The book, *Gene Anderson: Trailblazer to Tedim*, is an inspiration! Following God's leading, Gene Anderson, his wife Lois, and their children exemplified faith and courage as they traveled far from their home to do the Lord's work. What a pleasure to get to know the Andersons and the people they touched for the Lord in the Chin Hills! Readers will find themselves looking forward to witnessing the day when Christ returns to re-unite these long-time friends!

Thank you, Donna Faye, for sharing the family's legacy of devotion and life-long friendships!"

—*Lynal Ingham, Associate Superintendent of Education Northern California Conference*

Gene Anderson
Trailblazer to Tedim

Donna Faye Anderson

World rights reserved. This book or any portion thereof may not be copied or reproduced in any form or manner whatever, except as provided by law, without the written permission of the publisher, except by a reviewer who may quote brief passages in a review.

The author assumes full responsibility for the accuracy of all facts and quotations as cited in this book. The opinions expressed in this book are the author's personal views and interpretations, and do not necessarily reflect those of the publisher.

This book is provided with the understanding that the publisher is not engaged in giving spiritual, legal, medical, or other professional advice. If authoritative advice is needed, the reader should seek the counsel of a competent professional.

Copyright © 2022 Donna Faye Anderson

Copyright © 2022 TEACH Services, Inc.

ISBN-13: 978-1-4796-1421-9 (Paperback)

ISBN-13: 978-1-4796-1422-6 (ePub)

Library of Congress Control Number: 2022906228

All scripture quotations, unless otherwise indicated, are taken from the New King James Version®. Copyright © 1982 by Thomas Nelson. Used by permission. All rights reserved.

Dedication

To my amazing mother-in-law, Lois Anderson, who gladly faced incredible challenges as she stood by her husband's side, and to the dear people of the Chin Hills who want to know the whole story.

Table of Contents

Preface 11

Acknowledgements 13

Chapter 1 : *When God Calls, Answer* 15

Chapter 2 : *When You Make a Commitment, Keep It* 26

Chapter 3 : *When Adversity Comes, God Is Near* 35

Chapter 4 : *When Horizons Expand, The Big Picture Is Seen* 58

Chapter 5 : *When a Task Is at Hand, Do It* 71

Chapter 6 : *When an Answer Is Needed, Pray* 95

Chapter 7 : *When God Intervenes, Divine Appointments Happen* 107

Chapter 8 : *When Challenges Come, God's Grace Is Sufficient* 127

Chapter 9 : *When They Say, "Welcome," Your Heart Is Full* 140

Chapter 10: *When You Walk with God, Blessings Abound* 170

Chapter 11: *When You Trust in the Lord, He Provides* 184

Chapter 12: *When You Have Love, You Have Enough* 197

Epilogue When God Closes One Door, He Opens Another 209

Appendix 1 Gene Anderson's Adventist Ancestry 226

Appendix 2 Related and Supporting Material 234

Bibliography 255

Endnotes 259

About the Author 264

Preface

What an exciting day it was on March 18, 1973, when I sealed my love for David and became a member of the Anderson family. The Andersons had led such inspiring lives. I was awed by the thrilling stories they shared, especially those from the mission field of Burma (Myanmar). The unquestioning trust that Gene and Lois had in God instilled within my heart the knowledge that God delights in using ordinary people to do extraordinary things for Him.

David and I, along with our daughter, Vonni, had the privilege of visiting Burma with Gene and Lois in 2001. I found the people to be gentle, gracious, and generous—and easily understood how the Andersons had loved them.

David and I cared for Gene and Lois the last ten years of their lives, residing in their home with them for the final seven to provide the extra support they needed. The heart-stirring days they spent in Burma were the topic of many conversations. The last book we read aloud as a family was the journal Lois wrote about their life in Burma. We call it "The Burma Diary."

After their deaths—Gene on November 2, 2015, and Lois on December 19, 2016—David and I began sorting the volumes of diaries, journals, letters, and articles that had been stored in boxes. We were amazed at the priceless information they contained. I seriously doubt we have found it all.

Many of the letters were tattered and torn, yellowed and faded with age. Some of the four-year diaries contained minimal space for daily entries, and Lois had used every available corner. She wrote with pencil, ink, and a red pencil, but the words were barely legible due to the space constraint and the years of wear. The diaries began when she entered college. To be sure, she was not thinking then about anyone trying to read them many decades later.

My first thought was that this information needed to be deciphered, typed into a computer, and preserved for future generations. Enthusiastically, I embarked on a journey to preserve Gene and Lois's legacy.

I was immersed in reading, organizing, editing, and typing the rich tapestry of their lives when David and I were invited to attend a Zomi (Chin) Convention in Bowling Green, Kentucky, in June of 2019. A large gathering of immigrants from Myanmar (Burma)—primarily from the Chin Hills—came together from all over the United States. Some even came from Myanmar.

David shared the miraculous ways God had led his family to take the gospel of Jesus' love to the Chin Hills. We learned that many in attendance had never heard how God had guided the establishment of the first Seventh-day Adventist mission there. Their immediate response was, "We would love to have a book about this! Could you write one for us?" I returned home with renewed determination to fulfill this request.

Through character portrayals of each family member, I have sought to show the ties that bound them so closely together and to help the reader understand the deep, enduring desire that burned within their hearts to be led by God to those who were sincerely looking for Him.

If this inspiring story deepens your personal relationship with God, then I will have met my objective.

Acknowledgements

My first expression of gratitude goes to my wonderful husband, David, who has encouraged and cheered me on as I tackled this project. He is the only surviving family member able to verify details and reconstruct stories not documented by his parents. His brother Leslie died May 3, 2002, in a small-airplane crash while serving as a missionary in Papua New Guinea; Daniel was only twenty-two months old when the family left the Chin Hills; and Vernon was not yet born. David has been a tremendous support in the tedious task of editing and selecting the photographs for the manuscript. I will forever cherish his eagerness to pore over each chapter again and again. We have lost track of the number of times we have read through the manuscript.

Another family member who graciously edited each chapter was my sister-in-law, Mary Lane, who married Leslie—the other enthusiastic young missionary in this book. Additionally, she meticulously restored all the photographs. Working with her was a beautiful, bonding experience. Her insights and guidance greatly strengthened the manuscript. I will always treasure the joy she has brought me.

I want to extend a big thank you to Barbara Murrin of Silent Partner (silentpartner.ca) who provided copyediting services. She skillfully brought together the final pieces of the manuscript with such clarity and smoothness, creating a polished document to submit to the publisher. (Barb is Mary Lane's sister.)

I was delighted that my nephew, Sebastian Anderson (Vernon's son), readily agreed to design the cover for this book about his grandfather. Thanks for a great job, Sebastian.

Thank you to the Zomi people who specifically asked for a book about the Andersons and how God led them to the Chin Hills. Their interest in having a record of this for future generations fanned my zeal to accomplish the task.

I wish to acknowledge and thank the team who translated and printed the book for the Zomi people. Mungno Gualnam (Gin Sian Mung) was chosen to translate the book into the Chin language. (Mungno's parents were baptized in the first baptism in the Chin Hills. He sent me background information about his father, Phung Kai, which I have included in chapter 9.) The book will also be translated into Burmese by Thang Lam Mung, who is the nephew of Ngul Khaw Pau (first mentioned in chapter 7).

Thank you, family and friends who have taken a keen interest in this endeavor and prayed for me throughout the course of the project.

Most of all, I wish to praise God for guiding my steps to become part of the Anderson family and for blessing me with the vision and strength to record these stories. May He receive all the honor and glory.

Chapter 1

When God Calls, Answer

"And we know that all things work together for good to those who love God, to those who are the called according to His purpose."
—Romans 8:28

Gene Anderson looked around with delighted eyes at the beautiful campus of Pacific Union College in Angwin, California. On this late September day in 1949, he felt like he was coming home, for it was here in the mid-thirties that he had been blessed by the instruction of compassionate teachers and the fellowship of dear friends. Now, with a heart eager to meet the possibilities before him, he was returning to complete his degree in industrial arts. It was a day filled with promise, intrigue, and a major change in direction.

FIGURE 1.1 *Gene Anderson when he returned to Pacific Union College (PUC), September 1949. Photographer unknown.*

He and his wife, Lois, and their two sons—David, eight, and Leslie, five—found a tiny, green, dilapidated house on Cold Springs Road, a building original to the Angwin Resort. It had been tagged for demolition—but the Andersons managed to snag it for a monthly rent of eleven dollars before that happened. The rocky driveway to the house wound up the hill between boulders and pine trees.

FIGURE 1.2 *Lois Anderson when she returned to PUC with Gene, David, and Leslie, September 1949. Photographer unknown.*

FIGURE 1.3 *David (left) and Leslie (right) with Tippy at PUC. Undated photograph, circa 1949. Photographer Lois Anderson.*

The family soon settled into a pleasant routine. Gene was busy with his classwork, and Lois found employment in the college laundry. After school, David and Leslie waited for her at the laundry until she finished her work. David, fascinated by the big machines, learned how to press handkerchiefs. When they weren't in school, the boys built forts or played on the long rope swing with the neighborhood boys. They made a treehouse with their dad's help, and they sometimes pitched a tent and camped in the woods in their backyard. Near the end of November, Leslie announced, "Tomorrow is my precious day!" He had been anticipating his sixth birthday for weeks, but he refused to open his gifts or have his cake until evening so that he could celebrate by candlelight.

Before Gene had completed his first quarter, he realized his thoughts were in turmoil about his college program. He wanted, more than anything else, to change his degree to theology. This had been a dream of his since boyhood, but somehow, circumstances hadn't come together for him to pursue it. His teachers consistently advised him to stay with the industrial arts program, telling him that this was where he was naturally gifted.

By the end of the quarter, Gene finally decided to follow the yearning of his heart and switch to theology. The decision brought him a sense of peace and happiness. His grades improved, even though he was carrying more than a full load of classes as well as grading student papers for Elder Hartin in the Theology Department. He also drove to Benicia in the San Francisco Bay area once or twice a month, leading a group of his classmates in preparing for a summer evangelistic effort. Lois was happy that Gene would have an opportunity to preach at the meetings, since this had long been his desire.

PUC provided a valuable resource for the Seventh-day Adventist conferences to find theology graduates to fill pastoral positions. Usually, conference representatives visited the campus to get acquainted with the senior theology students. Gene, along with his colleagues, hoped to be offered a church in either the Northern or Central California Conference, but by spring graduation, neither conference had hired anyone from his class.

At camp meeting in Lodi, California, he accepted an invitation to be the principal of the church school in Fortuna, California—with the proviso that, if he was offered a pastoral position, he could be released from the assignment.

The very next day, a letter came from Elder J.I. Robison of the General Conference of Seventh-day Adventists (the world headquarters of the Seventh-day Adventist church) asking Gene if he would consider a call to the Burma Union Training School (also called Myaungmya Training School) as principal. Burma! *Am I reading this correctly, Lord?* wondered Gene. He answered the letter immediately, saying he would gladly accept a call to Burma.

He remembered his early-elementary teacher, Miss Lena Butler, reading mission stories after the noon lunch break. He had especially liked Elder Eric B. Hare's [1] exciting tales of his experiences in Burma. One of the stories that had touched Gene's heart was about Min Din, a young Burmese boy. Gene had wished he had been a part of that story and had set his heart on becoming a missionary—maybe even in Burma! Now, in his hands was a letter—tangible and readable—asking for a commitment to serve in Burma.

> *Burma! Am I reading this correctly, Lord? wondered Gene.*

Unknown to Gene, Dr. Paul Quimby, chairman of the Theology Department, had written to the General Conference recommending Gene and Lois for foreign service. In Gene, Dr. Quimby had recognized the same passion that had taken him to the mission field years before. He thought mission service would be a wonderful opportunity for the young family.

Dr. Quimby received a copy of Elder Robison's letter to Gene. With a big smile, he approached Gene after class. "I wish I were going myself!" he said.

David and Leslie were thrilled. "Daddy, will we get to see tigers and monkeys? What about big snakes, like pythons and cobras? Do we get to be missionaries like you?" The whole family took the mission opportunity seriously and began reading everything they could find about the country of Burma and its people.

Gene planned to graduate in the summer of 1951. To fulfill the requirements for graduation, he needed two years of Greek, but he was already in his senior year and had studied no Greek. He decided to take the first half of Greek I by correspondence during the spring quarter, then complete it during the summer while simultaneously taking Greek II in Dr. Leon Caviness's class. Many people had told him he just couldn't do it. Even Dr. Caviness had said, "You are doing the impossible, Gene, so don't expect a good grade."

About a week before graduation, he received his grade for Greek I; it was a B. Gene immediately shared the good news with his family. So much depended on his passing his two years of Greek; if he failed even one of them, he couldn't graduate. He wrote his final test for Greek II the morning of graduation. Just before it was time for the graduates to line up for the processional, he asked Dr. Caviness, "Did I pass the test this morning?"

Dr. Caviness nodded and said, "Oh, yes!"

Gene marched with his classmates on August 30, 1951, not learning until afterward that he had received a B in Greek II also. He had taken two years of Greek in five months and earned two B's! He was overjoyed, and Lois was extremely proud of him. This experience confirmed for Gene that if he set his heart on something and did his personal best to attain it, by God's grace he could accomplish more than he had ever imagined.

The official call to serve in Burma came just before Gene's graduation. A few days later, paperwork for medical exams for the whole family arrived. They took care of these details as quickly as possible.

The family received a letter from Elder Phillip Parker of the Burma Union of Seventh-day Adventists (the "Burma Union") outlining Gene's duties. He would be serving at Myaungmya Training School, filling the roles of principal, business manager, registrar, public relations director, outreach director, and purchasing agent. It sounded challenging but intriguing.

This experience confirmed for Gene that if he set his heart on something and did his personal best to attain it, by God's grace he could accomplish more than he had ever imagined.

"The school needs building up," Elder Parker wrote. "The enrollment is around 100, but it should be twice that." He concluded his letter by saying that he and his family loved the people and thoroughly enjoyed their work in Burma.

In September, Elder Robert Pierson, president of the Southern Asia Division of Seventh-day Adventists, visited the Andersons in their home. "Burma," he explained, "is an unsettled country. There are different groups who are rebelling against the Burmese government. They are not against foreigners—they are glad to have them—but it may be quite stressful at times. There have been several shootings near the school this year. When the bullets begin to fly, the students and staff get down on the floor—or protect themselves behind a brick wall—and wait until it's over." Despite the report of shooting, Gene and Lois felt it would be a joy to work under this sincere and godly man.

September passed, then October. Each month, the Andersons thought their visas would arrive and they would be sailing to their new home. Leslie began imagining celebrating his November birthday on board the ship. Family members prepared surprises for them to enjoy while celebrating a Christmas at sea. Gene picked up construction jobs, and the boys remained in school while they waited. Both Gene and Lois continued making lists of items to purchase or to get rid of because they wouldn't be needed. Still, the visas did not come.

Finally, a letter arrived from the Burma Union headquarters in Rangoon (Yangon). For the previous two weeks, President Cecil B. Guild had gone from one government office to another, asking about the Andersons' visas. They were finally located, filed away in a drawer. President Guild facilitated getting the process moving again.

In mid-January, the Andersons received a cable saying that their visas had been authorized and asking them to wire back the earliest date they could sail from San Francisco. Their immediate reply was, "Any time after February 1." This date allowed a two-week window for Gene to quit his current construction job and for the family to finalize packing and get ready to go.

The family waited anxiously for word about which boat they would be sailing on, but no word came. After a month, Gene contacted Mr. Raley—who was responsible for making the travel arrangements for the overseas mission workers—and asked, "Have you received any information about our sailing date?"

"Yes. I just received word from the General Conference that the visas sent were for only three months, so they were returned to be authorized for at least a year." The Andersons would need to wait some more.

Saying goodbye to family and friends was the hardest part of preparing for their new adventure. Five years seemed like a very long time to be separated from each other, and the family at home would miss watching the boys grow up. This reality brought with it a deep sense of loss. When the Andersons visited each grandma for the last time, it was difficult to watch their sweet old faces struggle between smiles and tears.

In the middle of March 1952, the family got word that their visas had finally been approved. They spent last moments with special teachers and neighbors at PUC. Gene had previously taken most of their provisions to Mr. Raley in San Francisco; now they scrambled to get the remaining boxes and bags packed. Their car was bulging as they pulled away from their home on the hill for the last time.

It was pouring rain when the Andersons arrived in San Francisco. They watched from inside the car as the wind turned umbrellas wrong side out, whipped overcoats around, and rolled hats down the street.

Their first stop was pier 48A to drop off the luggage they had brought for their ocean trip. The freighter they were expecting to sail on, the SS *Steel Artisan*, was due to arrive later that afternoon. Afterward, they checked into the Manx Hotel.

"Do you think they'll let us on the boat so we can explore it before it's time to sail?" asked Leslie.

"I'm sure they will, son," replied Gene.

Ivan and Gladys Jones, longtime friends of Gene and Lois, drove from their home in Mountain View, California, to spend the afternoon with the Andersons. They brought a box of surprise gifts for the family to enjoy on their long ocean voyage.

The rain had stopped, so the Andersons and Joneses decided to walk down to the pier and put the gift box with the other baggage. Gene and Ivan took it to the shipping office while the others waited outside.

Suddenly Gladys asked, "Is that it?"

Lois followed Gladys's gaze. Just coming into view from behind the next pier was an enormous ship. In a few minutes, they could make out the words "SS *Steel Artisan*" on its prow. The boys ran to call the men, and all four returned in time to see the freighter come into full view.

FIGURE 1.4 *The Anderson family watches the SS Steel Artisan arrive at the San Francisco dock, March 1952. Left to right: Gene, David, Leslie, and Lois. Photographer Ivan Jones.*

It was a glorious sight. The sun came out and lit the bay, the bridge, and the huge white clouds above the ship. The group continued to watch the ship as it slid to a stop, let down its anchor, then slowly swung alongside the pier.

The SS *Steel Artisan* remained at the pier for nearly a week, unloading and reloading, giving the Andersons time to explore the zoo and other interesting places in the city. It also provided the opportunity for family and friends to come and spend time with them.

Ivan and Gladys returned to the dock, along with Gene and Lois's mothers and several other family members. The group was granted permission to board the ship so they could see how the family would be traveling on the open seas.

First mate Ray graciously guided them on a grand tour. Everyone was impressed with the spaciousness and cleanliness of the freighter. The cabins were roomy, and the promenade deck had a strong railing to keep the boys safe.

FIGURE 1.5 The Andersons on board the SS Steel Artisan, March 1952. Front row: Leslie and David. Back row: Lois and Gene. Photographer Ivan Jones.

Friday, March 21, 1952, the Andersons moved from the Manx Hotel to their quarters on board the ship, where they began to unpack and settle in. Lois had just kicked off her shoes and was sitting on her bunk when the steward stopped by. "Could you please come see where your table is in the dining room?"

"You'll have to wait till I get my shoes on," she said.

The steward laughed. "That sounds just like my wife. She's always kicking her shoes off and running around barefoot."

The supper bell rang, and the family went down to their first delicious meal on board. Gene had previously spoken to the steward, explaining that they were vegetarians.

"You are missionaries. Seventh-day Adventists, right?" the steward asked.

"Yes," Gene replied.

"I have had many of your people on board during the last thirty years. Don't worry; we have lots of vegetables and plenty of other food. If there is anything that you would like that we haven't prepared, just let us know." The steward, like the rest of the crew, was pleasant and accommodating.

The captain was a character: short, stout, and often intoxicated. The crew thought him capable, despite his drinking problem. He was a good boss and knew the sea well. He was interested in his new passengers and wanted to talk with them about where they were going and why. He confessed a belief in God but didn't think biblical truth applied to him personally.

After supper, the family heard the tug, *Sea King*, chugging alongside their ship. They watched as the docking ropes were loosened and rolled up, and the tug began gently pushing first one side of the ship and then the other, slowly moving the SS *Steel Artisan* out into the bay. The captain directed the whole process from the bridge. When he made a sound like a policeman's whistle, the tug replied with one big *toot*. When the captain blew two *tweet-tweets*, the tug replied with two big *toot-toots*.

It was a lovely time of day to sail over to Oakland. The sun slowly sank behind the bridges, and San Francisco was clear and still. Lights twinkled all around the bay, making it a magical, enchanted evening.

At the navy base in Oakland, the tug eased the freighter up to the dock until it gently touched. Deckhands jumped onto the pier, caught the ropes thrown to them, then pulled the ropes taut until the huge boat fit snugly against the dock. Loading of the freighter kicked into high gear. Big cranes lifted boxes and crates and swung them down into the holds, loading four or five holds at a time. Though fascinated by the activity, the Andersons retired to their warm bunks when it got too cold to watch from the deck any longer. The hum of engines ran throughout the night.

At six the next morning, bells and whistles woke the passengers. Before the boys were dressed, the tug was busy again, moving the freighter away from the dock and over to the army base to load more cargo. This time, the captain didn't blow his little *tweet-tweets*. When he wanted to say something, he blew the ship's whistle with a *toot-toot* loud enough to rupture eardrums. The tug answered with a little *toot-toot*. It was entertaining to listen to their communications.

Outside, everything was clear and sharp, without a hint of fog. The horizon stretched all the way to snow-covered Mount Saint Helena. As the sun rose, San Francisco turned a rosy pink above the beautiful, shimmering blue and green of the water.

The Andersons made the acquaintance of the two single women who completed the six-person passenger roster. The ladies, headed for Bangkok, Thailand, were very pleasant to talk with. The older woman, they learned, was a teacher who had already spent thirty years in Thailand. The young woman was a nurse going to help start a leper colony in the interior. She was enthusiastic about her new adventure.

By mid-afternoon, a tug began to pull and push the freighter away from the dock until it was pointed in the right direction. The SS *Steel Artisan* was finally on its way. "I wonder if our family will be waiting for us on the bridge," Lois said.

Despite the cold wind, the Andersons stood watching from the deck. As the ship neared the Golden Gate Bridge, David exclaimed, "I see people standing on the bridge! They look like little black specks, but they are all waving."

"I think I see Nana," Leslie shouted, "and that's got to be Aunt Teddy beside her. It looks like they're waving bed sheets!"

Too soon, the huge ship passed under the bridge, and their loved ones could no longer be seen.

FIGURE 1.6 *The Andersons get one last glimpse of the Golden Gate Bridge as the shores of California recede into the distance, March 22, 1952. Left to right: Gene, Leslie, David, and Lois. Photographer unknown.*

There were no more tears; there were too many exciting things to experience. The sky flushed pink, and the wind sent veils of froth flying from breaking turquoise waves. They watched from the stern as hundreds of seagulls soared gracefully directly over the ship. Lois said, "They make me think of a cloud of angels hovering over us as we travel on our way."

At dusk, they passed the Farallon Islands with their jagged sea stacks.[2] The four Andersons, along with the young nurse, made their way to the prow to watch and feel the ship's rise and fall in the swell. Soon they began to sing hymns and choruses about the ocean: "Throw Out the Lifeline," "Will Your Anchor Hold?" and "Over the Sea, Over the Sea." They enjoyed a special time together on this, their first evening at sea.

Lois and David slept in the aft cabin, and Gene and Leslie in the fore cabin. The family felt more comfortable with this arrangement than with having the boys share a cabin by themselves.

The rocking movement of the ship seemed more noticeable inside, but once everyone was cozy in their bunks, the motion soon lulled them to sleep.

Gene and Lois were on their way to a foreign land—with no mission experience and two young boys. Gene was 34 years old; Lois, 33.

CHAPTER 2

When You Make a Commitment, Keep It

"Commit your way to the LORD, trust also in Him, and He shall bring it to pass."

—*Psalm 37:5*

Gene was born Arthur Eugene Anderson on February 14, 1918, at St. Helena Hospital, a health institution operated by the Seventh-day Adventist church. His mother was Helen Edith Anderson, *née* Chapman. His father, Arthur Eugene Anderson, was employed by the hospital as a painter.

FIGURE 2.1 Arthur and Helen Anderson (Gene Anderson's father and mother). Undated photograph, circa 1916. Photographer unknown.

Gene's grandfather, Alfred Anderson, and his wife immigrated from Sweden and settled in San Francisco, California, where Gene's father was born. Gene's first memory of his grandparents was visiting them in the house they had built in Napa. Grandfather Alfred had outlived five wives when he died at the age of ninety-nine, long enough for his great-grandsons to know and love him. (Alfred Anderson was a charter member of the Ukiah Seventh-day Adventist Church in California and no doubt helped build their first church on the corner of Bush and Henry Street.)

FIGURE 2.2 *Alfred Anderson (Gene's grandfather), with baby David in Ukiah, California. Undated photograph, circa 1942. Photographer unknown.*

When Gene was only sixteen months old, his father died from a ruptured appendix. This resulted in hardship for both Gene and his mother: he was without a father, and she had no marketable skills.

When Helen decided to take the nurse's course, she learned that she would be required to become a dormitory student at the nearby Seventh-day Adventist hospital and nursing school. She arranged for a sweet lady—known to all the neighborhood children as Grandma Rose—to care for baby Gene. Grandma Rose gladly did this until Helen finished her training.

FIGURE 2.3 Gene Anderson. Undated photograph, circa 1923. Photographer unknown.

Gene was five years old when his mother married Albert Lynn Roberts, who was known as Jack. Helen and Jack had two children: Edythe, affectionately called Teddy, and Calvin, who was a year younger. Gene's mother was heartbroken when she realized that her husband was not bonding with Gene, but she was unable to change those dynamics. Fortunately, Helen's father, Harry Chapman—who lived below the St. Helena Hospital in a community now known as Deer Park—welcomed Gene into his home.

FIGURE 2.4 Harry Chapman (Gene's grandfather, with whom Gene lived circa 1922–1929). Photographer unknown.

Many beautiful flowers grew around the house: roses climbing over and around the front door, violets, and lilacs. Their perfume hung heavy in the air. The apple, peach, pear, and cherry trees produced delicious fruit. There were also firs, an umbrella tree, a cork oak, and, of course, walnuts. It was a delightful, carefree place for Gene to live and grow.

Grandpa Chapman provided a strong Seventh-day Adventist environment for his young grandson. The two became very close and enjoyed each other's companionship. Helen did not sever her relationship with Gene—nor did she ever stop loving him—but he was unable to grow up with his siblings.

FIGURE 2.5 Gene and his mother, Helen, who lived with Gene and Lois during her last years. Undated photograph, Petaluma, California, circa 1974. Photographer Mary Lane Anderson.

Grandpa Chapman had a dozen milk cows and delivered bottled milk to community homes. He was out before daylight every morning, milking the cows. When Gene awakened, he would always find breakfast cereal staying warm for him in a double boiler on the stove.

When Grandpa Chapman came in with the milk, he would run it through the strainer and cooler, then bottle and store it in the basement. Every evening after milking was finished, he harnessed his horse, Dot, to the wagon and went on his milk route. Gene hopped off at each home to deliver the full bottles of fresh milk and pick up the empty ones. The empty bottles were washed and sterilized in readiness for filling the next day.

One time, Grandpa took a couple of carrying cases of milk to deliver on foot. He asked Gene to drive Dot and the wagon with the rest of the milk to the top of the hill and said he would meet them there. Having done this many times before, Gene went on his way, confidently trusting the gentle horse.

Suddenly, two older boys climbed up on the wagon beside him. They snatched the reins out of Gene's hands and, over his strenuous objections, urged Dot into a run. "Stop! stop!" Gene cried. "Don't make Dot run with the wagon! Grandpa said it could break the milk bottles or wreck the wagon!"

Soon the reins were tangled, and Dot was galloping up the road. The boys got scared and jammed the reins back into Gene's hands. Before he could get the reins straightened out and slow Dot down, the wagon crashed into a tree.

The troublemakers dashed away, leaving Gene to face Grandpa alone with a broken wagon and milk running everywhere. Gene felt terrible and so did Grandpa. It was not easy for Grandpa to get another wagon ready for the next day's deliveries, but somehow, he did.

Besides helping with the milk delivery, Gene gathered eggs from the nests the hens made in the hay barn. Grandpa also taught him how to plant and harvest corn. For the rest of Gene's life, the smell of young corn stalks took him back to the happy days of living with Grandpa.

It brought much joy to Gene's heart whenever he could do an anonymous act of kindness for someone. The Bray family were blessed by such an act. A big load of fire wood had been delivered to their front yard. Gene and one of his good friends moved the load of wood and stacked it neatly behind the house when the Brays were not at home. As far as Gene knew, the Brays never learned who did this labor of love.

The close neighborhood was part of his life. Across the street were the Websters; up the path were the homes of Willy White (Ellen White's son) and the Roses (where Grandma Rose had cared for Gene when he was a baby). Across the creek lived the Mathes, and over the bridge stood Mrs. Ellen White's barn and the James' family home. Mr. James was the manager of the White's farm. On a little hill stood Elmshaven, Mrs. Ellen White's home. (Ellen G. White was a co-founder of the Seventh-day Adventist church and had shared the biblical gift of prophecy during more than seventy years of public ministry.)

Gene often heard Willy White whistling as he walked past Grandpa Chapman's place on his way to his office behind Elmshaven. This habit earned him the nickname "Whistling Willy." Gene and his grandpa were frequently invited to have dinner at the Willy White home and to stay for evening worship. Gene never had the privilege of personally knowing Ellen

White because she had died three years before he was born. However, his mother, grandparents, and great-grandparents had known her well. In fact, his great-grandmother, Mary, had received a handwritten letter of sympathy from Mrs. White following the death of Mary's husband on February 20, 1882—just ten days after his fifty-fourth birthday (*see Appendix 2*). Mary's mother, Anna Colby, had died the day after her son-in-law, also of pneumonia.[3]

Gene's first paying job was picking prunes for five cents a lug.[4] These sturdy, high-sided wooden boxes were stacked after being filled with fruit. He also picked strawberries, raspberries, and grapes. He learned to swim in the old swimming hole in the Napa River—but even before he could paddle, he would dive in from the high bank and drift with the current to the shallow side.

On Sabbaths, Gene and Grandpa hitched Dot to the wagon and rode to the little church in St. Helena at the corner of Madrona and Oak Street for Sabbath school and church.

It was Grandpa Chapman who helped Gene develop a solid, personal relationship with Jesus. The desire to be led by his Lord shone from the young boy's heart. Grandpa Chapman arranged for Gene to attend Foothills Adventist Elementary School. Miss Lena Butler taught his first three grades and was an inspiration to him. It was while in her classroom that he decided to be a worker for God.

Gene lived with his adored grandpa until Harry's death in 1929. Gene was then eleven years old. After that, he went to live with Claude and Daisy Glassford on their ranch in Madera, California. The Glassfords did not have any children of their own yet, so they were delighted to share their love with young Gene.

He picked cotton and Thompson seedless grapes, laying them out on paper trays to dry into raisins. He irrigated the alfalfa fields and helped pitch and haul hay with a team and wagon, taking it to the barn where it was stacked. He and the Glassfords went to church and midweek prayer meetings faithfully. Occasionally, Gene was invited to take part in the prayer meeting. (Many years later, it was Gene and Lois's privilege to care for Claude in their home during the last years of his life.)

> *It was Grandpa Chapman who helped Gene develop a solid, personal relationship with Jesus. The desire to be led by his Lord shone from the young boy's heart.*

FIGURE 2.6 Gene with his classmates and teacher at Foothills Seventh-day Adventist Elementary School in St. Helena, California. Undated photograph, circa 1927. Back row, fifth from left: Miss Lena Butler. Back row, fourth from right: Gene Anderson. Photographer unknown.

During the summer of 1933, Gene heard positive reports about Laurelwood Academy, a boarding school in northern Oregon. This created a burning desire in him to continue his education at one of the Seventh-day Adventist academies where he could prepare himself for God's work. He wrote to the academy, letting them know he had no money but was willing to work to pay his school expenses if they would let him come. He told them about his experience with farm work. It was a happy day when he received their answer: he had been accepted as a student.

On his way to Laurelwood, Gene stopped at PUC to see a friend who was a staff member there. His friend persuaded Gene to stay at PUC for his schooling instead of going to Laurelwood. Gene received a warm welcome and lived in Grainger Hall, the college men's dormitory, while attending the PUC preparatory school.

He was able to pay his school expenses by working. Most young people develop work and study habits in a home setting with the encouragement of parents. At the tender age of fifteen, Gene was on his own—with no parental coaching or financial assistance. Because he had developed a daily relationship with Jesus early in life, he was now able to put his future confidently in God's hands.

Gene was assigned maintenance of the campus grounds, under the direction of Professor Noah Paulin. The grounds were a good place to work, but his employment there did not provide enough hours to pay for his schooling. With his experience on the Glassfords' farm to recommend him, he went to the college farm manager, Orville Baldwin, and asked if he could be transferred there. Mr. Baldwin told Gene he already had more fellows than he could use. Undaunted, Gene returned every few days to check again.

Many of the regular farm workers went home for Christmas. Since PUC was Gene's home, he stayed on campus during vacations, including Christmas and summer breaks. It was raining when Gene walked into the farm shed at the beginning of Christmas vacation. Mr. Baldwin was telling the fellows what to do when Gene joined the group with his winsome smile. Of course, Mr. Baldwin knew at once why Gene was there, and this time he handed Gene a shovel and said, "Go down and open the drain ditch by the septic tank." Gene grabbed the shovel and headed down the road to the septic tank, found the ditch, and cleaned it. And, just like that, he was on the farm crew!

He gained five years of valuable work experience, averaging sixty-two hours a week, in addition to attending classes and studying. He cared for the calves, chickens, and horses; planted corn and cut it for silage; planted, cut, and hauled hay; and pulled the binder with the D2 Caterpillar ("Cat") he had learned to operate. Often Gene would grab an ear of corn and place it, still in its husk, on the Cat's exhaust manifold. It was a perfect way to roast corn.

Gene made roads; plowed and cultivated the farmlands and orchards; helped to dig the hole for the campus swimming pool and a foundation for a new building; fixed fences; and herded and sheared the sheep and angora goats. He brought a trailer of wild horses from a range in Oregon and helped break them.[5] He was the lab assistant for the horsemanship class Mr. Baldwin taught. During these years at PUC, Mr. Baldwin became a treasured mentor and friend to Gene.

During the week, Gene rose at 4 a.m. to feed and harness the horses and get them ready for their work. Then he returned to the dorm, showered, ate breakfast, and went to his 7:30 class.

One day, Mr. Baldwin asked Gene to check on the hay in a certain field to see if it was ready to rake. Gene got on one of the horses, not bothering to take the time to put a saddle on her. One of the other workers jumped onto an old white horse, and they rode out together. Gene was ahead, when, suddenly, his friend took the lead at a full gallop. Gene's horse—high strung and not wanting any other horse to pass her—also broke into a gallop. The ground approaching the hay field sloped downhill, so Gene held his horse back, thinking it unwise to gallop bareback down the hill.

His mount responded by going stiff legged, pitching Gene off over her head. As he landed on his shoulders, he felt something snap in his back. Horrified, he saw the horse's front hooves right above his chest, but instead of crushing him, her knees buckled, and she rolled in a full somersault on the other side of him.

He wiggled his hands and arms, then his feet and legs, greatly relieved when they responded. After a few painful minutes, he slowly stood, got back on the horse, checked on the hay, and rode back to the barn. No one witnessed the accident; apparently Gene's friend had become completely enthralled with his galloping ride.

The horse was not injured, so Gene never told anyone about the accident. His back was sore for several weeks, but it eventually quit hurting. Although he had occasional pain in his back throughout his life, it never slowed him down and he never received any medical attention for it. Many years later, an MRI revealed that his fall had broken his back.

Chapter 3

When Adversity Comes, God Is Near

"But I will sing of Your power; yes, I will sing aloud of Your mercy in the morning; for You have been my defense and refuge in the day of my trouble. To You, O my Strength, I will sing praises; for God is my defense, my God of mercy."

—Psalm 59:16–17

Lois Lenora Dillon was born on January 4, 1919, in Visalia, California. Her parents, Lawrence Blodgett Dillon and Gladys Marguerite Dillon, *née* Roach, were dairy farmers. Lois enjoyed a carefree childhood, completing her elementary grades at the Venice Hill School, a Victorian-style, two-story building with a belfry.

FIGURE 3.1 *The Dillon family. Front row: Lois, Dorothy, and Joyce. Back row: Lawrence and Gladys Dillon. Undated photograph, circa 1927. Photographer unknown.*

Her first four grades were taught by Miss Lowery and her last four by Miss Parrigein. It was from the latter that Lois learned to figure out tunes using the "do-re-mi" (sol-fa) method, which she applied many times in future years. In Lois's autograph book, Miss Parrigein wrote, "To one of the sweetest girls I have ever known."

FIGURE 3.2 Lois (back row, fourth from left, in polka dot dress) with her schoolmates at Venice Hill School, Visalia, California. Undated photograph, circa 1932. Photographer unknown.

Lois's family lived within easy walking distance of the school, and her childhood was filled with the simple joys of playing with her two sisters—Joyce, who was two years older; Dorothy, who was two years younger—and baby Larry, who was ten years younger, along with dozens of neighborhood kids who were like one big happy family.

One day, Jack and Lily Sanders and their three girls—Helen, Arlie, and Ruth—moved in across the street from the Dillons. They were a Seventh-day Adventist family and invited the Dillon girls to join them for worship each day. Before long, the three Dillon sisters were going to Sabbath school and church with the Sanders, riding in the back of the Sanders's pickup truck.

"Since Joyce and I were the oldest of the girls," Lois remembered, "we always got to sit on the tailgate and hang our legs over the edge. Every week, Jack Sanders gave each of us a fifty-cent piece to put in the offering plate. That was a lot of money in those days."

A love for the Seventh-day Adventist message began to grow in the hearts of the three Dillon girls, along with a yearning to know God and His plan for their lives. Then Mother Dillon joined the group each Sabbath, also embracing the love of God's Word. Dad Dillon seemed uninterested and too busy with his farm chores to join them. Unknown to the family, however, he listened to many of their conversations about their newfound faith. The pastor made several visits to the Dillon family. He always sought out Dad Dillon, whether in the barn or in the field.

In December of 1931, evangelist Elder Boothby came to the church and conducted a series of meetings. Mother Dillon and her girls didn't miss one. One Sabbath morning, after the meetings had concluded, they went to church to be baptized. When Dad Dillon learned of their plan, he announced he was going with them. At the edge of the church yard, he gave his pipe a toss into a bush and went inside to tell the pastor he wanted to be baptized with his family. And he was. From that time on, Dad Dillon, who habitually sang as he went about his work, changed his choice of songs from popular tunes to hymns.

The Great Depression was in full swing. The bottom had fallen out of the economy, and many people were losing their homes and businesses. The Dillons had thirty dairy cows and sold the milk and cream every day. The prune orchard provided another source of income, but prices kept dropping until income from the dairy and the fruit crop no longer covered their mortgage payments. The bank was forced to foreclose on the Dillon farm, and the family had to move from what had been such a happy home into a tent on a vacant lot across the road. They stored their furniture in an empty building on the same lot. A few months later, the shed burned to the ground, destroying the remainder of their possessions. It was a terribly bitter experience for Dad and Mom Dillon, but somehow, they shielded their children from their distress.

The Dillons then left this area and joined the Sanders, who had already moved to "the island" in Central California. (The Kings River splits and encircles a large area of farmland before coming together again; hence, residents referred to this land as the island.) The Dillon girls attended the Seventh-day Adventist church school at Armona and soon made new friends.

> *A love for the Seventh-day Adventist message began to grow in the hearts of the three Dillon girls, along with a yearning to know God and His plan for their lives.*

The next few years were difficult and trying for Dad and Mom Dillon. Paying work was scarce, and the crop of gyp corn (sorghum) used for livestock feed that Dad Dillon had planted was a complete failure. Because he wouldn't work on the Sabbath, he often lost the small jobs he found. When that happened, he would begin looking for another job. He always found one, though the periods of unemployment were sometimes long and arduous. The family wore used clothing that had been passed along to them from friends and were thankful for even simple food. Yet, throughout these several years of struggling to survive, Lois never heard her parents express a discouraging word.

After two years on the island, the Dillon family moved to the Fresno area. By the grace of God, the three Dillon sisters were able to attend Fresno Adventist Academy, working at various jobs to pay their tuition. Lois drove them to school in their old family car, which often had to be cranked to get started.

FIGURE 3.3 *The three Dillon sisters during Lois and Joyce's senior year at Fresno Adventist Academy in Fresno, California. Left to right: Dorothy, Lois, and Joyce. Undated photograph, circa 1936. Photographer unknown.*

Since Joyce had contracted rheumatic fever during elementary school and had missed an entire year of school because of her illness, she and Lois were in the same grade. During their senior year, an academy faculty member encouraged Lois and Joyce to consider attending PUC for college. Even though the sisters both knew they wanted to be nurses when they finished their education, a thought of this magnitude had never entered their heads. They had also never been that far away from home.

Because the man was so encouraging, the girls felt it prudent to at least apply. Upon returning home from church one Sabbath, they found a long white envelope in the mail from PUC. Inside was an acceptance letter for both girls to begin school there in September. Lois was horrified. This meant she would have to leave her home and all her friends and familiar places! She had a good cry, but in her heart, she knew this was what she should do.

After Lois and Joyce's graduation from Fresno Academy, the Dillons moved back to the island, where they bought property suitable for farming cotton and alfalfa along the bank of the Kings River. Dad Dillon built a small two-bedroom adobe house from bricks he made himself. He never finished the plastering inside; nevertheless, the house was warm and comfortable. The family was content living there.

The girls found work during the summer: cutting apricots (to get them ready for drying), irrigating alfalfa, pitching hay, and doing other odd jobs on farms in the area. Life for the Dillons was gradually feeling more settled, and the family continued to enjoy happy times together.

Shortly before it was time for the girls to leave for college, the church people had a surprise shower for the girls that provided all the things they needed to furnish their room at school. They were bewildered as they stood in the center of the room—opening all the lovely gifts, hardly able to grasp that everything was for them.

On a bright, sunny morning, Jack Sanders drove the girls to PUC so they would have the month of August to work before school started. He stopped the truck at the front door of the girls' dorm, Graff Hall, where evening worship was in progress in the main parlor. Many eyes peeked out the windows to see who was arriving. Jack unloaded their few belongings and shook Lois's hand. He looked into her tear-filled eyes and said, "We are counting on you, Lois!" She determined, at that moment, that she would not disappoint him.

That same summer of 1936, Gene was talking with Bert Stickle—who worked in the registrar's office—when Bert mentioned he had seen applications from two girls who had very little money. The Dillon sisters, Lois and Joyce, planned to work for their school fees and would be arriving soon from Visalia, California. For some reason, Gene had a curious interest in who they were.

The sisters were warmly welcomed by a group of girls who were also working to help pay for their school expenses. It was not long before Lois and Joyce discovered a friend from academy days, Janet McClenaghan, whose bubbly personality cheered them on difficult days.

Lois and Joyce were assigned to work in the kitchen, preparing the vegetables, canning fruit from the school orchards, and doing other chores. Several boys were also working during the summer. Every day a group of them would come to eat at the table behind the kitchen, so they wouldn't have to change their clothes to eat in the dining room. There was always a great deal of happy chatter at their table.

Gene, who was one of those boys, was immediately attracted to Lois's sweet, friendly personality and her tall, slender build. He discreetly watched her whenever he went to the kitchen for meals.

FIGURE 3.4 Gene Anderson takes a break while working on the farm at PUC, summer of 1936. Photographer unknown.

As for Lois, her attention was soon captured by the handsome young man who would come striding into the cafeteria, his cap under his arm and a big smile on his face as he greeted friends on his way to the food counter. With his laden tray, he would join the others at the back table. Since Janet seemed to know everyone, Lois asked her what his name was. She thought

Janet said, "Arthur Temple," but she had already met so many people, it was difficult to keep all their names straight.

The first week passed, and Janet told Lois there was going to be a march at the gym Saturday night.

"A what?" asked Lois.

"A march," repeated Janet. "Let's plan to go!"

"What is a march?" asked Lois.

"Let's just go. You'll find out," Janet replied.

Saturday night, Lois and Joyce walked hesitantly to the gym where they found dozens of young people lined up along the walls. The two girls found an empty spot and tried to mimic the stance of the others.

Soon, march music poured from the loudspeaker, and the young people began to form a long line down the center of the gym. Evidently, they were going to march to the music. *Well, that might be fun if you had a friend to march with*, thought Lois.

Suddenly, standing in front of her was the young man she believed to be Arthur Temple. To her surprise, he introduced himself in a deep, rumbly voice as Gene Anderson, and then he asked Lois if she would be his partner. She said, "Yes!" What a smile he had, and what blue eyes! She had never dreamed marching could be so much fun.

Early the next week, Janet began planning for the next Saturday night. She, along with Gene Anderson and some of her other friends, arranged for the farm truck to take them on a hayride over the country roads, with a watermelon feed along the way.

Once again, Gene, his cap perched jauntily on one side of his head and a smile on his face, asked Lois to be his companion. It was a perfect evening. The air was balmy, the moon full, and the delightful ride wound along country roads through Pope Valley and back around by Conn Dam. The group sang, "Our college on the mountain, among thy fir clad hills …. P.U.C. is our school you know; we're P.U.C.-ites where'er we go."[6] They all sang like they loved the place. Despite her misgivings about coming to college, Lois decided she loved it too.

Five weeks of pre-school work flew by, and soon it was time to register for fall classes. Lois began to hear about a "handshake." What was that? Gene was busy signing up for his classes but asked Lois to be his date for the occasion. Wow! Three dates before school had even begun! She dressed up in a beautiful silk dress Mom Dillon had made for her after Lois left for PUC. *How did Mother know I would like a new dress for the handshake?* wondered Lois—but there it was in the mail, just in time.

The handshake turned out to be a get-acquainted activity for all the new students. After they shook an endless line of hands, Gene and Lois sat together to enjoy the program that followed.

School began with a full schedule of work and study. Lois learned that Gene had been employed at the school for several years already. He operated a small Caterpillar most of the summer. Whenever she heard the steady throb of the Cat engine, a picture of the young man driving it came to her mind.

FIGURE 3.5 *Gene and Lois getting better acquainted. Undated photograph, circa 1936. Photographer unknown.*

That first winter, it turned very cold with a pearly, gray cloud cover for several days. Professor Newton, the astronomy teacher and one of the pioneers of the school, went about sniffing the frosty air and prophesying, "It is going to snow. This is snow weather." It did start to snow—just a few flakes at first, then more and more great, soft snowflakes drifted silently down until nearly three feet of snow covered the ground. The college campus was transformed into a winter wonderland.

The snow shut down classes for several days. There was no electricity, but the steam heat still worked, so the buildings were warm. Roads were blocked and power lines were down. Mail made it as far as the college, but there was no way to get it through to nearby Pope Valley. Gene was asked to take a team of horses with a sled to deliver the mail and groceries to the stranded community. The road was a tangle of trees and limbs, but he got the mail and groceries through.

Snowball fights erupted all over campus, especially in front of the girls' dorm. Students poured outside to tumble, slide, or roll down the hillsides. When Gene returned from Pope Valley, he and Lois skipped the activity on campus, choosing to tramp through the storybook woods and nearby fields instead. It was a day they never forgot.

The spring term ended, another summer's work in the kitchen was finished, and it was time for a second school year. Lois had planned to enter nursing school at the St. Helena Sanitarium, but something else had become more important in her thoughts and heart: she and Gene had fallen deeply in love.

FIGURE 3.6 *An enjoyable day in the courtship of Gene and Lois. Undated photograph, circa 1937. Photographer unknown.*

Gene spent the 1937 Christmas vacation at Lois's home. In her diary, she jotted the following note for January 1, 1938: "Gene walked home with Daddy and talked to him about us getting married. Daddy said he saw no reason why we shouldn't. He'd like to see us go on with our schoolwork, but even that shouldn't stop one from having happiness."

On their way back to college, Gene and Lois rode in a rumble seat. "It got so cold, we covered ourselves with blankets, even our heads," she recorded. "We rode clear up to the girls' dorm that way. Gene kissed me, I don't know how many times."

Gene and Lois were engaged in the spring and planned their wedding for September 11, 1938. They finished the school term, but Lois let her teachers know she would not be back to begin the nurse's course the following year. She knew that the nursing program denied acceptance to married students.

Lois weeded a neighbor's onion field to earn the money for the fabric for her wedding dress and her sisters' bridesmaid dresses. Her mother sewed Lois's gown of white lace over satin, as well as Joyce's blue and Dorothy's pink taffeta dresses. In total, the three dresses cost less than twenty dollars.

The young couple had a simple country wedding at the island church. Elder Luther Hutchison conducted the service as Gene and Lois committed their hearts to each other and to the Lord. Unfortunately, by some strange happenstance, none of the wedding photos included the groom, which was a real disappointment to the young couple.

FIGURE 3.7 Gene and Lois's wedding day, September 11, 1938. Front: Doris Dunken, flower girl. Back row: Joyce, Lois, and Dorothy. Photographer unknown.

They had managed to save enough to buy a Model A roadster with a rumble seat into which they packed their few possessions. At nearly twenty-one years of age, they were independent and married.

Their first home was a camp in the woods in Whitmore, California, where Gene worked in the timber-falling business with Claude Glassford. To be close to Gene's work, the young couple moved into a tent on a deserted farm which had only a small cabin still standing. They were able to make the cabin usable, enlarging their living space.

As the third Whitmore year began, Lois occupied her spare moments making baby clothes and collecting all sorts of essential things—like a basket, diapers, blankets, and towels—in preparation for the arrival of their first baby. She and Gene enjoyed the long days of summer and ate from a garden that produced a wonderful abundance of food.

Gene's mother, Helen—with whom he had stayed connected over the years—came to help Lois in the camp before David's birth. On September 2, 1941, David Eugene was born at the Redding Maternity Hospital, which was about a forty-five-minute drive down to the valley. Since Helen was a nurse, she was able to assist with David's birth, but obligations at home prevented her from staying longer. Gene returned to his work, and Lois's mother, Gladys, helped after the birth. Mom Dillon stayed with Lois and baby David at the hospital in Redding for ten days before Lois and David rejoined Gene in camp. (In those days, no mother could return home for at least a week after giving birth. It was common for mothers to remain at the hospital even longer—especially if home conditions were compromised for a newborn.)

FIGURE 3.8 Lois and baby David at Whitmore, California, September 1941. Photographer unknown.

On December 7, 1941, Japan struck Pearl Harbor in Honolulu, Hawaii, and the United States became embroiled in World War II. The ugliness of the war made the future uncertain. Many men were being drafted. Gene did not want to leave his family to go off to war and struggled to find a way to contribute to the war effort without leaving home. He learned he could avert enlistment by working at Mare Island, a naval shipyard on a peninsula that jutted into the bay twenty miles north of San Francisco. So, the young family moved into a house that Gene's mother and her husband, Jack, had built on the corner of Grandpa Chapman's home place near Elmshaven. Gene commuted from there to Mare Island, where he made welding repairs on the war ships. However, the language of the other workers was so foul he didn't stay with this job very long.

Another way Gene learned he could avoid military enlistment was to farm, so the couple's eyes turned to Central California. He obtained a farm loan to purchase a herd of cattle, and he and Lois began a dairy business on the island. They rented a small cabin, dairy barn, and pasture from the Rosenfeldts, who lived in a house on the same site, and the property backed that of the Dillons. It was a blessing to be living near Lois's parents. Mom Dillon's consistently cheerful disposition made everyone happy to be around her.

FIGURE 3.9 Gene, Lois, and David with their car on the island after World War II started. Undated photograph, circa 1942. Photographer unknown.

On November 27, 1943, a second son was born to Lois and Gene in Dinuba, California. Lois remained in the hospital for three days. When Gene came to visit on the second morning, he announced, "I have thought of a name for our son. How do you like 'Leslie Earl'?" Lois loved it, so the name became official. Nana, as Gene's mother was known to David, helped care for the family for the first couple of weeks after Leslie's birth.

FIGURE 3.10 *David and Leslie on the Anderson's island dairy farm. Undated photograph, circa 1944. Photographer Lois Anderson.*

One day, after David had celebrated his third birthday, he decided to go see Grandma and Grandpa Dillon. He knew the way, so he went without letting his mother know. When he was missed a little while later, Lois began searching the barn, the fields, and everywhere else she could think of. The thought of him falling into the swift current of the river terrified her. She alerted Gene, who joined her search.

FIGURE 3.11 *David walks between rows of cotton on Grandpa and Grandma Dillon's island farm. Undated photograph, circa 1944. Photographer Lois Anderson.*

"Do you think he might have tried to go over to Grandpa's place?" Gene asked.

"He has never gone alone, but he goes with us all the time," Lois answered, tears in her voice.

They hurried down to the riverbank and ran along it toward her parent's place. About halfway there, they saw Dad Dillon walking toward them, holding David's hand.

Later, Lois wrote this poem about the event:

Two Little Boys

Now David and Leslie were two little boys.
They had lots of playthings, just tangles of toys.
They each had their freckles and stacks of blond hair,
Eyes that could sparkle and teeth that weren't there.

Their mother would give them a job just their size,
And if done correctly, they might get a prize.
But when they deserted and left it undone,
They found, to their sorrow, it was only begun.

But they were industrious (or usually so):
While one did the dishes, the other would hoe.
When David was little, he often would stray.
"I'll go see my grandpa; I'm sure of the way."

So down by the fence rows he toddled along,
Past orchard and pasture—he wouldn't go wrong—
Then upon the levy, past pools black and deep;
The angels were guiding those little bare feet.

His forehead got dusty, his cheeks pink and hot.
His little feet burned, but he noticed it not.
His thoughts were of Grandma, and how he would say
When he reached up to kiss her, "Got a cookie today?"

So on past the corn field, through sunflowers so high.
Yet, by looking above him, he could still see the sky.
At last, 'round the corner he came making his way
And there he saw Grandpa out raking his hay.

*But let us look backward and see what is there.
Does mother yet miss him, her face anxious with care?
Oh, yes! She has missed him. She is calling his name.
And how she is looking! But all is in vain!*

*She's searched every corner up high and down low.
Where could he have vanished? How could he just go?
The circle she widens—follows each little track—
Still calling and calling, but no one calls back.*

*At last, in a moment of worry and fright,
The answer came clearly: "Yes, I know I am right."
Then quickly she ran down the same dusty way
That David had taken much earlier that day.*

*"He's gone to see Grandpa, of course that is where,
But keep him from danger, Lord," was her prayer.
Had he reached there in safety? Had he passed those deep holes?
So many things happen; so many things told.*

*Her thoughts raced the faster as nearer she came
Without little David—but what's that in the lane?
Why, yes, it is Grandpa—he's coming this way,
And with him is David, his hair full of hay!*

*His face is just beaming; he's had so much fun!
But Grandpa knew mothers, so David's visit was done.
David returned with dust on his feet,
His heart full of love, and a cookie to eat.*

When Leslie was nearly two, a terrible accident almost robbed him of his eyesight. Gene and Lois had replaced their cast iron stove with another, moving the old one to the backyard to clean before selling. Lois had put the grates into a bucket of lye water to loosen the baked-on food residue overnight. She placed it on top of the stove, where she thought little hands couldn't reach it.

The next morning, the boys went outside to play. Leslie, always curious, saw the bucket and wanted to know what was in it. Since he couldn't see from the ground, he opened the oven door and used it for a stepstool. Unfortunately, his weight on the open door overbalanced the stove, causing it to tip over. The bucket of lye water hit him full in the face as he fell backward, and the heavy stove landed on top of him.

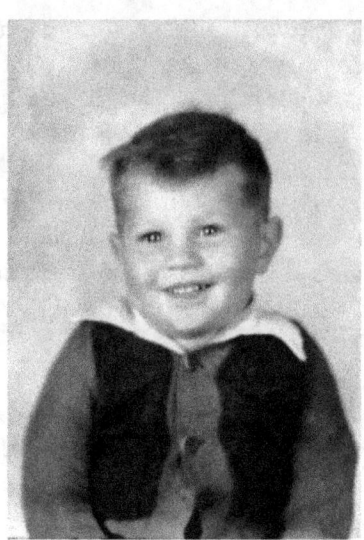

FIGURE 3.12 Leslie Anderson. Undated photograph, circa 1945. Photographer Lois Anderson.

Gene and Lois heard Leslie's screams of pain and terror and rushed outside, where they found him pinned under the stove. They lifted it off him, frantically poured water over his face, then rushed him to the hospital. By the time they arrived there, his eyes were swollen shut. Nurses immediately put vinegar poultices on his face and over his eyes. Not surprisingly, Leslie was still frightened, confused, and in a great deal of pain.

He was offered food several times but was too upset to eat. Finally, Lois asked him if he would like a cookie. Reaching out, he said, "Tootie! Tootie!" The cookie brought him some comfort, and he didn't cry much after that.

Lois stayed with Leslie in the hospital. He lay quietly in his bed, but he did not open his eyes. The swelling went down and the skin on his face began to heal. He still did not open his eyes, and his parents feared his eyesight had been permanently damaged. At the same time, they thanked the Lord that Leslie hadn't been crushed or killed by the stove when it fell on him.

Gene came to the hospital one morning after he had finished the milking. Lying in his crib at the end of the hall, Leslie heard his father greeting the nurses. He called out, "Daddy! Daddy!" His eyes popped open, and he could see!

Miraculously, the doctor couldn't detect any damage to Leslie's eyes. The whole church had been praying for him, and Gene and Lois were relieved and grateful that the Lord had spared Leslie's eyesight. Not only was his sight saved, but he never experienced problems with his eyes afterward. It was many years later during a routine medical examination that a doctor asked, "Have you ever had an injury to your eyes? I see evidence of some scarring."

Living on the island was a wonderful interlude in Gene and Lois's lives. The banks of the Kings River bordering their place provided lovely walks where they could watch the numerous birds and animals that lived there. The church—the same one they had been married in—was blessed to have many young families, and Gene and Lois spent most Saturday nights in sweet fellowship with these friends. The ultimate enjoyment, of course, was living next to parents, and many happy memories were made in the Dillon's cozy adobe bungalow.

FIGURE 3.13 Larry Dillon (Lois's brother) playing with David. Undated photograph, circa 1944. Photographer Lois Anderson.

Gene and Lois's dairy business prospered. In addition to their herd of dairy cows, they owned a tractor and other farm equipment. They received a cream check of thirty dollars a day but wondered if they should pursue this line of work indefinitely. They felt they would be more content employed in some branch of church work and prayed that the Lord would show them what He wanted them to do.

One morning a car pulled into the Anderson's driveway, and two men got out. Gene immediately recognized Jerry Johnson, a former classmate from PUC. With him was Elder Avery from the education department of the Central California Conference. Dinuba Junior Academy needed another teacher for the coming year, and Jerry—who was principal at Dinuba—had found Gene's name on the list of possible teachers at the conference office. Since Gene lived close by, the two men had driven out to see him. Elder Avery was not overly impressed with the young, unprofessional-looking dairyman standing before him; however, he knew that Jerry wanted Gene on the staff, so he offered Gene the position of teaching grades five through eight with a weekly salary of twenty dollars.

> *They felt they would be more content employed in some branch of church work and prayed that the Lord would show them what He wanted them to do.*

Gene and Lois were thrilled with how the Lord was working out the desire of their hearts, even though their income would be a big cut from what they had been earning. After prayerful consideration, Gene accepted the invitation. The Andersons sold the dairy, the horses, and the farm equipment, and paid off their debts. They left their island home the latter part of the summer and moved into the school building in Dinuba until the house they had purchased became available to them.

Labor Day, 1945, fell on September 2—David's fourth birthday. Since it was a special day, Dad Dillon wanted to drive into the hills to an area where he had worked in the lumber industry many years before. He seldom took time off, so Gene and Lois readily put aside their plans for the day.

Lois prepared a delicious picnic lunch, and the whole family piled into Gene's Graham coupe—Mom and Dad Dillon in front with Gene, and Lois, Joyce, and Larry in the back with David and Leslie. It was a delightful day, visiting the places where Dad Dillon had worked, listening to his stories, and enjoying their time together.

The sun slipped low over the farmlands and orange groves, then dropped below the horizon as they drove slowly toward home, singing and talking over the experiences of the day. Suddenly lights flashed from between the orange trees. A car streaked out of the darkness and rammed into the passenger side of their coupe with a sickening crash. Dad Dillon was thrown onto the pavement behind the car. Gene somersaulted over

Mom Dillon and landed on his feet on the opposite side of the car. Mom Dillon still sat in the middle seat, slumped over and badly injured. None of the passengers in the back seat were thrown out, though Lois received a severe blow to her head.

Other vehicles soon stopped and took the occupants of both cars to Dr. Brigham's clinic, where Joyce was working at the time. Mom Dillon was in the hospital for five weeks, but Dad Dillon was so seriously hurt he survived for only a few hours.

A highway patrolman questioned Gene about the accident. The officer asked him how fast he had been going. When Gene said thirty-five mph, the officer confirmed that Gene's knee had smashed the speedometer which registered thirty-five mph. Gene learned he had been driving on a side road that had a stop sign at the highway. The stop sign had been knocked down, and because the orange trees grew right to the very corner of the intersection, the highway hadn't been visible. The police were convinced that what Gene said was true; however, there had been a series of accidents in that vicinity recently, and they were getting tough on drivers. Gene received a citation for going through a stop sign and was accused of manslaughter because of Dad Dillon's death. Gene hired a lawyer for a fee of $250—a large sum for him—and after a thorough investigation, the charges were dropped.

Lois's thinking was foggy for some weeks following the tragedy—even though she could remember the details of that night and see the accident replaying in her mind. She felt like she was living in a bad dream, unable to realize emotionally what had happened. When Mom Dillon was released from the hospital, she came to stay with Lois and Gene for a little while until she was well enough to join Joyce in Paradise Valley where Joyce was teaching in the nursing school.

It was a horrendous way to begin a new job and a new school year. The whole family was grieving and traumatized. Gene prayed daily for strength to concentrate on his duties, and at the end of the year, he was asked to teach again the following year. At the same time, he was invited to become principal of Visalia-Exeter Junior Academy, a position he accepted. During vacation, the family spent several weeks at PUC while Gene attended summer school. Somehow, the change of location and duties relieved the terrible feelings resulting from Dad Dillon's death that had weighed them down for the past year.

After summer school, the Andersons found a house to rent in Visalia. It was only two miles from where Lois had grown up. Though her childhood home was gone and the land had been planted with oranges, the roads, rivers, and hills remained the same. The whole family began to feel settled and content. Unfortunately, the owners of the house changed their minds about renting it, so Gene and Lois were once again house hunting. They bought a lot along the Mineral King Highway and purchased a prefabricated house. With the enthusiastic help of the local church folks, the building was quickly completed.

The Andersons lived in Visalia for four years. Gene took classes at PUC during summer vacations, except for the summer he was asked to participate in a different project. Forest Smith from the Central California Conference asked Gene to direct a summer work program for teenage boys called the Sierra Foresters Boys' Club. The Club received a work contract from the California Forestry Department to eradicate the gooseberry bushes in the evergreen forests. The bushes had to be destroyed because their berries carried an insect that killed the evergreen trees.

The work program seemed like an interesting challenge, so the Andersons signed on. They joined the rest of the group at Lodi in early June and suddenly became the caretakers of twenty teenage boys from broken or single-parent homes. The boys had various behavioral issues that mandated their attendance in the summer program before they could continue their schooling. Three college students from PUC worked as team leaders under Gene, and Lois was the cook. She prepared large quantities of delicious food cooked on a wood range set up on a board floor under the trees. The boys were assigned kitchen duties—such as washing dishes and cleaning up—so Lois didn't have to do all the work herself. Still, with two small sons to care for, it was a challenge for her.

Everyone slept in tents. When one area of the forest had been cleared of gooseberry bushes, the group was transported by truck to a new area.

The days were full, with morning and evening worship, hard physical labor, good regular meals, and active recreation. Gene strove to guide the boys into a close relationship with Jesus and hoped, by filling the hours with activities, to keep the boys too busy to get into trouble. But, occasionally, they still did—which gave Gene opportunities to demonstrate his theory that discipline should be both redemptive and instructive.

On one occasion, one of the boys was blatantly disobedient. Gene sent him to the woods for a switch. The guilty fellow, expecting the switch to be used on him, came back to camp with a small branch. Gene sent him for a bigger one—and then again for yet a bigger branch. When Gene was satisfied that the size of the switch was equal to the size of the misdeed, he said, "Now I want you to whip me. I will take your punishment." Gene would not let the boy beg off or do a less-than-adequate job. Afterward, he explained to the heartbroken young man that this is what Jesus had done for everyone who did wrong: Jesus took our punishment and let us go free. It was a lesson no one in the camp ever forgot.

Two of the boys kept bullying and fighting each other. Their behavior was disrupting the whole camp, so Gene called everyone together, formed them into a big circle, and led the two boys into the center. "You want to fight," he said, "so fight! We'll stay here until you decide you don't want to fight anymore." Tentatively, the two culprits began poking each other. Soon they were punching, kicking, and rolling on the ground. They pummeled each other until they were so exhausted, they fell into each other's arms. For the remainder of the summer, they were best friends.

Gene also knew that energy-filled boys with a serious bent toward mischief needed active, rough games to occupy them during their free time. A favorite was called "hot seat." Participation was not mandatory, so only the bravest subjected themselves to its indignities. A boy—blindfolded[7] so he couldn't peek—would bend over with his hands on a tree while the other teens took turns swatting his bottom[8] with their hands. If he could guess who hit him, the named person would then be in the "hot seat."

Another game was a wild version of "drop the handkerchief."[9] The fellows, each with a belt in his hand, formed a big circle facing toward the center. The person who was "it" ran around the outside of the circle, tagged[10] someone, then raced ahead of the tagged person back to the empty spot, trying his best to stay out of reach of the swinging belt behind him. If he got hit with the belt, he had to be "it" again. The campers were always eager to play these games whenever they had time.

There was no town nearby, so the campers gave each other haircuts with hand clippers that Lois had brought to the camp. The "barber" would occasionally wreak vengeance on his customer's hair. Fortunately, the damage was never permanent.

By the end of the summer, all the boys and their leaders had earned a substantial sum of money. The campers were enthusiastic about returning the next summer, but the forestry project fell apart and was discontinued. Despite the challenges and surprises, Gene and Lois had had a marvelous time and were grateful for the experience. Several of the boys went on to become church leaders, doctors, and teachers, and many of them stayed in touch with Gene for years.

Gene practiced the same type of discipline with his own sons. David and Leslie, home on a vacation from VHS, were doing dishes after one meal when the Andersons were in Candy, Ceylon. Leslie was drying and repeatedly snapping[11] his dish towel at David. Finally, David threw his sopping wet dishcloth at Leslie—triggering out-of-control emotions for both brothers and resulting in a full-fledged scuffle. They knocked over the five-gallon glass water container that was on a stand and transformed the galley kitchen into a disaster area. For their punishment, Gene asked them to spend the evening in separate rooms where they were each to write research papers about anger, how to manage it, and how to behave toward irritating people. Their research sources were to be the Bible and Ellen G. White's writings.

That scuffle was their last.

At one family meal, David and Leslie were gobbling their food in great big bites. So, Gene told them they had to finish their meal, taking just one little piece of food at a time. The food happened to be rice, so they had to pick up one grain at a time. It took a long time to finish!

Many years later, Gene and Lois's two youngest boys—Vernon, four and Danny, nine—began a heated argument.[12] Furious words flew back and forth between them, but Gene, sitting in the living room with them, did not interfere. Instead, he reached over and pushed the record button on the tape deck. As the verbal onslaught quieted, he said, "Boys, I would like you to listen to this." Then he replayed their entire exchange. Vernon and Danny were appalled at how awful they sounded.

Gene had a great sense of humor, as well, but one time it backfired[13] on him. The family was going somewhere in the car, and it was raining. The wipers weren't keeping up very well, and visibility was poor. Gene stopped at a store to buy a plug of chewing tobacco to rub on the windshield to repel the water. For a joke, he came out of the store, pretending he had put some tobacco in his mouth and was chewing it. The thought that his father would do such a wicked thing so traumatized David that Gene never tried joking about anything like that again.

Gene and Lois attended a youth rally in Fresno one weekend. Several students from PUC participated in it. That night at home Gene said, "I would like to return to PUC and finish my degree. It will take so long to complete by just taking a course or two each summer. What do you think?"

"I think that is exactly what you should do," Lois agreed.

Gene and Lois had each signed a contract to teach again in Visalia the following year, so Gene asked the school board to release them from their commitments. The board agreed to do so if the Andersons could find suitable teachers to fill their positions. At about that time, a family moved to the area looking for work. Both the husband and the wife were qualified teachers, so they were hired—and the Andersons were free to go. Gene and Lois felt the Lord's hand directing this decision. They sold their home for the better-than-expected price of $6,500, making it possible for Gene to support his family while attending college.

Chapter 4

When Horizons Expand, The Big Picture Is Seen

"And do not be conformed to this world, but be transformed by the renewing of your mind, that you may prove what is that good and acceptable and perfect will of God."

—*Romans 12:2*

The Andersons could easily have lost track of time while they were at sea had they not kept a calendar handy. Some days it seemed all they did was eat and sleep. From the deck, they could see to the horizon in every direction. If it was too cold to linger outside, they returned to the warmth of the ship and the enticing smells wafting from the kitchen. They could feel the throb of the steam turbine engines under their feet.

When the wind lashed everything on deck and howled through the rigging, the family stayed inside where it was warm and dry, clamped down their portholes, and slept—trusting God to carry them safely across the ocean depths.

Unlike the present day when missionaries usually attend a Mission Institute training session before flying to their service destination, the Andersons had to learn about foreign cultures, climate, food, and customs on their own. As soon as their call to Burma had been confirmed, they had begun reading everything they could find about Burma. Now, on their two-month voyage, they continued to read, discuss, and try to find answers to their questions about the country that was to be their new home.

Even though no land was visible for sixteen days, not a day passed without the ship's passengers seeing birds of one species or another. Albatrosses[14]—whose powerful wings spanned an amazing seven feet— were the only birds that flew along with the ship, following almost to the

Mariana Islands.[15] The family enjoyed watching their graceful circling in and out of the wave troughs, over and up and down, always flying in the same pattern. One day, they suddenly all flew away and were not seen again.

On one occasion, the Andersons were standing at the prow watching the endless expanse of water and feeling the brisk sea air blowing against their faces when Gene suddenly exclaimed, "I see sprays coming up out of the water quite a ways ahead and a little to the port side." The rest of the family looked in the direction he pointed.

David and Leslie shouted, "I see sprays coming way up, Daddy!"

As they watched, a huge black form shot out of the water. The two ladies came running at the sound of the exclamations and were able to catch a glimpse of the whale before it slipped back into the sea. The whale spouted water several more times until it was even with their ship. Then, it disappeared as mysteriously as it had come.

Another day, hundreds of porpoises appeared on both sides of the ship, keeping pace with it for several miles. One after another, they leaped out of the water, creating little rainbows as the sun shone through the water droplets that fell from their fins. They continued leaping, jumping, and surfing the bow wake as though they were delighted to have a traveling companion. Finally, they swam away and were lost from sight.

One morning the family awakened to smooth sailing on a glassy sea. There was hardly a break, even where the prow cut the water. It seemed like a different ocean. When they looked out to the horizon, they felt as though they were looking at the vast blue prairies.

"It is so beautiful!" Lois exclaimed. "I have never seen the ocean look like this."

The crew on the ship was fond of the boys and often let them tag along to watch the work. David and Leslie delighted in the glorious freedom of being up on the bridge—especially when the helmsman took the ship off automatic pilot and let them test their strength by turning the enormous wheel.

The boys adjusted well to ship life and played together with what they had. There was one instance, however, while they were making chalk roads on the deck for their cars and trucks when a sudden spat ensued. David picked up one of his trucks—his favorite no less—and threw it at Leslie. The truck missed Leslie and sailed through the railing slats. Instantly, their anger was forgotten as the boys raced to the railing just in time to see the truck spiral downward and disappear into the dark water.

Every day, Lois put together a surprise package of things for the boys to play with or activities that would keep them entertained and teach them something new. At each port, there would be mail and packages waiting for them from family in the USA. Feeling such love and support was a priceless treasure. The Andersons always had their own letters ready to mail back at each stop.

From time to time, various family members struggled with nostalgia. This was especially true for Leslie. One day he told his mother, "I don't think I'll ever have as good a bed as the one I had at home. I used to talk to it." Lois knew it really was an awful bed—just a sway-bellied cot—but to Leslie, everything had a personality. He didn't want anything, not even a bed, to feel deserted because he had left it.

Then he added, "I miss our old green house too. I liked it better than any other house in the world."

Lois replied, "I know just how you feel, Leslie. I can easily put myself there—listening for you boys to come up on the porch; hearing Tippy barking; enjoying the sound of the wind blowing through the pine trees; listening to the bell ringing to announce it was time for church. What happy times we had there together!"

It isn't hard to get homesick, Lois thought—*although I can, with excited anticipation, turn my mind to what our next home might be like. Dear, sweet little boys! I hope we can make it up to them for what they have left behind.*

Elder Robert Pierson, President of the Southern Asia Division once said about mission service, "We know it is the children who often sacrifice the most. It is up to us to fill the places left vacant for them."

"What a wonderful thing it will be when we all get to heaven," Lois wrote in her journal. "Never will we have to leave our loved ones and friends. We can enjoy each other day after day and not have that ache and longing that fills our hearts when we are away from those we love."

They crossed the international date line on Sunday, March 30—making the next day Tuesday, even though they wanted to call it Monday.

At breakfast, first mate Ray told Gene a humorous story. "The last time we crossed the date line, we had a new crew member on board. As we neared the crossing, I asked him to come up on the bridge and watch for the string of buoys along the date line, as I wanted to know when we crossed it.

"Six hours later, the poor man gave up and reported, 'They must have taken them all in.'"

Ray laughed. "The joke was really on me when the fellow turned in his time card with six hours of overtime, and I had to okay it!"

As the ship came into the San Bernardino Straits, news spread that the Philippines would be coming into sight the next morning. The Andersons got up early and sat on the front deck to watch for the first glimpse of land.

Soon a long black streak appeared on the horizon. As they drew nearer, the streak became coconut palms lining beautiful long white beaches. Houses took shape, with tendrils of gray smoke curling up from cooking fires, and the peaks of several volcanos towered above everything else. The SS *Steel Artisan* passed close by a small island with a lighthouse and met two steamships going out to sea.

At last, the SS *Steel Artisan* docked in Manila. A military troop ship that had just brought wives and children to join their soldier husbands and fathers was docked at the pier directly across from them. The Andersons had a ringside seat to a moving scene as husbands, wives, and children flew into each other's arms. Tears of joy flowed freely.

Gene and Lois felt tears on their cheeks also. "Is this what heaven will be like?" Gene asked.

The family had a wonderful stay in Manila. Elders Warren and Dunton met them at the ship and took them to the mission compound for several days. They enjoyed meals at five different homes. All the workers were so warm and friendly, they made the Andersons feel as though they were visiting family. Gene and Elder Warren talked late into the night of their passion for serving God and the challenges it brings.

There were nine homes on the mission compound, all facing a lawn in the center. The cool and airy houses were constructed from mahogany, the cheapest lumber available. The office building, Quonset huts, and the stone church were also inside the walled compound, with the hospital located across the street.

The Andersons arrived in the Philippines with no definite idea of what the country would be like, since it was their first visit to a foreign land. Everything was different from what they had been accustomed to in America: the tasty cuisine, fragrant spices, trees, flowers, sights, and sounds. They felt like sponges, soaking up the novel impressions through their eyes, ears, noses, and taste buds.

They expected Manila would be a modern city. Maybe "modern" was the correct word, but Manila was unlike any city they had known in California. There were a few wide American-built streets, but just off the main avenues, the streets became so narrow, they didn't look like streets anymore—not even like alleys. There was scarcely room for two cars to pass each other.

There were no sidewalks in the residential areas, so people walked in the street, vehicles missing them by inches. Drivers constantly used their horns to warn pedestrians and other vehicles that they were close by. It was nerve-wracking and funny at the same time.

Elder Dunton took the Andersons to see the beautifully laid out Philippine Union College campus and its printing press. The press was modern and busy, meeting the constant demand for church literature. The school had an enrollment of about 1,000, but since it was vacation time, the students and staff were away.

In a letter to her family back home, Lois wrote, "We are different now than when we arrived. With such a quick glimpse, never again can we wonder why we send missionaries. Never again can we settle down in America and feel free of the call of duty. It is too big to describe all at once. Our minds are just whirling with the jumble of thoughts and things we have experienced, and we have not had time to organize them."

But the Andersons were sure of one thing: there was not a group in the world they would rather have joined than Seventh-day Adventist missionaries. It was not that missionaries were so wonderful in themselves—although any one of them was a vital, contributing person; somehow, they were all unified in their vision of what they had been called to do. They loved each other, and Gene and Lois knew it was not just this group in Manila; the Andersons had felt the bond of love between missionaries long before they left America.

Even when missionaries who had worked together were scattered to different assignments, ties stretched between stations and crisscrossed all over the world, holding the missionaries together. They were always so happy to hear from those they had worked with in other places. During their two-month journey, Gene and Lois had brought word to several people from other missionaries or family members who had heard that the Andersons would be seeing their loved ones or former co-workers.

With genuine affection, the Andersons said goodbye to their new friends and colleagues in the Philippines.

The ship's next stop was Saigon, Vietnam, sixty-five miles up the Saigon River. The land appeared quite flat and was just a foot or two above the riverbank. From the deck, the Andersons could see a patchwork of rice paddies stretching out from either bank, with water buffalos working in them. Palm-leaf houses dotted the countryside, and off in the distance, the impressive city skyline could be seen.

There were native fishing boats, a few sunken ships around the harbor, and freighters and troop ships passing up and down the river. Around a bend, just before reaching the dock, they saw about fifteen sailing boats with large woven bamboo sails, which made a beautiful picture in the sunshine.

The freighter docked on April 14. It squeezed into the last space left open by more than a dozen big freighters already tied up. Dock workers labored on the ships around the clock. They were dressed in all sorts of attire, but usually in baggy shirts and short pants. There was much chattering and waving of hands as they shouted directions to the crane operators. Most of the dialogue was in French.

The Andersons waited until the following day to contact the Seventh-day Adventist mission in Saigon. Communication was a challenge when Gene phoned, but he felt he had made himself understood. Sure enough, shortly after breakfast, several mission workers came to the dock and escorted the Andersons off the ship. One of these workers was Mrs. Wentland. She and her husband were the only Americans at the mission.

After searching for a taxi without success, Mrs. Wentland decided the group should travel in cyclos, which were three-wheeled cycles. Other than its two front wheels and the seat on the front that was wide enough for two passengers, a cyclo resembled a bicycle, with the driver sitting higher than his front load to be able to navigate through traffic. Cyclos didn't carry only people. They also transported all sorts of cumbersome loads—such as heavy baskets of fruits or vegetables, ducks and chickens, a stack of truck tires, or live pigs trussed on a sling. The mission group hired several of these conveyances to ride across town. They were a bit scary, making unexpected and sudden stops or darting between vehicles, but David and Leslie found the ride exhilarating.

The Andersons noticed a woman carrying two five-gallon cans of water on the ends of a pole that went across her shoulders. Later, they saw a small girl transporting water the same way and wondered how she could even lift the full cans off the ground.

It was a welcome relief for the Andersons to arrive at the Wentland home inside the peaceful walls of the mission compound. The mission house was a large two-story building with two apartments—one on the ground level and one upstairs. Spacious and airy, the apartments looked inviting after the wild ride across town. The building's rooftop was level and open with high walls around the perimeter, making it a safe place for the children to play. In the evening, the rooftop view and breeze were delightful.

Across the street was the mission office and a small press. The equipment was old but still operational. The indigenous worker in charge of the colporteurs was dedicated and energetic. They were selling $2,000 worth of books a month. A short time before, they had been told this could not be done—at least not in Vietnam—but they were proving otherwise.

The Andersons had a wonderful visit with the Wentlands in Saigon before Brother Wentland brought them back to the ship.

A couple days later, the SS *Steel Artisan* dropped anchor in the Bangkok Harbor in Thailand, avoiding the dock because of civil unrest. The freighter stayed far enough out for one barge after another to come alongside. Cargo of all sorts was unloaded onto each barge: small tanks, Jeeps, reinforcing steel, crates of food, and refrigerators by the dozens.

The ship was scheduled to remain at Bangkok for a week, so the Andersons had hoped to get off for several days—especially since the General Conference had notified each mission of the Anderson's ocean itinerary. Gene had made the necessary arrangements with the shipping company to disembark, but the captain refused to let them off, citing that it was too dangerous. They were disappointed to miss their anticipated introduction to yet another country.

Bangkok was the destination for the two Christian ladies who had been traveling with them. On disembarking, they were each assigned an armed guard to escort them safely to their land transportation.

The Andersons spent some time every day watching the dock workers. They were jolly as they labored together hour after hour. They lived on the barges and cooked big pots of rice, vegetables, and fish over small charcoal stoves that blackened their kettles. At mealtimes, they ate squatting down on the deck around their steaming bowls of food.

Bangkok was a busy harbor. Other freighters were being unloaded, and sailboats, rowboats, and launches were moving about. Sometimes, eight men manned the rowboats, their rowing perfectly synchronized like a nautical ballet.

After dinner one evening, Gene asked Lois, "Where are the scissors? I'll cut your hair."

He thought she would think he was just kidding, but she took him up on his offer, got the scissors and the razor, and told him what to do. He started right in and gave her a lovely, feathered hairdo. They were both pleased with the result. *What will he do next?* Lois wondered.

> *The family decided that having a lovely home and everything that one could want wouldn't bring complete and lasting satisfaction. They each expressed a desire to follow God's leading and be workers for Him.*

As a family, they spent hours reading, talking, and listening to each other. They discussed what it was that caused them to turn from the things that could have made them wealthy to choose, instead, a life that meant doing without many material things. The family decided that having a lovely home and everything that one could want wouldn't bring complete and lasting satisfaction. They each expressed a desire to follow God's leading and be workers for Him.

Lois wrote a poem during their long layover at Bangkok:

Sea Stars

Beside our ship where the foam turns under,
We stand to gaze on the scene with wonder,
Blowing curls of the wave tops breaking,
Gleam and swirl while a white trail making.

They pass us by in the velvet night
With soft sprays glowing in mysterious light.
Still, we look with searching eye
To see new wonders passing by.

A million lights are twinkling there
Like a spangled veil on jet black hair.
They twinkle and sparkle and glimmer and gleam
And dance and swirl in the eddying stream.

What beautiful sights pass before our eyes
On a moonless night beneath southern skies.

From the first time they met him, the family shared a strong liking for Ray, the first mate. He was the one who showed them all over the boat with their folks in San Francisco. He was a kind and consistent man, and everyone who met him loved him. One evening Gene went to ask Ray a question and found him mending his raincoat. Ray seemed to want to talk and invited Gene to share coffee with him. Gene replied that he chose not to drink coffee but would enjoy an orange instead.

That brought up the subject of diet, and Ray asked why Gene and his family did not eat meat. "I have always been told you had to eat meat to build blood. There's no other way. It is very necessary. But look at your boys! I have never seen two healthier children than those two, and they don't eat meat."

The conversation went from one subject to another, and Gene was thrilled to have this special time with Ray.

Later, as Gene shared the experience with the family, he said, "Ray is honestly searching for truth. He is afraid, though, because he's been told it's a sin to talk to a Protestant about religion or to read the Bible. Even talking to me made him nervous, and yet, he has always wondered what the Bible really says. We talked until one o'clock this morning, and he asked many questions that show he is a thinking man. We discussed all our main beliefs and doctrines, and he was most interested."

> *The family had prayed for the Lord to lead them to people who were earnestly searching for something better in their lives.*

The family had prayed for the Lord to lead them to people who were earnestly searching for something better in their lives. If their confinement to the ship at Bangkok meant bringing Ray closer to God, they were more than content.

The SS *Steel Artisan* left Bangkok and arrived at the harbor in Djakarta,[16] Indonesia, on April 25. It was directed to anchor outside the breakwater, since another large freighter was at the dock. While they waited, the crew took a lifeboat to shore numerous times. Leslie and David were occasionally invited to go with them and were sometimes given the chance to pilot the boat. After a week, the SS *Steel Artisan* was finally able to dock.

FIGURE 4.1 *The SS Steel Artisan anchored in the Djakarta Bay, waiting to dock, April 1952. Photographer Lois Anderson.*

Gene planned to get off the ship to contact mission workers in Djakarta, but he was told that both he and the shipping company would be subject to a hefty fine if he went ashore without a visa. Furthermore, the Seventh-day Adventist headquarters were in a town about five hours away. It appeared there was nothing to do about making any connections during the delay.

FIGURE 4.2 *David and Leslie steering the lifeboat of the SS Steel Artisan as it brings the crew back to the ship while first mate Ray looks on, April 1952. Left to right at back of lifeboat: David, Leslie, and first mate Ray. Photographer Lois Anderson.*

Then, suddenly, everything fell into place. Gene and Lois spotted a tall, blond man coming up the gangplank, asking for the Andersons. He was Pastor Klop, the man in charge of the Seventh-day Adventist work with the Dutch in Djakarta. He had come to take the family off the boat. He told them they needed to bring only their passports and freighter tickets. The Andersons quickly changed clothes and left with Pastor Klop.

Pastor Klop took them to his home to meet his wife and children. He spoke English quite well, but his wife understood very little. She served everyone a refreshing drink and then retired to her kitchen while her husband visited with the Andersons in the yard, which resembled a park with many different tropical trees and flowers. Afterward, they returned to the ship and boarded—without being questioned by the guards. The crew was surprised the Andersons had been able to disembark, but as Pastor Klop explained, "Missionaries can go places other people can't."

Pastor Klop planned to travel to the Seventh-day Adventist headquarters in Bandung the following day for an overnight visit, and he invited Gene to go with him. Gene had no trouble with the guards when he left early the next morning; they just looked at his smiling face and told him to go on.

The country was beautiful. The rubber plantations reminded Gene of the expansive walnut orchards back home. Tea grew on the sides of the mountains, going clear to the top in some places. Rice paddies were everywhere; some were small patches, others covered acres and acres in the valleys, and many more were terraced on the mountainsides.

Pastor Klop had phoned the mission at Bandung prior to their visit, so they were expected. The workers were disappointed not to meet the whole family, though. Gene was sorry too; Lois and the boys could easily have come with him.

The SS *Steel Artisan* steamed out of Djakarta on May 8 and docked at Surabaya, Indonesia, later that afternoon. A pleasant-looking man came up the gangplank and asked for the Andersons. The man was Brother Ansu. Having received word from Brother Brodeur at Bandung that the Andersons were aboard the freighter, Brother Ansu had come to take them off the ship for a brief visit.

The guards watched the Andersons come down the gangplank. Their expressions softened, they smiled, and then they let the family through the exit gate. A taxi drove them the five miles to Brother Ansu's church, which had a membership of about 300.

As the family sat in the church, Brother Ansu told them the story of an amazing experience the members had had during the war. They had been gathered for safety in the church one evening when suddenly, above the noise and confusion of fighting going on around them, they had heard the most beautiful singing. It was not coming from outside or from any of them. Then they had realized that angels were surrounding them with song. It had brought them such peace and comfort. It was also a moving experience for the Andersons to sit in the very spot where angels had once sung.

When the Andersons returned to the boat, first mate Ray asked, "Did you go ashore today?"

"Yes," Gene replied.

Ray shook his head. "I don't know how you do it. I just don't know. We once had a couple of tourists who had come only to see the country, and they couldn't get off the boat!"

One evening the family sat out on the deck watching the full moon and enjoying the balmy air. As she often did, Lois began singing. Gene and the boys joined her. For a long time, their music drifted into the night.

Leslie crawled into Lois's lap and tucked his head under her arm. "This makes me have a funny feeling, a feeling I never had before," he said. He often had feelings he didn't know what to do with, but homesickness was a new experience. Lois realized that many times she and Gene had failed to recognize the emotions their precious boys held deep inside.

On May 12, the SS *Steel Artisan* arrived in Singapore, an island city-state off southern Malaysia. Gene went ashore the next morning with the shipping agent to phone the mission compound. The Singapore mission personnel were expecting him, so someone came right away to pick him up. He cabled the Burma Union headquarters in Rangoon to ask about the possibility of the family completing their journey by air. Word came back the next morning for the family to continue by boat, as it would facilitate baggage clearance when they arrived in Rangoon.

In Singapore, the family transferred from the SS *Steel Artisan* to a small coastal steamer, the *Taksang*, to make the last leg of their journey to Burma by way of Penang, Malaysia.

David and Leslie were sorry to say goodbye to their good friend, Ray. In parting, they gave him four books: *Steps to Christ*,[17] *Signs of Christ's Coming*, *From Sabbath to Sunday*, and *Your Friends, the Adventists*. Ray thanked them and promised, "I'll be sure to read them. Believe me, I'll read them!" He would miss the boys, whom he had liked very much.

Gene and Lois hired a lorry to transport their luggage from the SS *Steel Artisan* to the *Taksang*. They said goodbye to all their friends on the freighter. It was strange how attached they had become to the whole crew, who had been so kind to them. The Andersons would miss seeing the crew members every day.

It was May 25, 1952, when the *Taksang* made its way up the Irrawaddy River and docked along the muddy riverbank at Rangoon, Burma. Finally, the Andersons had reached their destination. The gleam of the setting sun reflected off the gilded Shwedagon Pagoda, which rose high above the city like a beacon. It was after dark when the little ship finally got its mooring ropes cinched up. The Andersons cleared immigration and customs, all the while scanning the crowd for someone who might have come from the Burma Union Mission headquarters to welcome them. They completed the check-in process and claimed their baggage, but still no one had come. They were in a foreign land, an unfamiliar city, surrounded by strangers whose language they couldn't understand.

Gene certainly couldn't leave Lois and the boys in the dark with all the luggage. Neither was he happy with the idea of Lois going alone through the city at night. He decided to hire a trishaw (a bicycle with a small, attached sidecar) to take Lois and Leslie to the mission headquarters. He gave the driver the address—68 U Wisara Road—and sent them off through the dark streets.

At the mission, Lois found the workers in a meeting in the church. They were shocked to see her. Somehow, they had been given incorrect information regarding the Anderson's arrival, which explained why no one had been at the ship to meet them. Elder Cecil Guild, the Burma Union president, and Elder Bill Murrill, the Burma Union treasurer, dismissed themselves immediately and hurried down to the dock where Gene and David were anxiously waiting. What a relief it was for Gene to see them coming! Before long, the whole party was on its way back to the mission headquarters to join Lois and Leslie.

Chapter 5

When a Task Is at Hand, Do It

"And whatever you do, do it heartily, as to the Lord and not to men."

—*Colossians 3:23*

To compensate for missing the Anderson's arrival in Rangoon, the mission family threw a beautiful welcome party for them, complete with leis, a lovely program, and get-acquainted games.

FIGURE 5.1 Gene Anderson, principal of Myaungmya Training School. Undated photograph, circa 1952. Photographer Lois Anderson.

Francis and Catherine Scott, who had been administrators at the Myaungmya boarding school, were in Rangoon, ready to return home to the United States in a few days. Since Gene was replacing Brother Scott as principal, and school was starting in two weeks, Gene immediately assumed his new position. The two men flew to Myaungmya the next day so that Brother Scott could acquaint Gene with his duties. Afterward, Brother Scott flew back to Rangoon, and Gene remained on campus for his family to join him.

Lois and the boys were driven to the Rangoon airport several days later to catch a flight to Myaungmya. Barbara Wyman and her daughter, Emily, accompanied them. Barbara and her husband, Frank—who had been born in Burma—had been teaching at the school for several years.

As she walked into the low, open wooden building that served as the Rangoon air terminal on that dreary, muggy morning, Lois felt very much a foreigner and unsure of herself. With bags hanging from each shoulder and arms piled high with parcels, the missionaries made their way to the scales to weigh in. Lois glanced around the waiting room and noticed that almost all the Burmese passengers had similar piles of bulging cloth bags, brown paper sacks, and bundles wrapped in newspaper. Some Burmese ladies dressed in the typical dainty blouses and colorful longyis—lengths of cloth wrapped around the waist and extending to the feet—made room for them on the backless bench.

"Did you give the boys Dramamine[18] yet?" Barbara asked Lois. "From the look of those thunderheads, it could be rough today."

"No, I haven't. Do you think I need to?"

"Maybe. Sometimes we have a few bumps, and you don't want them to get airsick."

David and Leslie willingly took the pills, much to Lois's relief.

Lois watched the friendly faces, noticing the smooth skin and neatly coiled hair of the women. The soft, musical sound of voices speaking a foreign language flowed around her. She was part of the friendly chatter, yet she felt alone, and her mind was far away. What was Gene doing? How she wished he were with them to fly this last leg of their long journey.

She could see the darkening sky through the open side of the building. The air felt warm and oppressive, and the ominous, low rumble of distant thunder added to her apprehension. She wondered why people in Rangoon had pointedly told them how rough and frightening the flights could be during the monsoon season. Was it safe? Did the planes always get to their destinations? Had anyone been lost? She wanted to talk to Barbara about it but decided not to.

Lois watched Barbara as she chatted with the Burmese women. Her happy, carefree manner reassured Lois. No one else seemed anxious. *If they are not concerned about flying in a monsoon storm, why should I be?* she asked herself.

An announcement suddenly sounded over the raspy loudspeaker.

At once, the passengers grabbed bags and bundles and hurried to the waiting Dakota—one of the sturdy DC-3s still operating from the American efforts during World War II. Barbara led the way up the steps and into the plane.

"I see some empty seats in the third row," she said. "Come and sit here opposite Emily and me. Then we can all be close together."

Lois settled into her seat, with David and Leslie on either side of her. The boys immediately began checking all levers, seat belts, knobs, or whatever could be pushed, pulled, or turned.

Captain Baw Dee, the pilot, and Tin Shwe, the co-pilot, were in the cockpit going over their checklists. The captain, quite tall for a Burmese, wore a serious expression on his lean, handsome face. Tin Shwe, his round face creased with smiles, seemed more interested in sharing some amusing incident with the captain than in doing his job. He slapped his knee, leaned toward Captain Baw Dee, and burst into laughter—but the captain only nodded his head, his concentration unbroken.

Lois was anxious to be on the way. All seats were occupied. A thin Chinese man sat in the very front seat, making quite a commotion trying to get his baggage stowed. Just in front of Lois and the boys sat two women and a small child eating something with a spicy aroma out of a cone made from newspaper.

"Look! The propellers are turning!" Leslie announced with his nose to the window. The engines coughed, spurting puffs of smoke, then began to roar. Soon there was a surge of power as the two engines, under full throttle, gathered speed for the takeoff. The vibration of the wheels rushing over the rough pavement suddenly ceased as they lifted off into the gray, cloud-filled sky. Lois tried to relax, telling herself it was only a thirty-minute flight to Myaungmya.

They were just getting comfortable when Lois saw the co-pilot turn his head. With a frown, he stood up, leaned over the pilot, and peered out the window on the pilot's side of the plane. As Lois turned to follow his gaze, she felt the plane banking as it made a wide turn.

With a shock, she realized that the props of the engine on her side were visible. They had a dead engine! Lois searched Tin Shwe's face as he came to the cockpit door and made a loud announcement in Burmese. A gasp rippled through the rows of passengers.

"We are going back to Rangoon because of engine trouble," Barbara said from across the aisle. Her smile was as bright as ever.

Does this happen often? Lois wondered. *Do DC-3s fly well with only one engine?* Barbara didn't seem a bit disturbed. The situation must not be so unusual.

It didn't take long for the plane to return and touch down safely. The passengers filed back to the waiting room, their excited voices and waving hands betraying their feelings.

"They say another plane will be ready shortly," Barbara said.

"Well, let's hope our second try turns out better," Lois replied.

It was raining hard when it came time to board. Gusts of wind plastered their clothes against their bodies and drove rain into their faces. They claimed seats in the third row, as before. Up front, by the open cockpit door, the Chinese man was once again having problems getting his various bundles stashed to his liking.

The roar of the engines drowned all conversation as they climbed into the threatening sky. The point of no return whipped past, and Lois heard the welcome purring sound of the engines leveling off. The "fasten seat belts" and "no smoking" signs blinked off. Barbara and Lois exchanged smiles across the aisle. In thirty minutes, they would be at Myaungmya! Lois tried to visualize what it would be like. She wondered if she could make an inviting home in this new and different land.

The plane gave a sudden, violent lurch. Lois grabbed both David and Leslie as they pitched out of their seats. The "fasten seat belts" sign glowed red, and immediately the snapping of buckles was heard.

"Wow!" Lois exclaimed, looking into her boys' faces. "That was some bump, wasn't it?"

"What made it do that? Are we going to fall?" David asked, his eyes wide.

"No, we'll be all right. It's because it is so stormy," Lois answered. "We'll be out of it soon, I'm sure." But she was not a bit sure.

The plane began a crazy dance of leaps and jumps, the wings swinging up and down, tipping this way and that. Parcels from the overhead racks tumbled down around the passengers and skittered along the aisle. One minute they seemed to be floating, then, just as suddenly, terrific pressure pushed everyone down into their seats. Lois's stomach felt like it was wrapped with a cord that pulled tighter and tighter with every thud and jolt. She could sense the boys watching her. She knew they would mirror her reactions, so she tried to smile, but her face seemed frozen.

She made another attempt to ease the boys' tension as she reminded them how they had wished to ride a roller coaster. "Boys," she said, "here are your roller coaster thrills!"

The hands of her watch crept around the face. Fifty-five minutes had gone by, with each passenger locked in his own little cell of fear. She watched the muscles in the captain's face and neck as he struggled to keep the plane on a level course. The pilots opened their windows and peered out, frantically searching for a familiar landmark through the storm clouds below. The rain poured into the cabin and ran down the aisle.

To further heighten the tension, the Chinese man in the front seat turned around to face the passengers and declared in a loud voice, "We are lost!" Lois's mental anguish intensified. She felt pure, undiluted fear engulf her like a cold wave. Never had she felt such terror, and she fought against it. She remembered how the family had embarked on this journey, believing that God wanted them here, so why was this happening? *I don't want my life to end this way*, she thought. *Where are we, God? Where are You?*

> *To further heighten the tension, the Chinese man in the front seat turned around to face the passengers and declared in a loud voice, "We are lost!"*

More than an hour had passed since liftoff. The view out the windows seemed a little clearer. The terrible bouncing had eased. She raised her head just in time to see Tin Shwe suddenly stand up. He pointed excitedly through the front window, and a smile like the rising sun broke across his face. *Oh! Thank You, God*, Lois breathed. *There's a hole in the clouds! There is a way down!*

The plane descended through the little opening in the clouds, and in a few minutes, its tires splashed onto an airstrip. When they came to a stop, Barbara, Emily, Lois, and the boys made their way down the steps and stood with the others in the puddles beside the plane.

"Is this our place?" Lois asked.

"No," Barbara answered, "this is Bassein (Pathein). Myaungmya is a fifteen-minute flight from here."

In just a few minutes, the weather had cleared sufficiently for them to take off again. This time, it seemed the plane had scarcely reached cruising altitude before it was descending for its final approach into Myaungmya. The ladies caught a bus to the school.

FIGURE 5.2 *The bus that traveled between the Myaungmya Training School and surrounding villages. Undated photograph, circa 1952. Photographer Lois Anderson.*

Upon their arrival, Barbara confessed, "My legs have just about stopped shaking. How are yours?"

"I have to admit mine are still wobbly," Lois replied. "It is so good to be on the ground again! I don't know why the whole trip made me so uneasy. I knew all along the Lord could care for us just as well in the air as in the middle of a storm on the ocean." She shook her head. "It is something I can't explain. Fear got into me, and the more I struggled with it, the more it entangled me. I can sympathize now with people who are afraid of something that I may not be."

Gene took a break from his work to show Lois and the boys around the beautiful campus. The staff welcomed them warmly and were eager to ease the Andersons into their new life in Burma. There were four brick buildings on campus and several others attractively constructed from bamboo matting. The rains had begun, and the lawns were turning green. The grounds were tidy, with beds of canna lilies and other flowers. Many varieties of trees—such as mango, cashew, and guava—provided both shade and delicious fruit.

The girls on campus were planting gladiolus, which they hoped to sell when the plants bloomed. The boys were pounding crushed brick into the driveways to elevate them to keep the mud from accumulating during the monsoon season.

FIGURE 5.3 *David, Leslie, and their young friend, Emily Wyman, standing by the main gate of Myaungmya Training School. Undated photograph, circa 1952. Left to right: Leslie, Emily, and David. Photographer Lois Anderson.*

FIGURE 5.4 *David and Leslie in the yard in front of the Myaungmya Training School administration building. Front left (running): Leslie. Center (standing): David. Undated photograph, circa 1952. Photographer Lois Anderson.*

The tour concluded at their new house. With her first inspection, Lois knew she could make it homey and livable. She had brought yards of cheesecloth for making curtains. Starched stiff, they would look cool and airy. The baggage from the boat had already arrived; Pastor Wyman had brought it with some more of their things from Rangoon. Everything was stacked in the living room, waiting to be put away. The boys found a set of shelves. Under Lois's supervision, they scrubbed the shelves and unpacked the trunk.

FIGURE 5.5 *The Anderson's house in Myaungmya. Undated photograph, circa 1952. Photographer Lois Anderson.*

The first evening the family was together, they were invited to the home of Mr. and Mrs. Thra Peter, who served them a delicious dinner of rice, curry, and onion patties. Any reader of Elder Eric B. Hare's books about his mission experiences in Burma should recognize the name Thra Peter: he was one of the first converts in Burma. The Andersons felt very honored to be in the Peter's home and imagined themselves living one of the Dr. Rabbit[19] stories they had read as children. Mr. Peter had gone through some incredible experiences with Elder Hare.

FIGURE 5.6 *Student body and staff at Myaungmya Training School, 1952. Second row, far right: David. Third row, center (behind girl with the long braids): Gene and Lois. Sixth row, fifth from right (looking up at the sky): Leslie. Undated photograph, circa 1952. Photographer unknown.*

The campus was a busy place with an enrollment of 160 students. Most afternoons, David and Leslie watched the boys play soccer in the field across from the Anderson's driveway—and often went out to talk with the players. The school's sidecar also intrigued them with its two seats on the side of a bicycle: one facing forward and the other facing backward. They loved to catch a ride in it or on the ox cart. The oxen were as gentle as lambs, and the students drove or pulled them around. The school had four oxen and two carts. David and Leslie thrived in this lively campus environment.

FIGURE 5.7 *Gentle oxen on the Myaungmya Training School campus. Undated photograph, Circa 1952. Photographer Lois Anderson.*

FIGURE 5.8 *Leslie on the Myaungmya Training School campus with a python on his lap. Undated photograph, circa 1952. Photographer Lois Anderson.*

Worship for the students was every morning at six, with the boys meeting in the chapel and the girls in their dormitory a little farther away. Their singing drifted across the campus; it was a beautiful way to begin each day.

Lois heard one of the boys' groups sing at church and offered to work with them when they practiced.

The boys were excited about the idea. "When can you help us with our music?"

"Let's get together this evening before study period," she suggested.

Seven of the young men came. They chose a song from *Gospel Melodies*.[20] They knew practically every song in the book and sang a cappella. The leader gave the pitch, the rest hummed their notes, and away they went. They needed practice with starting the first word together and staying in time with each other, but their voices were strong and full. Lois didn't know how they had learned to understand music—but they knew how to harmonize, and that thrilled her.

One evening Lois was playing her accordion at home. Soon some boys were standing on the porch looking in the window. The next evening after vespers, they came again and told David and Leslie, "Tell your mama to play," while they mimicked playing the accordion. They were invited inside, sat on the floor, and sang along as Lois played her accordion. As they were leaving, they said, "Thank you, Mama."

Peddlers regularly came to the house, supplying them with eggs and bananas. The eggs were sold by sevens. Lois usually bought twenty-one for three rupees.

"Why do they sell them by sevens?" Leslie asked. "Don't they have enough hens to ever get a dozen?"

Once, a lady came with big stalks of bananas, selling them for five rupees a stalk. Lois bought one stalk, but the bananas did not ripen. The next time the lady returned with more stalks, Lois told her that the bananas had not ripened.

"Put a cloth around them and hang them over the charcoal fire," the banana lady said. Lois followed this tip and it worked, so the next time she bought two more stalks. The bananas were huge, and the family never tired of eating them.

One of several wells on campus had recently been reconditioned. Since the water was murky when first pumped, the family was advised to boil their drinking water. They also needed to scrub all their fruit with soap and water and disinfect the vegetables with a chlorine solution.

Lois hired two girls, Than Kyi and Maureen Montgomery, to help with the extra home chores. Than Kyi's parents had unofficially adopted her. She had never attended school, but she had wanted to for a long time. She used to beg to come to Myaungmya. This year, her parents had finally given their permission, but she had to start in the equivalent of first grade. She loved to sing as she worked in the kitchen. The second girl, Maureen, took care of the laundry and housecleaning. Both girls were faithful workers, and the Andersons felt blessed to have them.

Lois asked Than Kyi, "What do you want to do when you finish school?"

She replied, "I want to be a missionary."

"Where would you like to go?"

"Out to a village where no one has gone yet."

Some members of the Union Committee were expected to arrive soon. Maureen worked hard, scrubbing mildew off walls and polishing the floors with beeswax and kerosene, making everything clean and fresh.

"It is a big job to keep the house clean," Lois explained to those back home. "You really have no idea unless you have lived in a wet, warm climate. It more than doubles the work."

FIGURE 5.9 *Four female students (names unknown) on the Myaungmya Training School campus. Undated photograph, circa 1952. Photographer Lois Anderson.*

The Andersons were to host Elder and Mrs. Pierson and their fifteen-year-old son, Bob, and the Guilds were to stay with the Wymans. Everything seemed to unravel in the hours preceding their arrival. First, there was no water for two or three days—which meant all home chores took much longer than usual to complete. Then water got in the oil line for the kerosene stove, and the stove kept going out. Lois was cooking rice in milk. She planned to add bananas, coconut cream, and pineapple to the cooked rice to make a special pudding for her company—but every time she checked her rice, it was dry, and the fire was out. After adding more milk and re-lighting the fire again and again, the rice had expanded to the top of the kettle. She used about a third of the rice for pudding and incorporated the rest into a variety of dishes to serve her guests. Judging by the way the food disappeared at each meal, everyone was satisfied with her efforts.

A new generator had recently arrived from PUC, running 110V current to all the campus buildings and providing lights from 7-9 p.m. Everyone was happy for this new convenience.

At night, after the lights were out and darkness blanketed the campus, an unfamiliar and ever-changing night concert began. From a little village way off through the jungle came the beating of drums.

Lois described it in these words:

> The rhythm is certainly different from anything you ever hear in the States, and it changes often. To follow the accent in this drum rhythm seems impossible at first, although you can feel it easily. Sometimes the third count is strong, sometimes it's the fifth, and sometimes two or three different beats get the accent. It is really very complicated. Then, suddenly it stops, and you are left with both feet off the ground.

Or the Tuktoo—a fat, striped lizard that was everywhere—might be heard. After noisily clearing his throat, he would call his name *tuk-to-o, tuk-to-o, tuk-to-o*, in a startling and explosive manner, until he ran out of breath.

Sometimes the family awakened to the sound of wings beating close by. These were the bats or "flying foxes" that flew around the house every night. They were mammoth, having a wingspan of five or six feet. The family's eyes bulged the first time they saw dozens of them flying overhead. A trip into town revealed the bat's daytime hangout: a huge tree about the size of a cottonwood, thick with bats hanging upside down. At night, the bats feasted on the guava trees by the Anderson's house, which explained why there was seldom any fruit for the family to enjoy.

Lois recounted another night phenomenon:

> Once you decide to close your eyes, suddenly you detect a light moving about in the living room. Your hair begins to creep on the back of your neck. You raise your head to get a clearer view. Yes, a light is moving in the other room. Then it

goes off, and then on again. There's absolutely no noise. What in the world? Off again, on again. But, of course, it's a firefly.

At about four every morning, the ox carts began to pass by the entrance to the school on their way to work in the country. The horrendous screeching of their wheels always woke the family from sound sleep.

Lois said to Gene one morning, "I feel that I no sooner get up than it's time to go to bed again."

Gene wisecracked, "I no sooner get in bed than it's time to get up again!"

"It's all in your point of view," Lois countered. "But as soon as we start the day, there is no stopping till it's time to get in bed again."

Gene soon learned that principal of Myaungmya Training School (Myanmar Union Adventist Seminary) had a much broader scope than principal of a small school in California. He taught two classes to the eleventh-grade students: Denominational History in the first semester and Spirit of Prophecy in the second. He taught English both semesters.

Balancing the school budget was his responsibility, as was personally purchasing all larger, higher-priced items and approving various departmental requests. He oversaw student work assignments and the teachers who supervised the study hall, as well as four full-time hired personnel: a farm manager, a carpenter, a maintenance man, and a matron.

Every Sunday evening, he led out in the faculty meetings, counseled and encouraged the deans, and suggested better teaching and grading methods for the teachers. There were fourteen other teachers on staff.

FIGURE 5.10 The staff at Myaungmya Training School. Undated photograph, circa 1952. Photographer unknown.

Gene also handled the registrar's work, compiled students' grades every six weeks, authorized all absences, and processed the time cards. He arranged for weekly chapel speakers. If the teacher or guest speaker failed to appear—as happened on several occasions—he filled in for them. Planning for evangelism fell into his job description, as did meeting with government officials and showing interested persons around the campus. He also served on the Burma Union committee and school board.

While carrying out his daily duties, Gene studied ways to improve the operations of the school. He wanted to put in a tube well with a pump so they could irrigate and keep the campus and gardens green during the dry season and not have to draw up water in a bucket.

He also believed the farm could increase production by adding more gardens and setting out more fruit trees. He longed for a tractor as he watched the students digging up the ground with hand tools—or at best, with an ox team. If they owned a tractor, they could do so much more with the sixty-three acres the school owned.

His third dream was for an engine-driven sawmill, which would provide the school with a profitable industry, as well as materials to keep their own buildings maintained. Every piece of wood was so precious, the Andersons kept all their packing boxes and used them for tables and bookcases.

When Gene pulled a badly infected molar from his first patient, he joked that he had taken up a new profession, although the medical work performed was serious enough. Many times, he comforted people who were ill or facing difficult situations and needed assurance that God was able to keep them in His loving care.

Lois was also busy. She taught her own boys, as well as three classes for the school students: English for the seventh and ninth grades and sewing for the seventh- and eighth-grade girls. At first, it was difficult trying to organize her home while also preparing for classes. Once she got into a routine, it became easier.

The Anderson's day began at six, and the family ate breakfast at seven. Lois started David and Leslie with their first two classes, which went from a quarter after seven to a quarter after nine. Then she taught an English class at school and another class for David and Leslie, which was followed by chapel and another English class. That took them to noon. While she prepared lunch, the boys worked on their Bible lessons. After the meal, there was a brief rest period. The afternoon was spent writing letters or studying. Lois gave piano lessons to a student, trumpet lessons to David, and trombone lessons to Leslie—and somehow still fit in time for her own piano practice.

FIGURE 5.11 Lois shopping at the Maungmya market. Undated photograph, circa 1953. Photographer unknown.

One evening, she went to meet with her sixth-standard English class. The sixth standard was equivalent to seventh grade and was the first year the students had all their classes taught in English. It was difficult for them, and there were some who seemed to be having trouble understanding their assignments. Lois asked if they wanted to meet with her in the classroom for extra help. She thought maybe five or six might come, but everyone did! They were so earnest and eager to learn.

She enjoyed spending extra time with them. Never had any project challenged and inspired her like working with this group. She put a list of nouns, verbs, and adjectives on the blackboard, and they made sentences using them. When she left, they said, "Thank you." She told them they were a good class, and they responded, "Wonderful class." (She had used "wonderful class" once as an illustration.)

Lois loved dropping in on the students at mealtimes. They all came into the dining room and stood by the tables. The gong sounded and one of the students asked the blessing. Everyone responded with an "Amen" and hurried into line to get a tin plate heaped with rice, a steaming bowl of vegetable curry, and an onion or dahl cake. They chattered happily as they ate, then went back for more. They could eat all they wanted. Mrs. Ohn Myint oversaw all the kitchen and dining room details, which included preparing three meals a day for 160 students, as well as buying the food and necessary supplies. She seemed to rely on Lois a great deal. Lois really knew nothing of the local foods or prices but was confident she would soon be able to give helpful assistance.

FIGURE 5.12 Nora Guild and Mrs. Ohn Myint, the dining room matron, enjoy a meal together at the Myaungmya Training School. Undated photograph, circa 1952. Left to right: Nora Guild, Mrs. Ohn Myint. Man in background: name unknown. Photographer Lois Anderson.

FIGURE 5.13 The Myaungmya Training School kitchen staff preparing food. Undated photograph, circa 1952. Photographer Lois Anderson.

Sayama Assa was the dean of girls, and she wanted Lois to teach her how to be a better dean. She was a lovely young woman who had graduated from Spicer College in Poona, India, a year or so before. "Sayama" in the dean's name was a title identifying her as a female teacher. The male teachers had the title of "Saya," and the principal was called "Sayagee," which meant the "big teacher."

David and Leslie began taking Burmese lessons from Saya Aung Win, the boys' dean. He was a fine young man who had finished the ninth standard (eleventh grade) and planned to further his education.

The teachers supervised study hall in the library on a rotating schedule so no one person had to do it every night. Lois's turn came about every two weeks. The young people were so responsive and loving, it was a pleasure to work with them.

Lois and Barbara Wyman also took turns playing the piano for the various services. Lois played for vespers Friday night, for Thursday chapel, for choir practice, and for church. Barbara played for Sabbath school and Missionary Volunteer meetings.

It was a very busy program, with many random requests and special assignments, but Lois and Gene had never felt more content. Both were in awe when they realized how many people's destinies were being shaped on that campus.

The missionaries were often given the opportunity to share their faith through medical ministry. Half a mile down the road was a large Buddhist school. One of their men was sick, and they asked for help from the Adventist missionaries. They also requested a Bible and were willing for Gene and Brother Wyman to pray. In a room surrounded by young men with shaved heads and bright orange robes, Gene and Brother Wyman stood with heads bowed and prayed to the living God on behalf of the sick man. Their prayers were answered, and the sick man got better.

It was a very busy program, with many random requests and special assignments, but Lois and Gene had never felt more content. Both were in awe when they realized how many people's destinies were being shaped on that campus.

Another fellow from a village near the school compound came with a jaw so badly infected he couldn't open his mouth. Refusing to go to the hospital, he came to the school and said, "I want you to pray to your God, and I will get well." They prayed for him, and he did get well.

The Myaungmya boarding school played an important role in Burma as the place where Adventist teachers and lay preachers were trained to go out to the villages and carry on the church work. Overseas personnel were often not at liberty to go into the outlying districts, so the teaching and preaching needed to be done by national workers. Spicer College in

India was the only other educational institution in the region, but because of the cost of tuition and the difficulty of obtaining traveling papers, very few could go there.

At that time, there were eighteen or twenty jungle schools being operated by faithful young people, some of whom had no more than a fifth-grade education. When a student learned what he could in the jungle school and wished to continue his education, he was sent to the training school in Myaungmya. One dedicated young man and his wife oversaw two jungle schools a day's travel apart. The husband's was a small boarding school where he fed and cared for about forty students by himself. Gene and Lois hoped the young couple wouldn't have to start another year separated from each other but also knew that committed people like them would finish the work.

When it came time for the mid-year vacation, many students were anxious to go home to visit their families. They left the campus in small groups, as it was not wise to travel anywhere alone due to the civil unrest. A few rode away in sidecars, but most walked, carrying a rolled-up bamboo mat for their bed and a bag with all their other possessions over their shoulders. Some had to travel up to four days and nights to reach their families—only to discover that their homes had been burned down and their folks were hiding in the jungle. When the vacation was over, many of the students expressed how glad they were to be back at school.

There were two main religious groups in this area of Burma: Buddhists and Baptists. The training school had several Baptist students, even though there was a Baptist school just a few miles away. The faculty was particularly interested in Chit Hlaing, a Baptist boy who had spent almost two years at Myaungmya. His brother attended the Baptist school.

Chit Hlaing got himself into a minor difficulty and was restricted to the campus as a result. His brother came to see him before going home for a visit and urged him to come home too. Chit Hlaing replied that he was not at liberty to go, but at his brother's persistent urging, he finally went. That resulted in further restrictions for him. When mid-year vacation arrived, the faculty decided he should remain at school. He realized he had involved himself in a lot more trouble than he had intended and was willing to accept his discipline.

When Chit Hlaing's parents were notified that he was being kept on campus during the mid-year vacation, they demanded that he come home and immediately enrolled him in the Baptist school. Chit Hlaing was very unhappy about that and vowed he would return to Myaungmya as soon as he could. He felt that he would lose his Christian character if he stayed away from the Myaungmya boarding school, and he wanted to become a Seventh-day Adventist. He attended church the next Sabbath, so evidently, he meant what he said. The staff prayed that their influence would help Chit Hlaing stand firm for what he knew to be right.

Though the young people at the training school did not have the same opportunities as their counterparts in America, the Holy Spirit was speaking to their hearts too. When an invitation was extended to all those who wanted to be baptized, the staff was encouraged by the response. One of the older boys said, "When I saw so many choose to be Christians, I felt so wonderful and happy."

At another chapel service, a call was made for students to colporteur during the summer, and twenty-six responded. Selling books door to door was not easy in the heat, but they chose to go anyway.

Elder Ritchie from the Southern Asia Division was scheduled as guest speaker for Week of Prayer. He was to start with the church service on a Sabbath, but he hadn't sent word about what his theme would be. He did not arrive on the appointed day, and that evening, a letter came stating he couldn't come until Tuesday. He asked them to start the week without him and said he would finish it.

On the spot, Gene had to think of a theme, plan the sermon for Sabbath, and carry through with the morning chapel service and evening worship until Elder Ritchie arrived. Tuesday dawned, but Elder Ritchie did not show. On Wednesday, there was still no Elder Ritchie.

About noon on Wednesday, Brother Mya Pe, the educational superintendent from the Burma Union, arrived on campus. He said it had been impossible to obtain the required government travel permit for Elder Ritchie, so Elder Ritchie would not be coming at all. Brother Mya Pe took over Week of Prayer and finished it with excellent results. Gene's heart was thrilled as he listened to the students testify for Jesus.

After Week of Prayer, the school plunged into what the Burmese called Uplifting Work—or as it was termed in America, Harvest Ingathering. The school and Union were given a goal of 9,000 rupees to raise by means of donations from various businesses. Gene and the Missionary Volunteer Secretary for the Union—a fine Burmese fellow who lived on the school compound—took the lead. They began by going to the well-to-do merchants and rice millers, then took a group of students to Wahama, a village about four hours away by riverboat. They spent two nights in Wahama, and the next week, took a different group to Boisin for two or three days. The funds raised were used in mission work.

Rainy season—the monsoon—was in full swing and lasted from May through October. It began with sporadic rainstorms. One minute the rain poured so hard it seemed as though buckets of water were being turned upside down. Then, just as quickly, the day would be bright and clear, with blue skies and fleecy white clouds sailing over the coconut palms.

But when the rains began in earnest, the Andersons often did not see the sun for weeks. Unpaved roads became quagmires as patient oxen or water buffalo pulled their heavy wooden-wheeled carts through the chocolate-colored morass. The earth trembled as thunder roared and lightning stabbed spears into the ground. "Rivers of water poured from the raging sky, turning happy little rivulets into angry monsters—roaring, spitting, frothing, and snatching anything in their reach," was Lois's monsoon description in a letter she wrote to the family at home. Surprisingly, these oceans of water were absorbed by the many rivers, lakes, and ponds; so life went on without devastating floods.

Houses stayed damp, and mold grew on everything—not just a few specks, but in large amounts. If shoes had not been worn for twenty-four hours, they were blue with mold. It was warm but not unbearable. The Andersons never needed coats or sweaters and slept with only sheets for covers at night. Because mosquitoes were a big problem, Lois made nets for each of the beds from the yards of cheesecloth she had planned to sew into curtains.

The Andersons were aware that a civil revolt could flare up at any time, and one day an insurgent band burned villages out past the school. The displaced villagers streamed onto the campus, carrying baskets with their possessions and driving their cows before them.

A scout plane flew over just as the family was eating lunch. Gene said, "Listen. You might hear firing." He had no sooner spoken than the terrible sound of Bren guns[21] began. They kept up for some time, then all was quiet again.

The scout plane continued flying over, drawing more ground fire, and sometimes loud explosions shook the buildings. On several nights, the family heard gun shots close by, so they noiselessly rolled out of their beds and laid on the floor as the volley of bullets passed over their house. They remained on the floor until all was quiet again.

Lois summed up this experience in a letter:

The strange thing through all of this is that we have felt no fear at all. I am sure it is a gift from the Lord. I have been afraid twice since we came—once in the plane, and again the first time we heard a rumor of an attack. I prayed for the Lord to give me more faith and trust. I thank Him that He has. Most of the teachers are so afraid. I feel sorry for them. Gene has been encouraging them to keep their faith strong. He has been a rock of inspiration. We do not know what another day will bring. We can only leave it all in God's hands and let Him lead us each moment.

Many soldiers were stationed around the school property. Occasionally, one came onto the compound. A rumor had been circulating that the school was harboring the insurgents. Whether the head of the army believed that or not, the staff didn't know. The school body kept calm. They didn't miss a day of classes, and only a handful of the students went home for a few days when the conflict was at its worst.

Gene said, "We really do not know if the insurgents are quiet now or where they are. We do not ask. We just go on and live and work each day as though there was nothing different. The Lord has richly blessed in keeping our school safe and calm."

Lois humorously described an important event that she and Gene attended at this time:

> We were asked to come into town to join in a celebration to honor the army. There was a parade that would end at the high school where the festivities would be held. I hadn't planned on being seen in the big crowd. I was wearing my mismatched work clothes and did not take time to change. We went to the high school to find someone who could present our bouquet of asters to the army officers as a token of our thankfulness for the protection the soldiers had provided for our compound. We decided to wait there until the parade came back.
>
> Soon some of the women came and asked me to sit inside with them. I, of course, couldn't talk with them, but we smiled anyway. They were all dressed in their best longyis with plenty of gold jewelry on display.
>
> One lady, who spoke English well, came and sat with me. She told me she was getting the Signs[22] and liked the magazine very much. She also said she regularly listened to the Voice of Prophecy.[23] I really appreciated the opportunity to visit with this fine woman.
>
> After a while, she took me to the front row on the reviewing stand. I felt I was getting a little too far out in the front, but I couldn't refuse such graciousness. Another nice lady shared her umbrella with me, as it was getting hot.

Word came to me that I was to be the one to present the flowers at the proper time to the proper person. Me? In my old clothes and with a bandana on my head? But I couldn't back out now, so I tried to remain calm and hoped I would be able to pick up appropriate cues when it was my turn to be in the spotlight.

The soldiers came and formed three sides of a square, with the open side facing the reviewing stand. They were hot and tired after marching two hours around town. Following their demonstrations of martial maneuvers, a Burmese man gave a lengthy speech over the loudspeaker. I couldn't understand a word, except my name. I watched the district supervisor of police who was right in front of me. He seemed to be in charge. I decided he was not the one to receive the flowers, but who was?

I kept watching this same man closely. He nodded slightly, and I stepped out. He told me how far to go by a motion of his hand. An officer stepped from the center of the square, came to me, bowed, cameras clicked, and I presented our flowers to him. Then we both returned to our places.

I realized that I had been given a place of honor and felt very humbled. The ladies were so kind and gracious, treating me with respect and courtesy. They all waved and smiled as we left.

We were told later that they all appreciated very much our coming and joining in the celebration. The officer who received the flowers was the chief over all the soldiers, and he made the statement, "If there is anything we can do to help the people at the boarding school, we will surely do it."

We also learned that the kind woman who invited me to sit with her and told me she regularly listens to the Voice of Prophecy is the wife of the district supervisor of police. So, we were glad we went and showed them how we felt.

Gene had noted the areas in lower Burma that had been influenced by the Seventh-day Adventist church. For years, the work had been concentrated around Rangoon, Myaungmya, and the delta, but it was growing very slowly. Farther up the Irrawaddy River were Mandalay and Maymyo, and that was as far north as the mission efforts had reached.

FIGURE 5.14 Lois presents a bouquet of flowers as a thank you to the army commander during a large celebration at the Myaungmya high school. Undated photograph, circa 1952. Photographer unknown.

The Burma Union owned property due south of Mandalay at Meiktila, where they previously had a school. Some of the buildings were occupied by army personnel, though the church still owned the land. The number of churches in lower Burma could be counted on one hand. Gene wondered why there had been so little progress.

He was not the only one to see the problem. At the Burma Union year-end committee meetings in December 1952, plans were discussed at length for entering the northern part of Burma. A recent report had come that there were at least a thousand Nagas[24] who were calling themselves Seventh-day Adventists and keeping the Sabbath. The Nagas were a tribe who lived north of the Chin Hills, along the India-Burma border. Everything they had learned had come from one of their members—a former Baptist who had become a Seventh-day Adventist. He had been working for his own people who were accepting the Adventist message by the hundreds, but there was no one to help him. Willis and Helen Lowry were stationed in the Lushai Hills of India along the Burma border, where the people were also accepting the Seventh-day Adventist message and asking for more teachers.

The men of the Southern Asia Division had never seen this kind of interest and activity in the region, nor had there ever been a worker in the northern hills of Burma. With the people pleading for someone to come and teach them, the area seemed to be fertile ground for a wonderful outpouring of the Holy Spirit.

During the meetings, Elder Pierson and other division personnel focused attention on this part of the country. "We have had workers in lower Burma for years, but never have we sent anyone to upper Burma," the chairman said. "Is there anyone here who feels a burden to take our message to this remote region?"

Gene immediately rose to his feet. "I am willing to go—if this meets with the committee's approval and if the Lord wills it."

This sounded very similar to what occurred at the 1868 General Conference session when Elder James White had asked, "Is there someone here who would be willing to go to the faraway mission field of California?" *(See Appendix 1: Gene Anderson's Adventist Ancestry.)*

Elder Pierson was sitting beside Gene and watching him intently. He leaned over and said, "Brother Anderson, you have before you the greatest challenge open to anyone in the Southern Asia Division today!" Elder Pierson was committed to the opening of this new work, as was Elder Guild, the Burma Union president.

On his way back to the division headquarters in Poona, India, Elder Pierson visited the Assam Mission of Seventh-day Adventists in Nongthymmai, Shillong, Assam. He told the brethren there about the decision to send the Andersons to the Chin Hills. In response, Brother Lowry related thrilling stories of gospel-sharing opportunities in that part of the world and across the border into the northwestern regions of Burma. He told Elder Pierson that there were two Lushai workers who could be sent to assist Gene with the work of establishing a Seventh-day Adventist mission in the Chin Hills. While still at the Assam Mission, Elder Pierson conveyed this information in a letter to Elder Guild. *(See Appendix 2.)*

The more Gene and Lois thought about what was involved in their new assignment, the bigger it seemed and the smaller they felt. How could they ever accomplish what was expected of them? Gene's new position would be director of the North Burma Mission—but, of course, there was no mission yet. Whatever would be done was up to him to do.

The family remembered Elder Pierson's visit with them back at PUC when he asked them how they felt about possibly taking the message to a brand-new field. They had been open to the idea and responded positively. Quite possibly, the Union committee had thought about and discussed the idea of the Andersons going to North Burma for some time.

With a heart full of awe and praise for God's leading, Lois exclaimed, "So, it looks like a real adventure, with God going ahead and right along with us all the way. What more wonderful thing could anyone want?"

Chapter 6

When an Answer Is Needed, Pray

"Be anxious for nothing, but in everything by prayer and supplication, with thanksgiving, let your requests be made known to God."

—Philippians 4:6

How remote Myaungmya had seemed when the Andersons had arrived in Burma. Now they had the same thoughts about the Chin Hills. The Burma Union and Southern Asia Division would give them as much support as possible—and would expect to receive regular reports of their progress—but everyone knew it would be a difficult assignment. Gene and Lois reminded themselves that their first year of mission service had not been easy either, but it had taught them so much. They suspected that the new assignment would mean many more things to learn, beginning with facts about the people and geography of the area.

Gene recorded all the information he could find about northern Burma:

> Along the western side of Burma lies a vast range of mountains known as the Chin Hills. This area extends from lower Burma north to the Manipur State, which is the most easterly part of India. The peoples of these hills are known as Chins. They are peaceful, hardworking, honest, and dependable. It is said that there are approximately forty different dialects to be found within their race. In the northern section, the three most prominent dialects are the Haka, Lailo, and Kamhau. In addition to these numerous Chin groups are many Lushai people who have migrated into the Chin Hills from the bordering Lushai Hills of India.

The majority of the inhabitants are cultivators, their principal crop being corn, called vaimin, grown on the steep mountainsides. Sometimes their fields are located several miles from their home village. They have continued the age-old practice of burning their garden plots every year during the dry season, causing a pall of smoke to scarf the hilltops and settle in the canyons. The fire-scarred, denuded landscape is stripped of trees, presumably for firewood, and large areas are cleared for gardens.

The terrain is rugged, particularly in the northern section. The mountain ranges run from south to north, being cut or separated by deep canyons. The elevation ranges from near sea level along the Manipur River to over 9,000 feet on some of the mountain peaks. Travel is difficult throughout this entire area, being accomplished only on foot.

David and Leslie were excited beyond words about the upcoming move, but, of course, their initial thoughts were of adventure. Gene and Lois's personal feelings were not of elation but the realization of a tremendous job to be done. They would experience firsthand what it would be like to depend completely on the Lord to supply all their needs.

The division committee spoke with Dr. George Richardson and asked if both Gene and Lois could spend a few weeks in Rangoon to receive as much medical training as they could squeeze into a limited timeframe. Dollis Pierson directed the division's Home Commission, which provided information and resources for better homes and health. Once Lois arrived in the Chin Hills, she would be relying on Mrs. Pierson's support.

The Burma Union hoped to send more workers to join the Andersons as soon as possible, but, for the first year, the family would settle in and establish a mission presence. To Gene and Lois, the anticipated move seemed stupendous, and they prayed for wisdom and strength to rightly represent God in this part of the world.

When the school term at Myaungmya ended in March, the Andersons moved to Rangoon to prepare for their new assignment. Additionally, they were eagerly looking forward to another marvelous event: they were expecting to welcome a fifth member to the family by the end of May.

Lois was delighted. She had waited a long time for this baby, and although the mission field was difficult in many ways, she felt children were needed to help families be a happy unit. With the inevitability of Gene's frequent absences, she and the boys would be more than glad to have a little person to keep them entertained while he was away. Everyone hoped the baby would be a girl. It was so strong already, though, that Lois guessed it was a boy. The family would wait until the baby was six months old before they moved to the Chin Hills.

The arrival of a baby meant many extra preparations before their departure. Lois had found good-quality flannel for thirty-five cents a yard in Myaungmya and had bought many yards. While waiting in Rangoon, she used her treadle machine to sew a complete wardrobe for the baby, as well as the warm nightclothes the rest of the family would need for the colder climate of the Chin Hills.

Gene—along with Pastor Guild, Brother Robert Mya Pe, and Brother Freddie Batin—began praying for God's guidance as they planned the itinerary for an extended trip to the area. Their immediate goal was to find a suitable location for the new mission—preferably near an airport—and a place that could provide adequate supplies and regular mail service.

When the school term at Myaungmya ended in March, the Andersons moved to Rangoon to prepare for their new assignment. Additionally, they were eagerly looking forward to another marvelous event: they were expecting to welcome a fifth member to the family.

In early April, the four men left Rangoon on their exploratory trip. En route, they discussed how they would introduce themselves when they landed at Kalemyo. They decided to say, "We represent the *Voice of Prophecy*," since they knew that the *Voice of Prophecy* was broadcasting from Ceylon (Sri Lanka) to this part of the world. They were thankful that the plane would arrive early enough for them to find transportation up to Tedim that same day.

When the airplane landed and the door opened, they noticed a pleasant young man approaching the foot of the stairs. He held out his hand and greeted them with a smile. He introduced himself as Go Za Kham and politely asked who they were and where they were going.

FIGURE 6.1 Gene and the three Burma Union officers fly into Kalemyo on a DC-3 for their initial visit to the Chin Hills. Undated photograph, circa 1953. Photographer unknown.

FIGURE 6.2 Go Za Kham, who met the men at the Kalemyo airport. Undated photograph, circa 1953. Photographer unknown.

As they had agreed, Pastor Guild spoke for the group. "We are here to find the *Voice of Prophecy* Bible correspondence course students. Do you know of anyone who has taken this Bible course?"

Go Za Kham's face lit up. "The *Voice of Prophecy*!" he exclaimed. "I am a graduate of that school, the first one in the Chin Hills to receive a certificate of completion. I am so glad you have come!"

The visiting brethren felt this initial contact, made before they even collected their luggage, was a clear indication that God was leading them to the people they needed to see. Go Za Kham lived in Tedim and was the assistant pastor of a Baptist church there. He had been sent to Kalemyo to welcome a Baptist missionary who was to have been on the same flight. He had studied the *Voice of Prophecy* Bible lessons with keen interest and had learned that it was sponsored by the Seventh-day Adventist church, but he did not know that this church was active in Burma. He was astonished to learn that the visiting men were Seventh-day Adventist missionaries and was anxious to see them again when they came to Tedim. He hoped they could clear up some of the questions he had about things he had studied in his Bible lessons, though he knew he would face challenges because of such a visit.

> *Go Za Kham's face lit up. "The Voice of Prophecy!" he exclaimed. "I am a graduate of that school, the first one in the Chin Hills to receive a certificate of completion. I am so glad you have come!"*

The four men hired a Jeep and spent two weeks in the towns of Kalemyo, nearby Tahan, and Tedim, another fifty miles farther up the mountains. The people of the region were receptive to the visitors' proposed plans and the message they shared. The headman of Tedim was friendly and helpful and invited them to come again. His son also showed genuine interest. The government officer stationed at Tedim assisted them in many ways as well. In fact, everyone they contacted responded with an open and gracious spirit. Greatly encouraged by the results of their first visit, they prepared to return home.

They hadn't made plane reservations for Rangoon, so only Pastor Guild and Gene were able to purchase tickets for the outward-bound flight. They had just fastened their seat belts when the pilot tapped them on the shoulders and said, "I am sorry to have to tell you this, but the booking agent has miscounted, and we have room for only one of you."

FIGURE 6.3 Gene and companions stop on the narrow road to Tedim to take a photo of the steep terrain and distant mountains, April 1953. Front seat: Freddie Batin, driver (name unknown). Back seat: Gene Anderson, Robert Mya Pe. Photographer C. B. Guild.

Neither man wanted to leave the other to spend Sabbath in Kalemyo, so both disembarked and joined the other two members of their party, who had already planned to remain in the hot, dusty village until the next plane out, several days later. No one complained about the delay, because all of them felt that God had some purpose in it, even if they didn't understand what that purpose was. They did, however, make four reservations for the next Rangoon flight.

That evening, brethren Mya Pe and Batin felt impressed to go back to Tahan, a village about three miles away. When they returned, they brought the amazing news that they had found two young Lushai men who were keeping the Sabbath. The next day, these Lushai young people and half a dozen of their friends came to spend a delightful Sabbath with the missionaries. The missed flight resulted in a meeting that had far-reaching results.

The day for the return to Rangoon finally arrived. All four men were anxious to be on their way home to their families. They purchased their tickets, weighed in their luggage, and waited for the big Dakota to come thundering across the airstrip at the base of the towering Chin Hills.

Suddenly, the air agent looked up at Pastor Guild and asked, "Are you Mr. C. B. Guild?"

"Yes," answered Pastor Guild.

"Well," the agent continued, "I have a telegram for you."

FIGURE 6.4 Freddie Batin (on right) talks with a young man (name unknown) in Tahan. Undated photograph, circa 1953. Photographer Gene Anderson.

The telegram was from Elder Pierson in India. It simply read: "Willis Lowry will meet you at Rih Lake at the border."

The brethren looked blankly at each other. They were already out of the Chin Hills, ready to return to Rangoon. They wanted to meet Pastor Lowry, of course, but to do so would mean a drastic revision of plans. It was quickly decided that Pastor Guild and Brother Freddie Batin would continue to Rangoon, as planned, and that Brother Robert Mya Pe and Gene would stay.

When the plane was ready to leave, Gene and Robert bade their companions goodbye and began walking down the tree-lined street of Kalemyo, praying and planning as they went. Their first task was to find someone who could speak the Chin language and would be willing to accompany them as their interpreter. Suddenly, they spotted Rualchhina Vangchhia, one of the young men who had met with them in Sabbath school the day before. He had been a student at the Adventist mission school in Assam, India, and was a Lushai—the ethnic group who occupied the area of northeast India just west of the Chin Hills. The Chin and Lushai languages were different but had enough similarities that the speakers could understand each other to some degree. Rualchhina had come to Burma hoping to get a job in the ruby mines but had been unsuccessful. Gene asked him if he would be willing to accompany them to Rih Lake, and Rualchhina consented.

The three men were fortunate to find passage on a truck going to Tedim that same day. Since the fifty-mile road was quite narrow, the traffic between Tedim and Kalemyo was controlled: uphill traffic one day and downhill the next. In Tedim, Gene found two brothers, Thang Hau and Tual Za Do, who said they knew the way to Rih Lake. He hired them to carry his bedroll and supplies and to be guides on the trail. Plans went well, for which Gene was grateful. By nightfall, all arrangements had been made for the trek to the border.

Early the next morning, Gene and his four companions left Tedim for Rih Lake, a four-day, round-trip hike over steep mountain trails. The path descended from Tedim to the Manipur River, and by midmorning they crossed the river on the long, swinging-cable bridge and began the steep climb out of the canyon.

FIGURE 6.5 *Swinging bridge over the Manipur River. Undated photograph, circa 1953. Photographer Gene Anderson.*

As they approached the headman's house (at Muizwal), Gene noticed fresh, leafy branches over and around the entrance to the headman's yard. The young men and Robert walked right in, but for some reason, Gene hesitated. He did not enter the yard until the villagers insisted that he do so. Quite a few adults and children had gathered near the house. The two carriers and Rualchhina went to the corner where the food for the family was being prepared and began to cook rice over the chief's fire.

After some time, the chief sent a message to Gene via a village elder to the effect that they were having a special feast for the spirits. According to their custom, any stranger who came through the decorated gate was expected to pay for all the animals and zu (an alcoholic drink usually made from corn) that would be used for the feast. Therefore, Gene was expected to pay 300 rupees.

He hadn't realized that the leaves and branches at the gate were a warning for outsiders to stay away. By entering the village while spirit-worship restrictions were in place, he and his group had transgressed the villagers' sacrificial and spirit-worship laws. As a result, the villagers believed their sacrifices would not be accepted by the spirits and would have no effect or benefit to them. Therefore, the spirit worship would have to be repeated—and the trespassers were expected to pay for it.

Gene's mind began to whirl as he tried to figure a way out of this predicament without causing any ill feelings. He certainly did not want to pay for an animist[25] feast! At the same time, he wished to keep the goodwill of the headman, for Muizawl was one of the villages where he hoped to open a mission outpost.

The villagers explained to Gene that his party was not being treated any differently from others. The year before, government officers had come into the village on the feast day and they had paid the fine asked of them. While the travelers ate rice in the corner of the yard, they quietly discussed their problem and decided they would continue being friendly, praying all the while that their Lord and Guide would help them out of the situation into which they had unwittingly walked.

After visiting for some time with the chief, Gene asked if there were any who were sick at the feast or in the village that he might aid.

The chief answered, "Yes, there are many. We would like you to help us."

Gene opened his medicine kit and set up an impromptu clinic. He spent nearly two hours treating their sores and illnesses, all the while telling each person of Jesus' love.

Suddenly, Gene thought of something else he could do. He had his camera with him. "Would you like me to take pictures of your family?" he asked. Of course, the headman was pleased. Gene carefully positioned the chief, his wives, and his many children, then shot frame after frame of the family. When he was finished, he put his equipment back in the pack and hoped that now they could be on their way.

When the old village elder approached them, Gene was afraid that he would forbid them to leave until they paid for the feast. Instead, the elder said, "Because you have been so kind to us and have treated us like brothers, we are not going to ask you to pay your fine."

After thanking the villagers profusely, Gene and his companions bade the villagers farewell and hurried down the trail lest the elder should change his mind. The Lord had indeed made a way of escape.

FIGURE 6.6 *Gene meets a young man on the trail west of Tedim. Undated photograph, circa 1953. Photographer unknown.*

When Gene later developed that roll of film, he was shocked by what he found: the pictures taken before his Muizawl visit—and the ones after—were perfect, but the frames taken of the chief and his family were blank. A tingle went down his spine!

Toward evening, they arrived at the village of Laitui and found the local dak bungalow—a small building that had been constructed during British rule as a stopping place for agents patrolling the area. The bungalows were scattered throughout the hills. They were seldom maintained but were available for travelers passing through. The boys started a fire and cooked rice for their evening meal.

News spread quickly that there were visitors at the bungalow. It was not long before a group of people gathered. The travelers attended to the villagers' medical needs and told them about the love of Jesus.

The next morning, Robert Mya Pe found it impossible to continue the journey. His right knee was extremely painful, the result of a sprain he had sustained some time before. After Gene had tried every treatment he could think of, with no improvement to the knee, both men came to the difficult conclusion that it would be best for Robert to return to Tedim and home. Gene was sad as they parted, for he knew how much his friend had wanted to meet Pastor Lowry at the border.

"I stood there by the bungalow," Gene remembered, "and as Robert disappeared from sight, to say I felt alone is putting it mildly." He turned to the three young men, directing them to load up and start on their way. Two of them understood not a word of English and Rualchhina only a little, but they communicated quite well with gestures.

As they climbed higher, the main trail seemed to become more and more indistinct. There were no signs of any kind to point the way, so they kept walking, always taking the branch of the trail that seemed to be the most traveled. The pathway had become scarcely discernible when it abruptly branched out in four different directions. They followed one of the four paths for a quarter of a mile until they were confronted with three more trails, none of them much traveled. They did not know which way to go, and there was no one to ask. There hadn't been anyone else on the trail all morning.

Gene turned to the two young guides and through Rualchhina asked, "Which trail do we take?" They shrugged their shoulders and shook their heads. They did not know.

"What?" Gene exclaimed, "You don't know? Do you mean you have not been to Rih Lake before?"

No, they had never been to Rih Lake, and neither had Rualchhina.

> *Gene was astonished. Sure enough, two men sat beside the trail under a tree. They had walked past that very tree just a few minutes before, and no one had been there.*

"Lord," Gene prayed, "help us to know which way to go." They turned to the left and took the trail along the top of the ridge for about 400 feet. There, to Gene's consternation, it split again. He felt impressed to backtrack to where the trail had split into four. They walked single file with Gene in the lead, his head bowed in prayer, petitioning the Lord to send an angel, if necessary, to point out the way for them to take.

Suddenly, behind him, Rualchhina shouted, "Ask those men over there!"

Gene turned around quickly. "What men?"

Rualchhina pointed.

Gene was astonished. Sure enough, two men sat beside the trail under a tree. They had walked past that very tree just a few minutes before, and no one had been there.

Gene immediately asked the men for directions to the village of Haimual, and they answered, "Go back to the fork and take the lower path for three miles."

Gene thanked the men for their assistance and praised the Lord for His deliverance as they continued their journey.

Chapter 7

When God Intervenes, Divine Appointments Happen

"Trust in the LORD with all your heart, and lean not on your own understanding; In all your ways acknowledge Him, and He shall direct your paths."

Proverbs 3:5–6

The sun set, and darkness soon enveloped the travelers. Anxious to reach the lake, they pressed forward through a deep, over-hanging jungle with the aid of one small flashlight. To add to their concern, they could smell a strong, pungent odor, indicating the presence of a Bengal tiger. It was with joy and relief that they finally broke out into a clearing, and shortly thereafter, reached the welcome haven of the dak bungalow at Haimual.

They had not seen another person since the two men under the tree. Gene was certain those men were angels sent by God in answer to his prayers.

But Pastor Lowry was not there. Since Gene's communication with his three companions was limited, he couldn't express his disappointment or concern and felt very much alone. As soon as they had cooked a pot of rice and eaten, they wearily crawled under their mosquito nets and slept.

They had their first view of the beautiful, heart-shaped Rih Lake Thursday morning and were thankful to have reached their intended destination.

After breakfast, Rualchhina and Gene walked to the village to call on the headman, checking as they advanced to be certain there wasn't a spirit feast in progress. As they entered the large, thatched-roof hut, they stepped carefully to avoid the clutter on the floor. They could see fetishes[26] on the walls and in various other places: strings of tiger teeth, buffalo skulls with their widespread horns, and other charms used to pacify the spirits. The headman brought a small stool for Gene to sit on. Gene tried to concentrate on the conversation amid the clouds of dust being stirred up by members of the household who felt that they should tidy up for the visitors. He would have been much happier had they left the dust undisturbed.

FIGURE 7.1 *A typical village house in the Chin Hills. Undated photograph, circa 1953. Photographer Gene Anderson.*

Gene listened to the history of Haimual, then asked the headman if any of his people needed medical attention.

He nodded. "Yes, there are many sick people." He led Gene to his elderly mother who was lying on the floor. She was indescribably dirty, and her legs were covered with open, running ulcers. After dressing her sores and making her as comfortable as possible, Gene turned his attention to others who had come for treatment.

A lad of about sixteen hobbled into the hut on one leg, using a stick for a crutch. His left leg was drawn up and shriveled. He had had an accident when he was six years old and had broken his hip and leg. With no medical attention, the break had never healed properly. Gene's heart ached to leave him and others like him in such a pitiful condition. His desire was to be able to go through a town as Jesus did and not leave one sick person in it.

After caring for their medical needs, Gene began to tell the chief and his people about the wonderful love of Jesus and what He could do for them if they would let Him. He told them how Jesus died for them, so that someday they could live forever with Him in heaven. The villagers listened with solemn faces, pressing in closely to hear every word.

"Will you send someone to teach what the Bible says and tell us more about Jesus and the living God?" the headman asked, causing Gene's heart to thrill at hearing such words from the lips of this old man steeped in spirit worship. "We are just like a flock of little chicks whose mother has been killed. We are without a leader." The headman went on to promise that, if Gene could send a teacher, the villagers would provide a house for him.

Gene wished he could grant the request for a teacher, but he could only say that he would try to send one someday.

Friday dawned clear and bright, and with the new day came another request for help: Would Gene please come to a village three miles away, as some patients were too sick to walk to the bungalow? Gene was certainly willing to bring whatever relief he could to these suffering people, so he and Rualchhina followed the newcomers to the second village.

> *"Will you send someone to teach what the Bible says and tell us more about Jesus and the living God?" the headman asked, causing Gene's heart to thrill at hearing such words from the lips of this old man steeped in spirit worship.*

FIGURE 7.2 A spirit house along a trail in the Chin Hills. Undated photograph, circa 1953. Photographer Gene Anderson.

After paying their respects to the headman, Gene asked if any of the headman's people needed medical aid. The chief immediately went out to the center of the village and gave a loud call. In a few minutes, folks began to come, many of whom needed care. More than once, Gene wished he could tell them to step over to see the doctor, but there was no doctor to be found for miles and miles—or more accurately, for days and days. He could only do his best while silently praying for wisdom.

FIGURE 7.3 Gene holds a medical clinic in the Chin Hills. Undated photograph, circa 1953. Photographer unknown.

One man had been bitten on the finger by a poisonous snake about two weeks earlier. He had an ugly wound as a result. His finger and hand were grotesquely swollen and had turned black. A large section of decaying flesh ran through the center of his middle finger. He was suffering terribly from the pain.

Gene knew something had to be done immediately. Trying not to gag, he treated the wound as he thought a doctor would. When he finished with the dressing, he asked the patient to come to the bungalow the next day to have it changed. The man did come, and what a look of relief was on his face when he arrived! "My hand felt so much better after your treatment!" he said. "I could sleep last night. I haven't slept well for two weeks."

Over the following days, while Gene was still at the bungalow, the injured man came back several times, and each time the wound looked better. By the time the dressing was changed for the last time, the swelling was gone, and new flesh was growing over the wound.

Friday evening, as Gene watched the shadows creep across the lake, his mind was filled with questions and doubts. Had he misunderstood the directions in Elder Pierson's telegram? Perhaps Pastor Lowry had been delayed or was waiting at some other location. Sabbath settled around them, and still there was no Pastor Lowry.

Gene and Rualchhina took the flashlight and made their way to the head of the trail. As they sat on an old log, they tried to imagine what might have happened. Suddenly, Gene thought he heard voices off in the distance. As they strained their ears for the slightest sound, Gene saw a flicker of light beyond the north end of the lake. Someone was coming toward them. Oh, how he hoped it would be Pastor Lowry!

As the light bobbed closer, Gene's anticipation and hope grew stronger. Soon he could understand some English words. It had to be Pastor Lowry and his group. Gene's heart was about to burst with joy and relief as the hikers came into view. It was indeed Pastor Lowry; his wife, Helen; Lalkhuma; Zakhuma; and several carriers. Gene was thrilled to shake hands with this faithful missionary and his companions who had walked over rugged mountain trails for nine days from their home in Aijal, India, to meet him there at Rih Lake.

FIGURE 7.4 *Gene meets Willis and Helen Lowry at Rih Lake, April 1953. Left to right: Helen Lowry, Willis Lowry, and Gene. Photographer unknown.*

What a blessed Sabbath they enjoyed together, sharing how God had led each of them as they traveled. The Lowrys had brought Lalkhuma and Zakhuma with them, thinking that they could possibly become the first mission workers for the Chin people. With so much evidence that God was leading, these two young men agreed to stay in the Chin Hills to help start the new Adventist mission. It was a momentous decision.

FIGURE 7.5 These mission-minded men meet to share their goals. Left to right: Lalkhuma, Go Za Kham, Zakhuma, and Rualchhina. Undated photograph, circa 1953. Photographer Gene Anderson.

Despite the lack of modern communication, news of the arrival of foreign visitors and their medical expertise quickly spread from village to village. For the next few days, the missionaries were kept busy treating those who came for help, many from long distances. Being able to treat them physically opened the way to share spiritual topics with them. The missionaries were amazed by the people's questions and the depth of their interest.

The headman from a village twelve miles away asked, "Why do you keep the Sabbath? What is it that makes you different from other Christians?"

Gene replied, "Since I believe the Bible to be God's Holy Word, I choose to obey the fourth commandment. God blessed and sanctified the seventh day of the week to be a day to worship and remember Him."[27]

"There is a man in the village of Bukphir who also worships God on Saturday. The people say he is crazy!" the headman added.

"Where is Bukphir?" Gene asked.

"A day's journey that way," he indicated with a gesture.

"Do you know his name?"

"Yes. His name is Khawvel Thanga."

Gene was excited to hear about a Sabbath keeper deep in the Chin Hills. He recorded Khawvel's name and the name of his village in his notebook. Gene wanted to find this man but did not feel he could take the time on this trip.

The chief Gene had visited three miles up the mountain came down one morning with several of his village elders. They spent much of the day on the porch of the bungalow asking questions about Seventh-day Adventist doctrines. The men wanted to know and understand Adventist beliefs, and Gene explained with plain and simple words.

One of the men also told the missionaries he had two sisters who lived seven miles from the lake on the Indian side and that they had discovered the Bible truths from their personal Bible study. They had begun observing Saturday as their day of worship, thinking they were the only Sabbath keepers in the world. He also told them that his sisters had stopped using tobacco and wine,[28] as well as pork.[29] Pastor Lowry said he knew these two women and hoped to baptize them soon.

The missionaries spent four days together. Gene was amazed and inspired by the way God was leading in this remote corner of the world. It seemed almost prophetic of how the gospel work would be finished. "The last message will flow out in tiny streams," he wrote to Lois, "then spread far and wide and fill in the gaps, meeting in places where one little dreamed that it could. The Holy Spirit is going before us, impressing hearts to search for truth. May we have the faith, courage, and strength to follow His lead."

> *Before the Lowrys and Gene had gone their separate ways, Pastor Lowry had given Gene a letter he had received two weeks prior to their border meeting.*

The morning that Gene's group was leaving, they all decided to have one more swim in the clear lake. They had hardly gone into the water when a strong wind came up and rain poured down, creating a mysterious atmosphere. So ominous did it feel, they soon decided to get out.

Several months later, Gene received a letter from Helen Lowry that made his hair stand on end. "The day after you left for Tedim," she wrote, "I went down to pick some of the ripe raspberries along the lake just where we had been swimming. I suddenly heard a loud swishing sound coming from the lake. Startled, I watched as a huge whirlpool lowered the lake by about eight inches. What if that had happened while we were swimming there?"

Before the Lowrys and Gene had gone their separate ways, Pastor Lowry had given Gene a letter he had received two weeks prior to their border meeting. This letter had been written in pencil by a man who lived near Tedim, asking for information about Seventh-day Adventists.

The letter read:

> Dear Sirs,
> One time when I was in Calcutta, I was introduced to someone who was a Seventh-day Adventist. I would like to know more about the Seventh-day Adventists. Could you send me some books and literature that tell about your mission?
> Ngul Khaw Pau

When Gene reached Tedim after two long, hard days of hiking the mountain trails, he sought out Go Za Kham, the friendly young man who had introduced himself when they had first arrived in Kalemyo several weeks before. Gene showed him the penciled note from Ngul Khaw Pau and asked if Go Za Kham could help find him.

To Gene's surprise and delight, Go Za Kham answered, "Why, yes, of course. He is my cousin, but he is not at home. He is a patient in the government hospital. Someone was dismantling a bomb near his house when the bomb exploded, blowing that young man to pieces and severely injuring Ngul Khaw Pau. He was unconscious for three days but seems to be getting better. We can go see him."

The area around Tedim and down the mountains toward Kalemyo was the scene of heavy fighting during World War II. When the war ended, canteens, boots, bones, helmets, rusting vehicles and equipment, as well as hundreds of shells—both exploded and unexploded—were left behind. Occasionally the brush fires the villagers set to clear the land would detonate duds (unexploded shells which could be live or inert) with a muffled thump. It was one of these unexploded shells that nearly took the life of Ngul Khaw Pau.

Gene was unprepared for what he saw when he got to the hospital. The patient was wrapped in bandages from his hips to the top of his head, with just two small openings: one for his mouth and the other for one eye. Shocked at Ngul Khaw Pau's critical condition, Gene scarcely knew how to begin. Hesitantly, he introduced himself as part of the *Voice of Prophecy* Bible Correspondence School, then held out the note he had been given by Pastor Lowry. Gene asked if Ngul Khaw Pau recognized it.

With difficulty, Ngul Khaw Pau sat up in bed. "Yes! That is my letter!" Gene then explained that he was with the Seventh-day Adventist church, which was planning to open a mission in the Chin Hills.

Ngul Khaw Pau did not let his injuries deter him from his quest to learn more about Seventh-day Adventists. Almost his first words were, "Tell me about the Sabbath." Gene answered his questions about the Sabbath and many other Seventh-day Adventist beliefs. It was not a private conversation by any means. The window openings were crowded with faces; the doorways—and even the hospital room—were full of people. All the eavesdroppers were listening intently. Ngul Khaw Pau begged Gene to come back again, which he did that evening.

This marked the beginning of a close and wonderful friendship. Gene felt God had spared Ngul Khaw Pau for a definite purpose. Satan had tried to take his life, but God had overruled. Still, the bandaged eye had been badly injured.

FIGURE 7.6 Ngul Khaw Pau and his wife, Ciin-Ngaih Man. Undated photograph. Photographer unknown.

Ngul Khaw Pau was a language teacher and highly educated. As soon as he was well enough, he began to translate the book, *Bible Doctrines*, into the Tedim-Chin dialect. It was the first Adventist book printed in the Chin language. He was baptized and became an ordained Seventh-day Adventist minister. For the remainder of his life, he faithfully took the gospel to those in his homeland.

While still in Tedim, Gene also called on a young man the four Union workers had previously visited. That night, he came to see Gene and they spent an evening reviewing Seventh-day Adventist beliefs. The next day, the young man brought five other young men with him. They spent a second evening discussing the main points of Adventist teachings. These young men were the leaders of the youth of Tedim. Among them were the eldest son of the headman, a shop owner, a government employee, and the head of the largest church group in Tedim. As they left, they bade Gene a warm farewell and expressed the hope that he would return soon.

FIGURE 7.7 *Villagers in the Chin Hills pound grain. Undated photograph, circa 1953. Photographer Gene Anderson.*

FIGURE 7.8 *A Chin Hills woman weaving a blanket. Undated photograph, circa 1953. Photographer Gene Anderson.*

One morning, Gene saw Go Za Kham approaching the bungalow. After Gene invited him in, Go Za Kham shared that he had been studying about the Sabbath for eight years. "I have many arguments with my friends. They tell me that Saturday is not the Sabbath, but I can show them from the Bible that it is. I think you can help me understand some of the problems I face." Go Za Kham did not stay long that morning, but said he would come again in the evening to tell how he had learned about the Seventh-day Adventist message. With a twinkle in his eye, he added, "I don't think it would be wise for people to see me coming to visit you."

"I understand," Gene replied.

Very late, after the other visitors had gone home, Go Za Kham knocked softly at the door.

"I have been eagerly anticipating your visit, Go Za Kham," welcomed Gene. "Please, come in, and we'll sit together at the table while you share your story with me."

"This might take a long time," Go Za Kham warned with a smile, then began his story.

> My parents became Christians before I was born. When I was twelve, my father, Kam Zam, relocated our family to the Lushai Hills across the border with India, because the Japanese had invaded the Chin Hills, destroying villages, and creating fear and widespread suffering.
>
> Life was not as hard in our new home. My father made a fair living as a trader. There was plenty of food and cotton to spin for our clothing. The people were friendly, and the war became a distant memory.
>
> One afternoon, I found a group of my friends in earnest conversation. I asked them what they were talking about.
>
> One of them placed a small tract in my hand. I stared at the title. It read, "Saturday the True Sabbath." I had no idea what it was talking about.
>
> I asked my friend where he had gotten the paper. I was curious about what it contained. He told me a man had come from Aijal the day before and brought it. He also said there was a new mission at Aijal, but he couldn't remember the name of it. He just knew that they taught that Saturday is the true Sabbath, not Sunday.

I didn't know what to think. I had never heard of such a thing before, but I was determined to learn more. That evening I went to the house of the man who had the pamphlet and asked him what the message of this new mission was.

He repeated what I had read on the pamphlet, that Sunday is not the true Sabbath, and that God never changed the Sabbath from Saturday to Sunday.

When I questioned if this meant that when the Bible spoke of the Sabbath, it meant Saturday, the man assured me that was exactly what the new mission was teaching.

I couldn't go to the new mission, but I wanted to learn more, so I asked him if he had any other literature. He showed me a book he had bought—Bible Doctrines—and offered to loan it to me.

I borrowed the book and became so interested in what I read that I purchased my own copy.

When the war was over, I said goodbye to my parents and walked back to Tedim near my home village to attend a private school. I took my book, Bible Doctrines, with me.

As the school days passed, I continued learning new things from my treasured book. I had never heard of Nebuchadnezzar's dream, the story of the dark day, or the falling of the stars. Nor could I find a biblical mandate for Sunday worship. I told my classmates they were not worshiping on God's rest day but on the day of the sun, a pagan holiday which Constantine incorporated into Christian worship. They responded with the usual comments, such as, "If Sunday were not the right day, then surely God would have sent a message to someone so that everyone would know it. Besides, one day in seven for worship is the important thing."

When the mission to which I and my family belonged started a Bible school, I was among the first to attend. One day I was writing at my desk when the missionary's wife came in and picked up the well-worn Bible Doctrines lying at my elbow. She glanced through it and quickly saw that it was a Seventh-day Adventist publication. She told me it was not a good book and took it away with her. Later, when I had finished my classwork, I was able to retrieve the book and hide it once again in my box.

I applied myself diligently for four years, and when I had completed my studies at the Bible school, a friend and I were sent on tour to hold Bible classes for the people. We would spend a few days in a village, or longer if there was a good response, then move on to another village. We were bringing God's message to villagers far removed from the influence of schools or Bible teachers, just as I had dreamed of doing.

One night I noticed an army officer in the Bible study group. He listened with rapt attention and came forward at the close of the study to introduce himself as U Khup Za Neng. He said he was a Christian, and as we talked together, I noticed that some of the things he mentioned sounded like the Bible truths I had found in my Bible Doctrines book.

A few evenings later I spoke with him again, commenting on his interest in Bible study. I asked if he studied by himself at home. He assured me that he did, using a set of lessons that came to him through the mail from the Voice of Prophecy Bible Correspondence School. They had answered many of his Bible questions.

My interest was aroused. When I asked what the Voice of Prophecy was, he explained that it was a radio program that sent Bible lessons[30] to those who wanted them. He had attended evangelistic meetings in Rangoon, and at the close of one of the meetings, attendees were given cards they could sign if they wished to receive the courses. The lessons were free, so he had turned in his name and had been receiving his lessons at home ever since.

This was good news. Anything that would help me to understand the Bible better was just what I wanted, so I sent in my name with a request that all the lessons be sent to me at once. I finished the entire series in two months to become the first person in the Chin Hills to hold a Voice of Prophecy certificate of completion.

I had just begun working on the advanced course when I was appointed to work in the office at the headquarters of the Baptist mission at Tedim. I was thrilled with what I was learning and was completing six lessons a day. One day I was so absorbed in my study that I forgot about getting the mail. My pastor went to the post office and picked up my mail with his own. He couldn't help but see the bold print "Voice of Prophecy Bible Correspondence School" stamped on each of the big brown envelopes that were handed to him.

I looked up when I heard someone enter the room. There stood my pastor. My heart sank when I recognized the familiar Voice of Prophecy envelopes in his hand. By the look on his face, I knew he was fully aware of what I was doing. He handed the envelopes to me with the remark, "Here are your lessons—if you are still making contact with your friends."

I suddenly realized that I was spending too much time with the lessons and decided I must be loyal to the old way, so I abruptly quit studying them. It was not long before the Voice of Prophecy headquarters wrote to me to find out why such a diligent student was suddenly so silent. They encouraged me to continue my study, since I had been so successful thus far. The battle became intense. The truth was gripping me. At last, I could deny my spiritual hunger no longer, and I finished the course.

My pastor came to me and told me this was a snare of the devil! He warned me to have nothing to do with it.

I decided I must talk with the Adventist missionary, so here I am, coming to see you at night, just as Nicodemus came to find Jesus.

The two men talked about how God had directed Go Za Kham's life and discussed the Ten Commandments, the Sabbath, the state of the dead,[31] and many other doctrines until long after midnight. Finally, Go Za Kham stood up to go.

"I think you are right," he admitted, "and I hope that you and your family come to Tedim to live very soon. Do not be surprised if someday I decide to join you."

"We certainly hope and pray that you will clearly see God's plan for your life," was Gene's response. They said goodnight, and Gene watched Go Za Kham disappear down the dark path.

> *"I think you are right," he admitted, "and I hope that you and your family come to Tedim to live very soon. Do not be surprised if someday I decide to join you."*

FIGURE 7.9 Go Za Kham. He spoke five languages fluently and several of the Chin dialects. Undated photograph, circa 1953, Photographer unknown.

Almost a month had passed with no word from home—not because the family hadn't written, but because the letters were lost somewhere. Gene was anxious to return home, yet his heart was thrilled in a way he had never experienced.

Many times, he had witnessed the direct guiding of God's hand. He had entered a new country—unfamiliar with its language and customs—and had been led to those who were seeking to follow God's will. He couldn't explain why their first request was, "Tell me about the Sabbath," or "Tell us why you are different from other Christians." There had been no prior church work in this field, so what was pressing them to come miles to ask questions of those just passing through? Educated people, such as those in Tedim, were studying the Bible on their own to learn what it said—and in the mountain villages of western Burma where there were no schools and many of the people could neither read nor write, the gospel story was passed by word of mouth.

Gene sensed the Spirit of God working among the men and women who lived far removed from the modern world. With a feeling of awe, he renewed his commitment to his new assignment.

On the next day for downhill traffic on the controlled road between Tedim and Kalemyo (a "down" day), Gene left Tedim for Kalemyo. He had become better acquainted with Rualchhina while on the Rih Lake trek and was impressed with his abilities. Gene had decided to help send the young man to the training school at Myaungmya to finish his high school. Once he reached Kalemyo, Gene reconnected with Rualchhina, as previously planned, and purchased tickets for them both. They would fly together as far as Mandalay, and from there, Rualchhina would continue to Rangoon by train.

On the appointed day, they went to the airstrip and were standing beside the pile of luggage when the ticket agent approached Gene and said he had miscounted. There was only one seat available, not two. This meant that Rualchhina would have to stay behind and come later. It was a keen disappointment to both men. Gene had planned for Rualchhina to travel with him to be sure Rualchhina wouldn't change his mind about going to school. In any case, they couldn't argue with the agent, so Gene bade Rualchhina goodbye and boarded alone.

In front of him was an empty seat. The last of the passengers sat down, the door closed, and the seat remained empty. Gene was upset. Why was Rualchhina not allowed to have that seat? he wondered. Couldn't the agent count? The seat remained empty, not only to Mandalay, but all the way to Rangoon. But why?

As Rualchhina watched the plane take off and disappear, he, too, wondered why. Why hadn't he been able to go with Pastor Anderson? What about his plans to attend school? A wave of loneliness washed over him. He considered his options and decided to go back to the village of Tahan to stay with friends. All his belongings were rolled up inside his bedroll, and it was too heavy to carry three miles in the midday heat. Scanning the street, he saw a man standing nearby with a bicycle that had a carrier on the back. Rualchhina approached him and asked if he would be willing to carry the bedroll on the back of his bike to Tahan.

"Why sure," the man answered at once. "I would be glad to, if you are a Christian."

"Yes, I am a Christian. My name is Rualchhina."

"I mean a real Christian," the man countered. "One who keeps the seventh-day Bible Sabbath."

Rualchhina could hardly believe his ears. Nobody in Kalemyo had ever heard of the seventh-day Sabbath, much less kept it. "I do! I keep the seventh-day Sabbath. What is your name?"

> *The man was so overcome with emotion he could hardly speak. "My name is Khawvel Thanga, and I live in Bukphir. I keep the seventh-day Sabbath too."*

The man was so overcome with emotion he could hardly speak. "My name is Khawvel Thanga, and I live in Bukphir. I keep the seventh-day Sabbath too."

Now Rualchhina was really surprised. This was the very man that he and Pastor Anderson had heard about in Haimual—the man whose name Gene had written in his notebook and hoped to visit one day. From his private study of the Bible, Khawvel Thanga had determined that the seventh day, Saturday, was the Sabbath and had been keeping it as his day of rest. Until that moment, he was not aware that anyone else in the whole world was doing the same. He had also stopped using tobacco and eating pork.

Rualchhina spent several hours talking with Khawvel Thanga, who was thrilled to find that he was not alone in his new faith. He had come to Kalemyo, many days' journey from his home village, to get a parcel waiting there for him at the exact time Rualchhina was prevented from getting on the airplane. Both men felt that their meeting had been divinely arranged. When Gene heard the rest of the story, he praised God for the empty seat that had been in front of him all the way to Rangoon.

In due time, Rualchhina continued his education and became an ordained Seventh-day Adventist minister who provided strong leadership for many years.

FIGURE 7.10 Rualchhina, as a young pastor, with his wife, Zo Tin Khumi, and the first of their six children. Date unknown. Photographer unknown.

On February 14, 1998, he wrote the following letter to Gene:

Dear Pastor A.E. Anderson,

On this, your 80th birthday, I do not have sufficient words at my command to express what is at the bottom of my heart and in the deepest depths of my feelings.

My mind quickly goes back to 1953 in Tahan, where you, C.B. Guild, Freddy Batin, and Robert Mya Pe came to look for a place to set up missionary work in upper Burma. You picked me up to join you in the Lord's work, making the greatest turning point in my life direction.

The event, though insignificant as it may seem at the time, turned out to become a beginning of an important church history, for which not only I, but also over 7,000 people, are grateful for your missionary work for us.

Being together with you and under your care as a young and ignorant worker, your fervency in the spirit, love, and goodwill to the people, greatly inspired me and my fellow workers who followed. The Spirit of the Lord overflowed everywhere in length and breadth.

Many are still fervently keeping the ministry in the Chin Hills and Kabaw valleys today. As a matter of fact, a large number of Burma Union workers, today, are composed of the people from the Chin Hills. In the Union, the Bible seminaries, and the local missions, people from the Chin Hills today fill many important positions. In upper Burma itself, over 80% of the workers are from the Chin Hills.

Even one soul was very important to you, and we walked together for days and days, up and down great mountains, deep valleys, and gorges to meet a single soul. You never forgot the names of the people who were interested to learn from the Bible. You met them where they were, and you told them about the Bible and God's love.

Because of who you were for us and for your kindness of heart, on behalf of my family, over 7,000 strong in the Chin Hills, and 20,000 strong members in Burma, I take this opportunity to send you a most Happy Birthday greeting.

With best wishes and love,
Rualchhina

Back in Rangoon, Gene's family stood by the fence overlooking the Mingaladon airport. For many nights they had watched planes land, always hoping that one of the disembarking passengers would be Daddy. They did not know when to expect him, so they had met every flight coming from Kalemyo. When he did not come, they would drive the ten miles back to Rangoon in their little Jeep and begin counting the days until the next plane from the north was due.

Now they watched again, searching the dark sky for the blinking lights of a plane. At last, they saw two little bright spots winging in from the north, and their hearts beat faster. Would Daddy be on this flight?

The DC-3 landed and taxied to the terminal where they were waiting. In the darkness, they could just make out figures of people as they came down the steps. One of the boys gave a shout, "There he is! See? The tall one. I know that's Daddy!" A man, head and shoulders above the crowd, walked toward them carrying a bundle in each hand. The boys ran to meet him, while Lois forced herself to follow at a more dignified pace.

Oh, how glad they were to have him safely home! He was weary, dirty, thin, tanned, and needed a haircut—but bursting to tell them about his thrilling adventures. They tossed his bedroll and satchel into the back of the Jeep and drove back to the city.

"It's so good to be home!" Gene exclaimed, as he came into the kitchen after a shower and shave. "This seems like a palace!"

That was stretching the point,[32] as they had very little furniture, but their house was clean, and it was home. Lois studied him and saw the lines in his cheeks and the cords in his neck. She wondered if he had been ill or if it was a lack of food that had taken the pounds off his frame.

"Sit down at the table," she said. "You look like you haven't had a meal for quite a while. What have you been eating?"

"Rice," Gene replied. "Then more rice, and after that, more rice."

"Don't they have any vegetables?"

"They are pretty scarce," Gene admitted. "I had cabbage at one man's house. He had someone bring it from a village five miles away. Sometimes, I had white pumpkin. When we were in the jungle, I hunted for banana buds."[33]

"Well, it's no wonder you are thin. Is that all we will have to eat when we get there?" Lois began to worry about taking two growing boys and a new baby to a land with a shortage of food.

Gene tried to reassure her. "I don't believe food is always so scarce. It is the dry season, and there are very few things growing. They tell me after the rains start, it will be better. It is true that there is very little variety, but don't worry. It will be all right." With a smile he continued, "Just wait until I tell you everything about it!"

Then he turned to David and Leslie, who were both leaning over the back of his chair. "What fun you boys will have! You can roam over the hills to your hearts' content. [34] It is safe there."

"Do they have horses?" the boys asked.

"Yes. I guess you could call them horses. They are very small."

"Can we get one?" came the inevitable question.

"We will surely try—if we can find one and have a place to keep it and enough to feed it. I warn you, though, that feed will be hard to get."

Gene pushed his chair back from the table, grabbed a boy in each arm, and started into the other room. "Come on, Mother. Let the dishes go. I've got lots to tell you!"

"And we are eager to hear about everything too," Lois said.

"It won't be easy up there in the hills," Gene said, "but I am sure when you get there, you will just love it, and the people will love you. Many have asked us to come to Tedim to set up our mission, but we do not know yet if that is where the headquarters will be established. What I can tell you is they want us to come, and that means a lot. Well, I guess I might just as well start at the very beginning. I suppose we can talk all night."

"Of course," Lois answered. "When we get tired, we can just go to bed and keep on talking."

Watching the wide-eyed, eager faces before him, Gene began. "A highlight of our trip was the way we were met at the plane in Kalemyo by a young man named Go Za Kham."

As Gene told the exciting story of Go Za Kham, Lois marveled at the many ways in which God had opened doors and influenced decisions. When the four men had set out on their exploratory trip, they had had no idea where they would find interested people. It was clear to her that God had prepared the way before them; all they needed to do was follow His leading.

It was late when Gene said, "I told Go Za Kham goodnight and watched him disappear down the dark path."

He hugged David and Leslie. "On that note," he concluded, "I think it's time for us to go to bed and get some rest. There will be more stories tomorrow!"

Chapter 8

When Challenges Come, God's Grace Is Sufficient

"He said to me, "My grace is sufficient for you, for My strength is made perfect in weakness.""

—2 Corinthians 12:9

The fifth member of the family, Daniel Lawrence, was born in the Rangoon Adventist Hospital early on the morning of June 2, 1953—the coronation day for Queen Elizabeth II. The Andersons thought their baby was every bit as royal as the new queen since he was a child of the heavenly King. As Lois watched her precious baby sucking on his fingers with his eyes wide open, she thought he resembled Leslie. But, in a few days, he simply looked like himself. At three and a half weeks, he smiled at his mother for the first time. How happy she was!

David and Leslie began another school year the day after Daniel was born. Miss Lockie Gifford, principal of the church school in Rangoon, taught the missionary children, as well as English to the Burmese students. David and Leslie continued with their Burmese language study and became quite fluent.

Lois made weekly trips to town to buy food for the family. The market was located on a narrow street scarcely wide enough for two vehicles to meet. If it had rained recently, the road was thick with mud. On either side were booths and stalls filled with produce and household items. The proprietor of each did his best to shout louder about his wares than his surrounding competitors, attempting to attract a steady stream of customers.

When Lois reached the market's vicinity, she inched the Jeep along so as not to run over a bicycle, a cart, a beggar lying on the ground, or any pedestrian. Even before she could park and get out of her Jeep, little boys would come running with their big baskets, begging to help her with her shopping. No matter how many times she told them, "No," they kept coming, each one hoping to be chosen.

Lois usually went first to her favorite place, one of the smaller shops. While she was there, the little boys waited for her outside. As she continued down the street, more and more boys tagged along calling, "Good morning, Mama," saluting her, and pointing to themselves as they tried to take her basket. She didn't choose any of them; she was waiting for a certain boy.

She didn't know the boy's name—names in a foreign country are confusing and difficult to understand or remember—but she had chosen him because he was older, had proven trustworthy and helpful, and didn't hound[35] her like the little boys did. She was hoping that by choosing the same boy every time, she could escape the constant demands of the ones who followed her, hoping for her favor.

Soon the boy she wanted saw her—or someone told him she was there—and he came running. Somewhat taller than David and a few years older, he put Lois's big basket on his head and helped her by pointing out the best produce and translating whenever necessary. She really appreciated his assistance.

Ever hopeful, the parade of little boys stayed right with her until she returned to the Jeep. They waited as Lois paid the big boy four or five annas, then all the little boys saluted her, said, "Good morning, Mama," and watched her leave.

Lois found bargaining for every purchase tiring, but she knew it was customary and necessary in her new home. She would lose many rupees if she did not watch carefully to be sure she was not being overcharged. Sometimes the merchants raised prices when they saw her coming, but other times, they asked the regular price first. Lois didn't want to be unfair, but if she paid too much, they thought she was foolish. Since she didn't know what the prices should be, she could only do her best and hope she was not cheating either the merchants or herself.

Gene left for his second tour of the Chin Hills the first part of August. After he had been away for nearly a month, Lois slipped into postpartum depression. The strain of her temporary living situation, compounded by the arrival of Daniel and all the extra work that came with a new baby, seemed overwhelming. Vexed by her inability to meet her own expectations, she found herself snapping at David and Leslie for no reason. She did not want to feel this way, so she pleaded for God to carry the burdens for her—and He did! She no longer felt impatient, her depression left her, and her heart was filled with an incredible peace.

Danny, as the family had taken to calling Daniel, brought much joy to the family. One day, as Lois sat on the porch holding him in her lap, he laughed and "talked" to her. "It must be Burmese," she quipped, "because I can't understand it." At three months old, he learned to turn over onto his stomach. His big brothers delighted in trying to make him giggle. When David knocked over a bamboo ladder, Danny laughed, so David knocked it down several more times just to hear him laugh again.

FIGURE 8.1 Lois and Danny. Undated photograph, circa 1953. Photographer unknown.

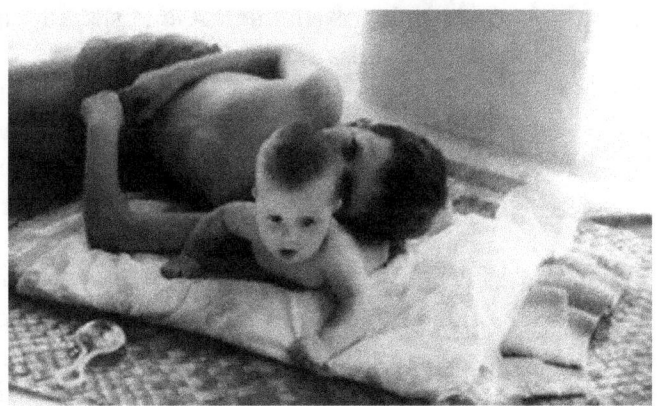

FIGURE 8.2 Leslie plays with Danny in Rangoon. Undated photograph, circa 1953. Photographer Lois Anderson.

When David and Leslie weren't in school, they spent many carefree hours rowing on Inya Lake, always at the end of the lake closest to the house where Lois could keep a watchful eye on them. They became excellent oarsmen and boasted healthy tans from the outdoor exercise.

Just below their yard along the highway was a row of small bamboo houses and shops with rice and oil for sale. The people used the lake for bathing as well as fishing, so there was always a great deal of activity along the shore. What a colorful sight it was to see a long row of umbrellas bordering the edge of the lake, with a fisherman squatting beneath each one, hoping to catch his dinner.

At last, the day came when Lois expected Gene to return. As she and the boys neared the airport, they saw a British Overseas Airways Corporation plane landing, and right behind it, a Dakota DC-3. They thought the DC-3 must be Gene's plane, so they hurried even more. They sped along between thirty and forty miles an hour with Leslie in the back seat, trying to keep Danny from bouncing out of his basket, and David in front, gripping the Jeep's canvas top tightly to keep it from flying off.

Passengers were disembarking by the time Lois parked. She and the boys watched until it seemed everyone had climbed down the steps. "Guess we'll go home alone." She had scarcely finished speaking when they saw Gene's tall frame in the doorway of the DC-3. David and Leslie raced to meet him.

"Daddy was up in the pilots' compartment," Leslie explained to his mother when the three of them walked back to where she was standing. The family was overjoyed and thankful to be together again. On the ride home, Gene told Lois he had never felt more fulfilled.

After the initial homecoming excitement, Gene shared experiences from his latest trip to the Chin Hills.

One evening in Tedim, he stood by the local dak bungalow contemplating the tremendous challenge presented by the vast, unentered territory. Dusk was creeping in, slowly blotting out the distant mountain peaks. Out across the deep valley, evening fires began to glimmer in the villages.

Suddenly, he realized he was not alone. Five men were coming up the pathway. After greeting each one, he invited them to come into the bungalow. He lit a candle, and when all were seated, the men began to talk among themselves. Although Gene couldn't understand their language, he caught the names of other mission groups who had large followings in the region. Uneasily, he tried to guess what their visit might mean.

Then the speaker for the group turned to Gene and asked, "What is your scheme for the Chin Hills?" Gene hesitated, afraid that perhaps these men had been sent to ask him not to come, despite the warm welcome he had received thus far.

Before he could reply, the spokesman continued with a request that turned Gene's foreboding into joy. "Our village is a four-day journey by foot from here. Our people are in great darkness; they need help. We have come this evening to plead with you, that by the grace of God, the Seventh-day Adventists will remember the people in our village. Please send us a teacher and establish a dispensary to care for our sick."

Gene wanted to say he would send someone immediately, but he could not. He did promise, though, that as soon as possible, he would come to help their village. Many times that evening, the spokesman begged Gene to remember his people.

Gene accompanied Lalkhuma and Zakhuma to Darkhai to assist them with their evangelism. It was usually a four-day hike, but since they were on a tight schedule, they pushed themselves to make it in two. It was difficult walking at the best of times, but much worse during the rains when the trails became as slick as glass. Gene would have been more comfortable if his hiking boots hadn't rotted from so much moisture. He bound them with heavy shoestrings but wearing them that way caused blisters.

During the four days the men were in Darkhai, they conducted two meetings a day in the schoolhouse with its old hand-hewn log desks. The teacher and his students were pleased when Gene took a picture of them in front of the school.

Before each meeting, Gene rang the school bell, and soon the people filed into the building. They brought pine-pitch torches to the evening meetings to light their way home in the dark. The listeners had many questions, and Gene always began each reply with, "The Bible says."

The villagers noticed he had a Scripture for every query. "This is what we want!" they declared.

> *Our people are in great darkness; they need help. We have come this evening to plead with you, that by the grace of God, the Seventh-day Adventists will remember the people in our village.*

FIGURE 8.3 *Gene talking with villagers in the Chin Hills. Undated photograph, circa 1953. Photographer unknown.*

Most evenings he had visitors until midnight. One night, twenty men came to discuss the Sabbath. When they left, a young man lingered behind. When he and Gene were alone, he said, "I have been studying the question of the Bible Sabbath for over a year. I am convinced this is the truth, and I am going to keep my first Sabbath with you tomorrow!" And he did.

The family planned to leave Rangoon for the Chin Hills in October. A week before their scheduled departure, Gene heard that the official who issued permits was looking for him. This man informed Gene that the family would need a permit to live in the Chin Hills. The men at the Union office had understood no permit was necessary.

"We must stop our packing," Gene informed his family. "The application for the permit has to go to the Chin Ministry, and who knows how long that will take. Hopefully, we will be able to leave within a week after we get the permit."

The Andersons received their permit one month after the date they had originally planned to leave. They felt everything was finally coming together for them to complete their move.

Miss Gifford had a farewell party for David and Leslie on their last day at the church school.

The next morning as dawn was breaking, Lois left Danny with Miss Mann, one of the nurses at the Rangoon Hospital who had offered to care for him. The family had a big day of packing ahead and wanted to get an early start. David and Leslie worked like troopers until the packing was finished. One of their jobs was to paint the name "Anderson" on all the boxes. That afternoon, the truck that would take their freight to Mandalay arrived. The Jeep was sent by train the next day.

Pastor and Mrs. Guild took the Andersons to the airport. They had a lot of extra baggage, as the boys and Lois planned to stay in Maymyo for several weeks while Gene took the Jeep and their household goods from Mandalay to Kalemyo on a riverboat. The boys carried their pet rabbit, Daisy, in a wicker basket.

Even at 8 a.m., it was uncomfortably warm in the rambling buildings of the air terminal, so the family found a bench under a slowly moving ceiling fan where they could wait. Danny, now five months old, was stripped down to his diaper. A crowd of people moved about them, waiting to board planes bound for different parts of Burma: Moulmein to the south, Myaungmya to the west, and Mandalay to the north. Slim Burmese ladies with colorful swaths of silk wrapped smoothly around their hips walked by on their simple strap slippers. The bright flowers tucked into the coils of their thick black hair and their dainty white blouses made them appear cool and fresh in the languid heat of the building.

FIGURE 8.4 Gene and family waiting at the Rangoon airport to board the DC-3 for Maymyo. Undated photograph, circa 1953. Left to right: Gene, David, Leslie, Lois, and Danny. Photographer Cecil B. Guild.

The Andersons heaped their hand luggage around them: lunch basket, drinking water, and Danny's supplies. They didn't know if they would be allowed to take the rabbit on the plane, but were determined to try.

In due course, their larger luggage was transferred to the cargo hold of the plane and their tickets were checked. An announcement in Burmese came over the loudspeaker. They recognized "Mandalay" and "Maymyo," and realized it was their flight being announced. As the Andersons gathered their things, Pastor and Mrs. Guild smiled a farewell and said, "God bless you."

FIGURE 8.5 *The Andersons board the Union of Burma Airways bus to take them out to their airplane on the tarmac. Undated photograph, circa 1953. Left to right: David, Lois, Danny, Leslie, and Gene. Photographer unknown.*

To their delight, the boys were able to take Daisy on the plane with them. David carried the rabbit basket and put it on the floor between his legs, in front of his seat. The family settled themselves in their seats and fastened their seatbelts. Lois looked reassuringly at David and Leslie. "Remember to smile at Danny. He doesn't know what this is all about. The roar of the motors might startle him." She hoped Danny wouldn't get too much pressure in his ears and start to cry.

The plane taxied to the end of the long concrete runway, paused to test the motors and brakes, then, with a roar of the engines, rose smoothly into the air. They were headed north to the hills, north to a new country, north to a new assignment. Questions of every kind raced through Lois's mind, but she would have to wait for the answers.

Toward the end of the two-hour flight, the plane passed over the ancient Burmese capital of Bagan, also known as the "Land of a Thousand Pagodas." Below them, the family saw hundreds of pagodas—all sizes and shapes—spread over the countryside. It looked much different from any place they had seen before. Like Mandalay, Bagan was situated along the Irrawaddy River. Just before landing, they noticed that two spans of the bridge over the river had been destroyed by insurgent activity.

When they boarded again after a fifteen-minute stopover in Mandalay, the plane was almost empty. In just a few minutes, they landed on the grassy strip in Maymyo. Mr. Gerling, from the Adventist mission at Maymyo, met them.

Everything about Maymyo felt different from Rangoon. The air was cool and invigorating; the sun, warm. A paved road ran through small sections of woods, past neat gardens with rows of pineapple plants, and beside fields with blue and pink asters that would be sent by air to Rangoon. Gigantic poinsettias, ten feet tall and covered with huge blooms, lined the road to the mission. The sky was bright blue, the vegetation green and fresh, and tidy gardens spread over the hills. It was a gorgeous sight.

The mission, "Brightlands," consisted of seven acres, a big two-story house, and a Quonset hut for a church building. Fred and Peggy Gerling, with their two small children, had been in Maymyo less than a year. Since Peggy was a nurse and Fred a lab tech, they had expanded their ministry to include a clinic.

Early the next morning, Gene returned to Mandalay to complete the arrangements for him to accompany their Jeep and freight on a boat to Kalewa, the nearest river port to Kalemyo. Kalemyo was where the family would arrive by plane and where the road to the Chin Hills began. Before he had left Rangoon, he had reserved boat space—but, not knowing how long the river trip would take, he was not able to tell Lois when he would return.

Gene was dismayed at the discouraging news he learned at the shipyard. Neither the train bringing their Jeep nor the truck with their household goods had arrived from Rangoon. As he walked down to the riverbank, his dismay intensified when he saw heaps of cargo waiting to be loaded onto a boat. With all that was waiting to go, Gene wondered if their things would ever get on.

The shipping agent told him, "The backlog of freight has been piling up daily, as there are not enough boats to carry it all. Since the rains have stopped, the water level of the river has dropped to the point that many boats are getting stuck on sandbars. This is delaying shipments." Still, he promised Gene that if his freight arrived by the next morning, it would be put on the boat the same day.

The household goods did not arrive in time, but the Jeep did, so Gene purchased a deck ticket and boarded the boat to see that the Jeep got to Kalewa. He tossed his bedroll into the Jeep. He could be spending three days—or ten—crowded in with the rest of the throng that had pressed on board to find their way up the Chindwin River. At least he had the Jeep to sit in, which made his prospects a little brighter.

Gene watched as every available space on the deck filled. Mats and bedrolls were spread out, surrounded by baskets of food and small aluminum containers filled with rice and curry. Bunches of bananas and papayas lay on top of most of the food baskets. Babies and small children scrambled about, unmindful of the dirt and trash that gathered as the crowd increased. Some of the weary travelers, already settled for the long trip, stretched out on their mats and dozed, oblivious to the noise and activity about them. The whistle blew, and the boat—loaded far beyond what the law allowed—moved out into the current.

The day Gene left, Leslie went into the house to get a drink and quickly ran out again. "Daisy's had her babies!" The family had expected her to give birth after they got to Tedim, but the month delay in Rangoon had upset the schedule. Lois and the boys had been putting the rabbit under a basket in the grass during the day, and in a big box in the house at night. Daisy had six kits lying in the box when Leslie found them. She had pulled out some of her fur to cover them, but it was not enough; the newborns were already cold. The boys found old rags and a hot water bottle to put in with the newborns, and soon they were all snuggled in their nest. Daisy was a gentle mother and paid no attention to the boys. They planned to sell the rabbits to earn money for the much-desired horse.

One day, Lois and the boys received a letter from Gene.

> I am sitting in our Jeep alongside a large diesel engine which is pounding away, turning the stern paddle wheels that are pushing this boat up the Chindwin River. About an hour and a half ago, I left Monywa. I have already been two-and-a-half days on the Irrawaddy River. I have another two days or so to get to Kalewa, then I will get off the boat and try to get to Kalemyo.
>
> I would judge the boat is about 50 feet wide and 150 to 175 feet long, and it is carrying approximately 100 tons of freight. Our freight was supposed to come on this boat too, but for some reason, it didn't get to Mandalay. So, I have come on with the Jeep.
>
> Besides the freight, there are 250 passengers sprawled out all over. The Jeep is my anchor. It is anything but clean on the boat, and as far as facilities are concerned, there are nearly none. My food choices have been limited——bananas

and more bananas. This morning I bought a couple of small loaves of bread and some onions. From time to time, we pull in beside the bank at a village. Food peddlers wade out to the boat with baskets of prepared food on their heads. Sweet fried cakes, crisp fried sparrows, steaming rice in thin bamboo tubes, and of course bananas and peanuts, are available for a few pyas. I usually buy the bananas and peanuts.

The slower pace of river travel gave Gene an opportunity to study the country that drifted by. The land was flat, and the Irrawaddy River was wide—as much as half a mile in some places—but at times, so shallow that the boat scraped bottom.

The surroundings changed as the boat passed through a sort of gate with green, rocky bluffs on either side. The river narrowed considerably, and Gene could easily see the activity on either bank. Some folks were cutting and loading wood into sampans.[36] Farther along in a little village of bamboo and thatch huts, women came down to the river to get water, carrying big clay pots on their heads. At a larger village, naked children ran along the bank. Some people were fishing, and a man was plowing his field with a team of oxen.

Soon the riverbanks steepened, rising nearly forty feet straight up and covered with dense jungle. Gene saw a wild animal built like a member of the cat family, about the size of a German Shepherd and reddish in color. He guessed it might be a young tiger. There was a pair of smaller animals, about the color and size of raccoons, but he was unable to identify them. The many different birds were also new to him.

The banks gradually flattened to a gentler slope. Gene watched two men cutting grass that was about twelve feet tall, perhaps to clear land for a hut. There were many native boats plying the river—from small dugout canoes to big sampans—the largest being about fifteen feet wide and fifty feet long.

When the water level was too low to use the motor safely, the crewmen poled the boat. If the passage was both shallow and narrow, they jumped to the riverbank and pulled the boat forward with ropes.

Gene was fascinated by the teak log and bamboo rafts they met as they chugged up the river. The rafts ranged in length from 100-200 feet long and were about 75 feet wide. A grass hut had been built in the middle of each raft to house the six to eight men who guided the raft downriver.

Later, he watched twenty men building one of these rafts. Because teak logs are too dense to float, large bundles of bamboo poles were lashed on top of the logs to make the raft buoyant. Only the bamboo bundles were visible above the water. He learned that the rafts were made solely for transporting the teak logs to the sawmill and that it would take eight months to a year to float them all the way to Rangoon.

The river was not always shallow; much of the time, it was very deep. Two men stood on the prow of the boat and continually called out the depth in a singsong chant.

Gene wrote his letter sitting on a bamboo stool behind his Jeep while seven or eight men squatted on the deck watching him. A little boy hung over Gene's shoulder, totally absorbed in the writing. Being watched—or more accurately, being stared at—wherever they were or whatever they were doing, was something to which the whole family was becoming accustomed. Not only were they white, but at six feet three inches and five feet nine inches respectively, Gene and Lois towered over the Burmese's average height of five feet five inches.

"I hope to get to Kalewa today," he wrote. "If the road between Kalewa and Kalemyo is open, which I have heard it might be, I will try to get to Kalemyo this evening. The scenery has been really grand, but the weather is very cold. Tomorrow will be Thanksgiving Day, but I guess we will celebrate it when we get to Tedim."

Eventually Gene reported, "Believe it or not, I am on solid ground again. Whew, what a mess! The boat pulled in alongside the riverbank at 2 p.m., and three hours later, I was finally able to get my Jeep off the boat. It was first one thing and then another. So, I won't get to Kalemyo tonight.

"Besides, the bridge is not in yet. I will have to drive some distance, then load the Jeep onto a small motorboat, travel about eight miles, and then drive again. I am going to try to leave early in the morning in order to catch tomorrow's plane back to Mandalay. I am afraid that I won't make it. I will sleep here in the Jeep again tonight."

He knew the letter would probably not reach them before he did, but he wanted his family to know they were always in his thoughts.

Gene traveled the last eight-mile segment of his river journey in a sampan with a very old auto motor that knocked and rattled alarmingly. Water had to be bailed out every little while. Suddenly, there was a loud *clang, clang*, and the sampan headed for shore. A few bolts were tightened, and away they went again. Every time Gene checked his watch, the hands seemed to be going around faster and faster;[37] the day was disappearing, and he was still far from his destination.

Finally, he saw the river landing ahead. Fifty feet from the bank, the captain cut the motor, followed shortly thereafter by a horrendous noise. The prop and its shaft had broken off, and water was gushing into the boat. One fellow dove into the water to try to plug the hole.

Fortunately, the boat was still moving toward the bank, so Gene grabbed his case and sleeping bag and jumped off the deck to a dugout alongside. The dugout took him to shore, where he scrambled up the bank.

He found a fellow with a transport truck who was willing to take him to Kalemyo. The truck needed water and had to be cranked before it would start, but finally—with a clank and a rattle—they chugged up the road. All the while, Gene was praying that somehow his Jeep would make it off the sinking sampan and that it would be waiting for him when he returned. He was anxious to get the flight back to Mandalay to pick up the rest of the family. The folks in the Chin Hills were planning for the Andersons to arrive on a specific date, so Gene couldn't delay; flights from these isolated locations only went once or twice a week. There was nothing he could do to help with the unloading or further transport of the Jeep, so he left it in God's care.

When Gene reached Kalemyo, there was one seat still available on the second flight out. He flew into Mandalay that evening, only to discover that taxis to Maymyo weren't running because the police had blocked the road for security reasons. The following day, he finally arrived at the mission and was joyfully reunited with his family.

The Andersons spent another week at Maymyo. Gene and Lois drove forty miles down the mountain to Mandalay to make reservations for their flight to Kalemyo on December 6. When they inquired about their freight, they were told that it had arrived from Rangoon, but the next boat to Kalewa was not ready to leave yet. They decided this was just one more delay to teach them patience.

Burma was a country of amazing contrasts. It could be lovely, pleasant, and enjoyable—then uncomfortable, hard, and unpredictable. The Andersons constantly relied on God's strength to maintain a positive attitude.

Chapter 9

When They Say, "Welcome," Your Heart Is Full

"'You have made known to me the ways of life; You will make me full of joy in Your presence.'"

—Acts 2:28

The Andersons left Maymyo for the drive to Mandalay airport just as light was beginning to creep through the trees. With blankets about their shoulders and scarves tied around their heads, they managed to squeeze in on top of all the luggage. All the members of the rabbit family were doing well.

As the Andersons made their way through the sleeping town, they came upon Ngul Khaw Pau waiting for them by the roadside. He, too, was wrapped in a blanket to keep out the chill. He had come to Maymyo to earn money to buy glasses. His eye that had been injured in the bomb blast hadn't been destroyed, but it had been badly damaged. He wished the Andersons God's blessings as they began their ministry and gave them a letter to take back to his people in Leilum. He assured the family that, as soon as he had bought his glasses, he would return to Tedim. Thanks to God's marvelous healing power, he eventually regained 20/20 vision.

It was an hour's flight from Mandalay to Kalemyo. Gene had been to the airstrip several times before, but this was the first visit for Lois and the boys. They peered eagerly out the windows of the airplane for the first glimpse of their new home. The town was situated in a fertile river valley where rice paddies flourished between low mountains and the skyscraper walls of the blue ranges that comprised the Chin Hills. When the family arrived in Kalemyo, the peaks were hidden in fog that hung over them like billowing white skirts.

As Lois stepped out of the plane, her eyes turned to the mountains. She couldn't see how far they reached into the sky but knew that somewhere up there was her new home. She shifted her attention to the scene around her. Villagers had come to see the plane arrive, and beyond them was the central street running parallel to the air strip. Large spreading trees lined both sides, and buildings—which appeared to be the main part of the village—clustered at one end. Traffic consisted of a few old army trucks, a Jeep or two, bicycles, and the inevitable ox carts that navigated their way around cows, goats, chickens, and dogs.

Gene touched Lois's arm. "Here comes the headman of Tedim." Lois looked in the direction Gene indicated and saw a well-built man, a little taller than most of the crowd, coming through the gate.

He approached the Andersons with a welcoming smile and greeted them in his native Chin. "*Na dam uh hiam?*" (How are you?)

Much to Lois's surprise, Gene answered, "*Dam mah ingh ei!*" (I am fine, thank you!) *He sounds like a native*, she thought.

Gene turned to Lois. "This is U Pau Za Kam, headman of Tedim," he said. Lois shook U Pau Za Kam's outstretched hand. Judging by the firmness of his handclasp and friendly tone of his greeting, she had no doubt he was glad they had come.

U Pau Za Kam motioned the family toward his Jeep. It was then they realized he had come in his own vehicle to meet them and take them to his place in the village. As they made their way past the crowd, many of the villagers greeted them with smiles and friendly handshakes.

When the family arrived in Kalemyo, the peaks were hidden in fog that hung over them like billowing white skirts. As Lois stepped out of the plane, her eyes turned to the mountains. She couldn't see how far they reached into the sky but knew that somewhere up there was her new home.

"You would think we were coming home, not just arriving for the first time," Lois whispered to Gene.

His face beamed. "I told you that you would get a royal welcome, didn't I?"

They smiled back at everybody and climbed in the Jeep. A cloud of dust followed them as they drove down the tree-lined street. U Pau Za

Kam pulled up in front of a two-story wooden structure. There was some type of shop on the street level and living quarters upstairs with a veranda overlooking the street. Gene told Lois that this was U Pau Za Kam's headquarters whenever he was in Kalemyo. He owned a truck and a Jeep to transport goods and passengers to Tedim.

FIGURE 9.1 Main Street in Kalemyo, the village where you look toward Tedim to the west. Undated photograph, circa 1953. Photographer Lois Anderson.

U Pau Za Kam led the way upstairs and showed the Andersons where they could sleep for the night. They put down their bedrolls and suitcases, then followed him back down the stairs and out the back door to the room used for cooking. A big pot of water was standing on the porch.

"Is there a room for bathing?" Lois asked Gene.

"There is none. You just put on your longyi, stand there on that little porch, and take a bath," he answered with a grin. She knew he was visualizing how funny it would be to see her there in a longyi with a crowd of people standing around watching.

Lois had seen the Burmese ladies bathing like that many times at the wells or beside the water hydrants on the streets. With bare shoulders and a longyi tucked tightly around their bosoms, they poured water over themselves. Then they slipped a dry longyi over the wet one which fell off underneath. With a graceful twist, they were once again wrapped in a fresh, dry longyi. Lois knew it was much harder to do than it looked. Imagining the crowd that would enjoy watching her, she decided to take her bath upstairs after dark.

"What do we do first?" Lois asked as she looked around the room. They had had a filling breakfast at four that morning and lunch along the way, but it would soon be dark and they were tired and hungry. Fortunately, Danny had proved to be a good traveler, even with a bad cold.

"I'll go next door to the tea shop, order some rice and vegetable curry, and ask them to boil some drinking water for us." Gene said. "We need to get a good night's sleep. We have plenty to do tomorrow."

While Gene went to order the meal, Lois arranged the beds and mosquito nets. She had enough powdered milk and boiled water to make Danny a bottle of milk. After emptying the bottle and eating some prepared baby food, he fell asleep.

Soon the waiter from the tea shop came and called them to eat. They sat at a table in the tea shop, asked the blessing, and passed around the steaming rice and bowls of cauliflower curry seasoned with cinnamon.

"This is good," Leslie said, and they all agreed with him.

Gene had learned that his Jeep was at Tahan, so after supper, he and U Pau Za Kam went to get it. Gene never did hear the particulars of how the Jeep had arrived; he was just thankful it hadn't ended up in the river. Now that he had his own vehicle, he felt more independent.

Early the next morning, Lois walked down the street to see what she could find to cook for the family. On the street corners, women were squatting beside their baskets of eggplant, gourds, okra, potatoes, and onions. In the shops, she found rice and yellow peas. She bought what she thought she could prepare easily on the camping equipment she had.

"What are you going to do today?" she asked Gene when she got back.

"I plan to leave as soon as possible for Kalewa to see if our goods have come. I am hoping we can go to Tedim tomorrow. We cannot go the next day, as it's a downhill-traffic day and Sabbath. By the way, there is someone downstairs I want you to meet. He brought a letter from Go Za Kham with good news about a house."

"What do you mean?" Lois asked. "Do we have a house to live in when we get there?" For some reason, she had been expecting to arrive on the mountain with no place to spend the first night.

"Believe it or not, we have two houses," Gene replied as he reached for his cap. "I think we should accept them both, as the folks concerned have worked really hard to get them for us."

Gene started toward the stairs. "Come on and meet this man, and I will finish the house story later."

Just inside the shop's entrance was a gentleman wearing a long gray overcoat and a soft-brimmed army hat. When he saw Gene and Lois, he turned toward them, and his face broke into a wide smile. He spoke no English, but they soon were able to converse through an interpreter.

Go Za Kham had sent word to the Andersons, explaining that U Khup Za Neng was a former army officer who was now serving as one of the village elders in Leilum. He had made the trip down the mountain at his own expense to welcome them. Gene and Lois felt their hearts expanding to embrace these people who were going out of their way to show how much they wanted the Andersons to live in their hills.

Gene and Lois invited U Khup Za Neng to ride back up the mountain to Tedim with them, and he readily accepted their invitation. They planned to leave in the morning if they could get everything ready.

After U Khup Za Neng left, Gene and Lois returned to their temporary lodgings upstairs. "Now I'll quickly finish the house story before I go to check on our goods at Kalewa," he said, knowing she was eager to learn about their new accommodations.

"U Pau Za Kam felt terrible that the house he had arranged for us when I was in Tedim last August did not materialize. He felt responsible for providing another in its place, which he has done, paying a month's rent in advance.

"But Go Za Kham has also been concerned about lodging for us. His sister and her husband have moved back into their little mud hut from the wooden house they were building so we can have a place to live."

Lois's heart was touched. "What should we do? Obviously, we can't live in two houses, and we certainly don't want to offend anyone or appear ungrateful for such kindness." As with so many other problems, they decided to trust God to work out a solution.

David and Leslie accompanied Gene on the short trip to Kalewa to pick up their goods. They looked like rugged mountain boys in their Levi pants, billed caps, and heavy shoes slightly too big for their feet. As they scrambled into the Jeep, Lois asked, "Do you have a good supply of drinking water?" Out the boys tumbled, clomped up the stairs, and soon returned with a big can of drinking water.

After they had gone, Lois stood on the veranda watching the stream of people and animals moving up and down the street. It looked the same as any street in any Burmese village, but Lois sensed a difference in the people. She noticed the hill people had stockier bodies, heavily muscled legs, darker brown skin, and rough, homespun clothes that set them apart from inhabitants of the valley and plains.

She was also interested in the packing and preparation for travel going on around her. Kalemyo was the gateway to the distant mountains with their many isolated villages. As she watched, passengers found places to sit on top of the overloaded trucks that moved slowly out of town. She felt those mysterious places calling her too.

Late in the afternoon, her family returned, as well as U Pau Za Kam in his truck, piled high with the Anderson's boxes. They unloaded quickly since there was still one more load to bring. It was almost dark as Gene and U Pau Za Kam left.

Lois fed the boys, and soon they were fast asleep. To escape the mosquitoes, she crawled under her net and waited for Gene to return. It was quite late when she heard the truck pull up in front and decided, from the sound of their quiet voices, that everything was all right. Much later, after making further preparations for the trip in the morning, Gene came upstairs.

"For a while, I was afraid I was not going to get back at all tonight," he said.

"What happened? Kalewa is only two miles from here, isn't it?"

"Yes," Gene answered, "but sometimes two miles can be awfully long. When we got to the checkpoint, we didn't see any soldiers or roadblocks. U Pau Za Kam should have stopped, but he didn't seem concerned. We loaded the rest of the stuff and were coming back about nine o'clock when, suddenly, soldiers jumped out into the road with guns and bayonets pointed straight at our windshield. We quickly stopped. They approached the door of the truck, shouting at the top of their voices. I couldn't understand what they were saying, but there was no doubt they were plenty angry. I didn't feel very safe with a bayonet right under my nose and an angry soldier at the other end of it.

> *Gene and Lois knelt together and thanked the Lord for His protection thus far, trusting that He would continue to be with them. Gene felt as though he could reach out and clasp his angel's hand.*

"U Pau Za Kam tried to explain what we were doing and that we had no intention of disobeying the law. They said they had called to us to stop on our way out, and we had not responded. It is a wonder they didn't fire at us then. They felt we had disregarded their orders and didn't want to listen to us, but after a while, they quieted down and let us go on our way. Both of us felt shaky and would have liked to pull off the road to get our nerves quieted down, but we felt it best to keep going.

"What a day! Everything is here now and am I glad! You should have seen the female workers lifting and carrying our big boxes off the boat and up the steep bank, then loading them onto the truck—women with babies tied on their backs! I could hardly stand to watch them do such heavy work. It was amazing. I don't see how they do it."

Gene and Lois knelt together and thanked the Lord for His protection thus far, trusting that He would continue to be with them. Gene felt as though he could reach out and clasp his angel's hand.

By eight the next morning, everything was on the truck and ready to go. They piled their bedrolls and cooking equipment into the Jeep. U Khup Za Neng sat in the back with the baggage. David perched on top of the bedrolls where he had a king's view of everything. Leslie was squeezed in the front between his parents, and Danny had the softest seat of all on Lois's lap. Because it was not too hot this time of year, they left the top down so they could enjoy the ride to its fullest.

Smiling and waving to the watching crowd, they started up the road. The sun shone clear in the valley, but the mountain tops were still hidden. They passed many small bamboo houses set in banana gardens. A few water buffalo wallowed in the ponds, and cows grazed along the stream flowing by the road. Small, naked children played in the front yards, and older children—wearing only shirts—chased each other about. Mothers nursed their babies, and wrinkled old grandmothers sat winnowing rice. Everyone seemed busy in an easy sort of way.

At the foot of the mountain, they entered a teak forest. Tall, straight trees with huge leaves over a foot in diameter towered above all the undergrowth. Through a clearing, the Andersons caught sight of the river bounding over the rocks.

"Can we come here and camp sometime and go swimming in the river?" the boys asked.

"It's a promise," their parents replied.

At a bend in the road, a small stream fell from the rocks above and made a pool. Gene stopped to fill the Jeep's radiator for the steep grade ahead, and everyone washed the dust from their hands and faces.

"Now we really begin to climb," Gene announced as he started the Jeep again. "Everybody ready? Sit tight and hang on. I'll have enough to do without worrying about somebody falling out."

Back in their places again, they went around a curve, and what Gene had just told them was truer than the rest of the family could have imagined. Up, up the road went, twisting around hairpin turns and blind corners in rapid succession. The road was narrow, just wide enough for one vehicle in most places. On one side, the mountain rose straight above them; on the other, it seemed to drop straight down.

FIGURE 9.2 *The one-way road from Kalemyo to Tedim. Undated photograph, circa 1953. Photographer Lois Anderson.*

Sometimes the family was able to look down on both sides of the road. At other times, the range across the canyon was covered with fog, and they felt as though they were traveling on the edge of the universe. When they caught glimpses through openings in the fog to the blue shadows beyond, it seemed like they were looking out of the present world into a vast unknown.

FIGURE 9.3 *The blue hills to the west of Tedim, looking toward India. Undated photograph, circa 1953. Photographer Lois Anderson.*

The Jeep was proving it could handle the steep grade, and Gene was getting plenty of practice shifting gears up and down as the pitch of the road demanded. With her eyes glued to the road and her ears tuned to the whine of the motor, Lois found herself thrilling to the excitement of the ride.

FIGURE 9.4 From their Jeep, the Andersons catch a glimpse of Tedim in the distance. Undated photograph, circa 1953. Photographer Gene Anderson.

Beautiful, green forests stretched away below them. Tangled vines clinging to great, white tree trunks that thrust their tops high above the bamboos and ferns made the family realize they were truly in the jungle. Sometimes, as they looked up a dark canyon with majestic trees holding their branches high over graceful clumps of willowy bamboo, they thought of the first beautiful garden God gave to man.

They would later learn that this cool, green forest, now ringing with bird calls, presented an entirely different character during the hot, dry season. Then, the teak trees would shed their leaves, and foliage that still clung to the branches would become faded and dusty. Fallen leaves would cover the dry ground, and the heat would press in more and more as one descended to the valley. But, for the moment, they drank in the beauty of the forest.

They climbed the mountain, passing through different areas of growth as the road followed first one side of the ridge and then the other. Here and there, a wild cherry tree stood in a burst of bloom like pink smoke against the dark green of the other trees.

The wind whistled and turned cold after they crossed the highest point on Kennedy Peak. The family wrapped up in blankets they had left out for that purpose. On every side stretched the blue ranges with deep canyons between. Suddenly, Gene pulled to the side of the road.

FIGURE 9.5 *A small village sits on the cliff at the edge of the road in the Chin Hills. Undated photograph, circa 1953. Photographer Lois Anderson.*

"There it is," he said, pointing away to the west. "The first village on the left is Leilum. Scattered along that ridge are the new houses beside the road going into Tedim—and that thick cluster of specks is Tedim itself."

FIGURE 9.6 *The Anderson's first view of their new hometown, Tedim, with Leilum in the foreground. Undated photograph, circa 1953. Photographer Lois Anderson.*

As they neared Leilum an hour later, they saw several boys sitting on the bank waiting for them. Smiles broke out on the boys' faces. They leaped up and raced down the road, suddenly diving off the side and disappearing down the slope.

Gene began to explain that they had gone to tell the villagers of their arrival, when Go Za Kham appeared from the side of the road where the boys had gone headlong out of sight. He was dressed in his suit and was puffing from hurrying up the hill, but he, too, smiled his welcome.

"Ah, you have come. You got here very early. We saw you driving around the bend over there, but I couldn't make it up here to the road before you arrived." His outstretched hands told the family he was glad to see them.

He indicated a turnoff. Gene drove onto the side road winding down through the bushes. He realized that it had been worked by hand—boulders removed, and holes and gaps filled—so that the Jeep could come down into the village.

In a few moments, they stopped at Go Za Kham's house and met his mother, Cing Za Huai, and his father, Kam Zam. His mother was a petite woman—straight and thin, with snapping black eyes and a laughing face. His father was tall and strong with curly, black hair. Go Za Kham's parents shook hands with the Andersons and welcomed them in Chin, then led them to stools on the open porch. The Andersons were served cold fried eggs, which they ate like finger food. All of them were hungry after their long ride in the mountain air, and the food tasted good.

Cookies and Ovaltine—a hot drink made from milk and a flavoring product of malt extract, sugar, and whey—completed the refreshments.

After they had eaten, the Andersons went to see the house Go Za Kham's sister and family were offering them. When they realized the huge sacrifice that had been made, they felt they could not accept so generous an offer and declined as politely as possible.

The family then made their way to the house U Pau Za Kam had arranged for them. They noticed hedgerows on both sides of the winding road, the shrubs reminiscent of wild roses. Homes in Leilum were spaced far enough apart to allow each family to have a vegetable garden beside their house.

The Andersons turned back onto the main Tedim road, which entered a pine forest. It was one of the few places where the trees hadn't been cut down, and the family learned that the forest had been preserved by the government. After they passed through the woods, they came to a cleared area and saw new houses along each side of the road.

The very first house they came to was the one reserved for them. Heaps of bricks were drying on every side. It was evident that many people were camping here to make bricks.

All brickmaking ceased as Gene stopped the Jeep and the family got out. When they opened the door and stepped inside their new home, they were surprised to find several young men— students at the local high school—in residence. As soon as they realized the Andersons had arrived to live there, they rolled up their beds and moved downstairs.

The Anderson's new home was one big room with no cupboards, no closets, and no heat source. The walls were finished with pine boards, and there were windows with panes of colored glass. The family had entered by the only door on that level. In Chin fashion, the kitchen was separate from the house. Since the house was built on the side of a mountain, their kitchen was at a lower elevation, and the room the students had moved to was like a daylight basement.[38]

Soon the truck with their belongings arrived. Lois swept the floor, the family moved their things in and set up their beds. One of the students took them along the hillside and down into a canyon where a small stream of water ran through a pipe and into a hand-hewn trough. This was the nearest water supply. The only sanitary facilities available were the woods. It was not a very satisfactory arrangement, but the family didn't worry about it this first evening.

About the time darkness brought a close to their first day in the Chin Hills, the Andersons were surprised by five visitors. With warm handclasps, they addressed the Andersons in Chin. Gene pulled out some boxes for the men to sit on. While he conversed with them through one of the men who could speak a little English, Lois quickly made a pot of Ovaltine. She had already learned that it was customary to offer a drink to guests. She wanted these first guests to be welcomed properly, even if they had to take turns with the cups. The men finally left, after saying how happy they were to have the Andersons living in their village.

Gene and Lois looked around the room heaped with boxes and barrels. The lantern hissed on top of one of the boxes. Shadows played up and down on the board walls as Gene and Lois pushed containers here and there, trying to identify which ones they should open first. The room was cold, and they were tired. Morning seemed so long ago and Kalemyo so far away. The boys were asleep on their beds.

"Do these people live all around us?" Lois asked as they listened to the voices outside.

"I think most of them are folks who have come to make bricks. They evidently sleep up on the hillside in those little brush lean-tos."

Lois thought about the warm clothes she was wearing. "It seems like they would freeze. I noticed that most of the men and women working this afternoon had no extra clothing on and everyone was barefoot."

"Come and look," Gene said, as he opened the door. They stepped across the ditch in front of the house.

On the hill across the road were many little fires burning. Figures wrapped in blankets were squatting beside each one. From all around them came the sounds of singing in unfamiliar and haunting minor keys.

As Gene and Lois stood quietly listening, it seemed time and space had transported them to some far-away village of long ago, where people sang about the success of the hunt or victory in battle. It was not a time for dancing—just the ceaseless passing of time by the fire on a cold winter night, singing quietly together of things that used to be.

At three in the morning, Lois could still hear the music, and the flickering fires still burned.

The local people expressed the hope that the newcomers would remain in the Tedim area. Accordingly, the Andersons located a house in the village of Lawibual, which was more centralized than Leilum. It had four rooms upstairs for the family, as well as a large room downstairs for visitor accommodations, weekly church services, and temporary mission headquarters. After a month in the rental, they moved into their new home.

FIGURE 9.7 Gene and his boys by their house in Tedim. Left to right: Danny (in the Jeep), David, Leslie, and Gene. (The building on the left is their house; the one on the right, the kitchen. The deck area between the two is their innkaa.) Undated photograph, circa 1954. Photographer Lois Anderson.

Every evening since the Anderson's arrival, there had been a guest sitting at their table. Sometimes it was only one, but often it was two, or five, or even ten. Teachers from the high school stopped by, one of whom was their next-door neighbor. The man in charge of the physical education classes for all the schools came and brought the director of the high school with him. The public relations man for the government, a young fellow, visited almost every day. He brought the family a table and four chairs. Most of the guests—well-educated leading men of the villages—were taking the *Voice of Prophecy* Bible lessons, and it was rewarding to have them stop in with their questions.

Go Za Kham confessed his convictions about the Seventh-day Adventist faith to his superior, Reverend Hau Go. He told the Andersons, "Everyone is talking about me, but I am burning my bridges with the Baptists and coming along as fast as I can."

On Friday evenings, interested villagers gathered around the family fire for vespers. Among those present one evening were two men from Darkhai who had accepted the Adventist message when Lalkhuma and Zakhuma were preaching there. They still had much to learn, but their hearts were open to God's leading, and they stayed for several hours after vespers to ask many questions.

The men from Darkhai were fascinated by the music playing on the tape recorder. Evidently, word about the music spread, because a whole crowd came in to listen. To be perfectly honest, it was so cold outside that the warmth of the room was a great attraction. (The Andersons brought their camp stove downstairs whenever a meeting was planned.)

Gene asked Lois to organize the weekly programs for Sabbath school. She was glad to be assigned a specific ministry. The first Friday and Sabbath evenings of her weekly programs, people came when they heard Lois playing her accordion. They loved to sing along with it, and she played until she couldn't hold the instrument any longer. They held three services in their home each week.

One Sabbath morning, the ground was white with frost, and the people, wrapped in blankets, were shivering when they came in. There were seventeen Sabbath school members and quite a few visitors. Almost half of those who attended regularly had studied their *Voice of Prophecy* lessons every day.

The Andersons had scarcely settled in before Gene started preparing to leave for year-end workers' meetings in Rangoon. Lalkhuma and Zakhuma, who planned to attend the meetings with him, soon arrived from the villages where they had been evangelizing and stayed with the Andersons. In the evenings, the three men enjoyed discussing Bible topics, while David and Leslie read their books.

Lois was very busy in her kitchen, preparing food for everyone. The warm, crusty, homemade bread[39] that she served with milk and jam was a favorite. She was able to purchase a good variety of local produce from peddlers who came to the house every day: cabbage, corn, mustard greens, pumpkins, sweet potatoes, green beans, tomatoes, bananas, oranges, and peanuts. She ground corn for mush and bread. Following the example of the local ladies, she also dried mustard greens to store for use in the dry season.

Danny had gotten a cold in Maymyo and was still coughing and congested after their arrival. Lois was afraid he had pneumonia. She applied several hot compresses[40] to his chest to try to break up the congestion, but he showed no improvement until she put a tent over his bed and gave him medicated steam inhalations. He recovered quickly and became his usual happy, healthy self.

FIGURE 9.8 *Danny discovers his reflection in a mirror at Tedim. Undated photograph, circa 1953. Photographer Lois Anderson.*

It was nearly Christmas time, and the whole family was busy with secret projects. The cozy mountain cabin with the glow of kerosene lamps, a Christmas tree that the boys had decorated with garlands of popcorn, the warmth of their little camp stove, and Christmas songs playing on the radio all helped to create the perfect holiday atmosphere.

The night before Gene left for the committee meetings in the south, the family celebrated their first Christmas in the Chin Hills. Gifts magically appeared beneath the lovely tree. David and Leslie—the "big" boys—had made an elephant for Danny, some little towels with embroidery in the corners for their dad, and potholders for their mom. Leslie had made David a shoeshine box, and David had made Leslie a pair of bookends.

The present that brought the most enjoyment to everyone, though, was another homemade gift for Gene from his boys. It was a board like a toboggan[41] that was padded on one side.

"What's this? A tombstone?" he joked, making Lois and the boys laugh.

"It's for you to lie on under the Jeep when you're working on it, Daddy," Leslie said.

Gene had made a playpen for Danny. Danny had been scooting all over the floor, putting everything he found into his mouth, so now he could safely sit inside his own little house and look out at the world.

There were a few more gifts: books and T-shirts for the big boys, toys for Danny, and popcorn balls for everyone. They all wished the special evening could last forever.

After Gene left for Rangoon, Lois went to Leilum to give a hot compress treatment to Suak Khaw Kai's wife. The woman had lost a baby two years before and had been in pain since then. Gene and Lois both thought she might have a displaced, inflamed uterus. They decided applying hot compresses could do no harm, and knee-chest exercises might help. Gene planned to ask Dr. Richardson about her condition while he was in Rangoon.

When Gene retuned home, he confirmed that Dr. Richardon had agreed with their treatment plan for Suak Khaw Kai's wife. After several more weeks of treatments, her symptoms disappeared.

Suak Khaw Kai had been keeping the Sabbath. He had quit smoking and was no longer eating pork. "If Pastor Anderson can get along without those things, I can too!" he declared.

Gene and Lois began to search for a location they could develop as mission headquarters with enough space to include a mission house, a school, and a church. They found an ideal parcel among pine trees on a hill at the south end of town. The property sat on a ridge, overlooking the Manipur River Canyon on the west and a beautiful valley on the east. It had good soil for a garden and enough building sites for the necessary facilities. They wondered if this was the place the Lord had in mind for them and prayed for His direction.

Upon inquiring, Gene was told the land was reserved for a new government high school and was not available. Gene and Lois began looking elsewhere. One day, a man from the government office—who knew the Andersons had been looking at that property—came to their house and told them that the land had been released and was now available. Gene immediately went to the office to ask if this was, indeed, true.

"Yes," he was told. "You may stake out what you would like and make application for the same."

So, Gene placed the stakes and filed a request to obtain the property. In a few days, he received a reply that said he could have the plot for a ninety-nine-year lease for the fee of one kyat (less than one-tenth of a US penny). However, as details unfolded, it was not as simple as he had been told.

Gene priced lumber and drew a house plan—a simple design, but adequate for their living quarters on the main level, with enough rooms beneath for storage, meetings, and an office. When they received appropriations from the Burma Union with the go-ahead to build, they took it as God's answer to their prayer for guidance.

Several weeks later, when Gene went to see if his request to lease the property had been processed, he learned that it had to be posted for thirty days prior to approval. After the posting period, the assistant superintendent of the district and Gene would re-examine the property. The assistant would then send his recommendations to his superiors—who would approve them or not, as they deemed appropriate. The assistant superintendent had finished almost three-fourths of the *Voice of Prophecy* Bible lessons and told Gene he would do all he could to facilitate the lease.

It was fortunate the Andersons did not know it would take close to nine months before the process was complete, or they might have become discouraged. (The family arrived in the Chin Hills on December 8, 1953, and the lease permit was not issued until September 20, 1954.)

Lois felt she was making progress toward establishing a routine and organizing her home, but it came slowly. Besides caring for Danny, she homeschooled David and Leslie—though, in her words, "the school situation went steady, by jerks." The boys certainly did their part, but it was so unlike traditional school, it was challenging to keep them focused on their work. The continual interruptions did not help, but the boys were learning many things that couldn't be found in a textbook.

Once the gas-powered, wringer washing machine was set up, David took over laundry duties. He became adept at the chore, even though water had to be carried from a distant spring to fill the washing machine and two rinsing tubs. All the laundry was line dried.

Because there was no indoor plumbing, a metal tub was used for personal bathing. It was big enough to sit in if bathers bent their legs up to their chests. Using cups of water from a heated kettle on the wood range and adding enough cold water to make the bath water a pleasant temperature, bathing was accomplished with less than a gallon of water per bath.

FIGURE 9.9 Leslie and David saw the firewood into lengths that will fit in their wood stove. In the background is laundry David did. Undated photograph, circa 1954. Photographer Lois Anderson.

Gene made a windmill that generated electricity whenever there was enough wind. The family also had a gasoline generator that provided light for the house, but it was too expensive to use often. They relied on kerosene lanterns that were moved from room to room as the household activities changed throughout the day. The only heat source was the wood range in the kitchen, which was a separate building. When it was cold in the house, everyone wore sweaters and coats—and sometimes even wrapped themselves in blankets.

There was no refrigeration for perishable foods, necessitating frequent buying from the food peddlers who came by every morning. These girls carried baskets on their backs. The baskets hung from a broad band that passed across the top of their heads. The loads were heavy, and Lois noticed one little girl with a crease in her skull from the weight of her basket. Many carried firewood about three or four feet long and two to four inches thick, sticking up lengthwise in their basket. The wood strips fanned out over their heads, like gigantic, elaborate headdresses.

The girls dressed similarly: a loose gray or black flannel-type shirt and a knee-length skirt made from a straight piece of purplish-black cloth that wrapped around them and overlapped a few inches in the front. The skirt was secured at the hips with a belt. Numerous strings of brightly colored beads hung around their necks, and their hair was usually done in three braids—one on each side and one down the center of their back. When it was cold, they wrapped up in blankets to go about their work.

FIGURE 9.10 Three young Chin villagers bring firewood from the forest in their baskets to sell to the Andersons. Undated photograph, circa 1954. Photographer Lois Anderson.

Mothers carried their babies in slings that they fashioned from long strips of cloth. A mother would hold her baby against her front or side, then wrap the cloth around and under the baby before tying it around herself. This bucket-shaped sling fit differently for each child, depending on its size. A mother of a toddler would put it on her back, wrap the cloth around the child, pull the ends of the cloth over her shoulders, and tie it in front of herself. Sometimes, the mother would swing the toddler around, under her arm, and carry it on her hip. Regardless of the method used, the mothers' hands were free, and the children were secure—whether awake or asleep. When it was cold, the mothers wrapped another blanket around their little ones.

Cecil B. Guild, president of the Burma Union, and his wife, Nora, arrived from Rangoon—along with Dr. Richardson and his family. The Guilds, Dr. Richardson, Lalkhuma, Zakhuma, and Ngul Khaw Pau then accompanied Gene on a ten-day tour through the mountain villages. It was the first time any physician or missionary had been to many of them. Nellie Richardson and her girls—Sharon, Bonnie, and Nancy—stayed with Lois and the boys while the others were away. David and Leslie were delighted to have playmates.

Early one morning, after a night of heavy frost, Lois went over to talk with Sian Za Kham, the teacher who lived next door. His wife had had a baby son the evening before. When Lois felt the newborn, his hands, feet, and legs were cold. She went home, got a hot water bottle, some undershirts, and a nightie, and went back to warm him up. She rubbed oil

FIGURE 9.11 *Two young Chin women carry loads on their heads, while a third carries her young child in its sling. Undated photograph, circa 1954. Photographer Lois Anderson.*

FIGURE 9.12 *The Guilds and Richardsons arrive to help the Andersons at Tedim. Front row: Nora Guild, Nellie Richardson, Nancy Richardson, Dr. George Richardson. In doorway of DC-3: Bonnie Richardson, Sharon Richardson. (The Richardsons were missionaries in Rangoon.) Undated photograph, circa 1954. Photographer Cecil B. Guild.*

on his skin and bundled him in warm flannels. Sian Za Kham asked Lois to pray for the baby and for them, which she did. He also asked if she would choose an English name for the baby. She chose Paul.

Lois returned home to make breakfast for her family and the Richardsons. A few minutes later, Sian Za Kham arrived with Suak Khaw Kai, for whom he was acting as interpreter. Suak Khaw Kai wanted medicine for his sick wife, the same woman Lois had treated for residual pain following childbirth. He thought she might have pneumonia. Lois was hesitant to dispense medicine without checking the patient in person. So, after breakfast, Lois and her boys—along with Nellie and her girls—drove to Suak Khaw Kai's house. As soon as Lois saw his wife, she realized the woman was very sick. She was sitting up on her mat, groaning, coughing, and wincing from pain.

A young man who had interpreted for Sabbath services on previous occasions was in the house and helped Lois communicate with the patient, whose temperature was 102.4°F (39.1°C). Lois had brought sulfa medicine and hot compress cloths and decided that both were needed. She asked for hot water and gave the woman a treatment. The woman was in such pain, it took three people to help her lie down. Lois prayed for the sick lady before she left and promised to return later to give her another treatment.

When Lois returned that evening, she took the woman's temperature and could hardly believe her eyes. It was normal! The woman was resting quietly—no groaning or coughing. Lois applied more hot compresses. Before she left, everyone knelt, and Lois prayed again. Suak Khaw Kai and his wife kept repeating how grateful they were. "If you hadn't come today, I think I would have died," she told Lois.

The next morning when Lois went to give another treatment, she found the woman's temperature was back up to 101.5°F (38.6°C), but she was not coughing and seemed much better. The young man who had interpreted the night before came back to see how the woman was. He gave Lois a note he had written, expressing heartfelt thanks for what she had done and praising God for the patient's improving health. He addressed it, "Dear Mother," and signed it, "Your loving son."

The day before the expected return of the tour group, Ngul Khaw Pau arrived and told Nellie, who was sitting in the yard, "They're here!"

Surprised, she turned around and asked, "Who's here?"

"Pastor Anderson," he answered.

The women and children jumped in the Jeep and drove to where the mountain trail joined the road. They had just arrived when Pastor and Mrs. Guild came up the trail. The Guilds had left Muizawl early that morning, leaving Gene and Dr. Richardson to treat more patients. The whole group walked back down the trail and sat by a spring where the ferns were taller than their heads, waiting for the remainder of the trekkers. After a while, Lalkhuma, Zakhuma, and the pack horses appeared, followed a few minutes later by Gene and Dr. Richardson, who both looked tanned and happy.

FIGURE 9.13 Gene (left) and Dr. Richardson (right) hiking a mountainous trail in the Chin Hills. Undated photograph, circa 1954. Photographer Cecil B. Guild.

Everyone had a great time visiting around the fire that evening. While on the trail, the travelers had smelled the strong, pungent odor of tigers—distinctly different from the odor of other wild cats—but they hadn't seen any. The next afternoon, the Guilds left by Jeep for Kalemyo, hoping to catch a plane to Mandalay, and from there on to Maymyo for a few days. Since he was the Burma Union president, Pastor Guild and his wife, Nora, were taking this opportunity to visit the Gerlings on their return to Rangoon. They planned to sail for the United States at the end of February for furlough.

Lois continued treating the sick woman for another week. The woman improved so much that Lois was able to join Gene and her boys on their overnight excursion to take the Richardsons to Kalemyo for their flight to Rangoon.

Kalemyo was at the base of the fifty-mile road to Tedim. Once they were off the mountain, the Andersons and Richardsons decided to camp for the night, instead of staying in town. The campsite they chose was the place the boys had seen on their journey to Leilum—the one their parents had promised to take them to. It was a perfect spot in a lovely grove by the river that flowed through the gorge. There was plenty of wood, a clean, gravelly beach, and clear water rushing over the rocks. It was too cold to swim, but the youngsters waded, threw pebbles in the water, and helped gather wood for a fire. After supper, they all sang around the campfire.

The Andersons said goodbye to their dear friends the next day. As the plane rose into the air, the realization suddenly swept over Lois that they were now all alone. Tears filled her eyes. The Richardsons were leaving for America in April, and the two families would not see each other again for a very long time, if ever.

The family hurried with their shopping, so they could get on their way home well before dark. Though the road was solid, it was also narrow and steep. In some places, it was just a small shelf clinging to the mountainside with a cliff going straight up above them on one side and straight down to the valley below on the other. By the time they arrived at Kennedy Peak—8,868 feet above sea level—the wind was fierce, chilling them to the bone. They wrapped themselves in blankets, which protected them from the worst of the cold until they reached home.

One morning, a woman and her daughter from a village two miles away came to the Anderson's door and offered Lois two lovely hands of bananas. Lois wondered why they were giving her a present.

She called Sian Za Kham, the next-door neighbor, to come and translate.

After listening to the woman, he said, "This woman would like you to hire her daughter to care for your boy child."

Lois did not feel ready to tackle the job of training a girl, so she replied, "I want to care for my boy child myself."

Sian Za Kham told Lois he was acquainted with the family and knew that they needed food and clothes. The father was a teacher but had been too ill to work for many years, and there were nine children in the family, the youngest only two years old.

Lois began to think that maybe this would give her an entry into the women's lives. Most of them hadn't gone to school and had little opportunity to learn new ways. Many of the young men spoke English well enough to converse, but it was challenging to communicate with the young girls and women. Lois wanted so much to make a difference in their lives!

So, contrary to her first inclination, Lois hired the woman's daughter, Ning Go Cing. She came each morning and went home in the evening—an hour's walk each way. It was not long before Ning Go Cing asked if she could stay with the Andersons, and Lois consented.

FIGURE 9.14 Ning Go Cing standing on the Anderson's innkaa in Tedim. Undated photograph, circa 1954. Photographer Lois Anderson.

Ning Go Cing was a sweet girl and learned quickly. Lois was able to turn much of the routine household work over to her. This freed Lois to supervise David and Leslie's schooling, tend to Danny, make clothes for the family, write letters, assist Gene with his ministry, and help the women learn how to care for their families.

A woman arrived who was having a difficult time feeding her baby from a bottle. The baby cried and cried. Lois told the mother she would help fix the milk for the baby if the woman brought her the milk and sugar. When Lois went to put the milk in the bottle, she found the nipple was split a half inch at the end. No wonder the baby couldn't drink from it! Lois put one of Danny's bottles in the baby's mouth. He didn't like it at first but soon finished all the milk and fell sound asleep. When his mother said he was drinking half a cup twice a day, Lois advised her to give him three times that amount.

One morning, Go Za Kham and his cousin Ngul Khaw Pau came to ask Lois to evaluate Ngul Khaw Pau's baby nephew. As soon as Lois finished cutting Leslie's hair, she took her hot compress cloths and rode a bike to Leilum. The baby did not look too sick, but it was so hoarse it couldn't make a sound and had difficulty breathing. Lois applied hot compresses. She wanted to give steam inhalations, but there was no way to keep the water boiling.

Lois returned in the evening and found the baby much worse. It was breathing in gasps. Lois had brought her small kerosene stove to do a steam inhalation, as well as a tin can so she could direct the steam better. She put a blanket over two chairs and had the mother hold the baby under the covering. Lois wondered if the baby would live through the night.

She asked the family if they would like her to pray. "Of course," the baby's father responded. For a while, he had regularly attended the services the Andersons conducted in their home, but it had been a long time since they had seen him. He rode home with Lois and the boys to get cough syrup. Lois left her kerosene stove with them, hoping they would give the baby more steam inhalations. Lois prayed the Lord would heal this baby for His honor and glory.

The baby was quite a bit better the next day. He still couldn't breathe easily, though, so Lois continued the steam inhalations. By the third day, the baby was much improved. Lois was relieved and thankful to the Lord for answering her prayers.

One day, Khawvel Thanga from the village of Bukphir came to visit the Andersons. He was the Sabbath-keeping man Gene had heard about at Rih Lake months earlier—the man who had carried Rualchhina's luggage to Tahan when Rualchhina had been prevented from boarding the flight with Gene.

When the Guilds and Dr. Richardson had accompanied Gene on his most recent tour, the missionary group had visited Bukphir, Khawvel Thanga's village. He had not been home at the time, but his wife had insisted the group stay and hold a meeting. More than sixty-five people had attended, and they had expressed the desire for Adventists to start a school there. The villagers had emptied and cleaned a house for the group to stay in overnight.

Now Khawvel Thanga had come to the Anderson's house to meet them for the first time, bringing with him a letter from Lalkhuma. Khawvel Thanga told the Andersons that he had been keeping the Sabbath for nine years, after reading about it in the Bible. His people laughed at him and called him a fool, but he had been preaching about the Sabbath all over the Chin Hills. His belief in the state of the dead, the second coming of Jesus,[42] the millennium, and the destruction of the wicked[43] matched the Anderson's beliefs, all of which he had learned from reading his Bible. As a compounder, he traveled widely, selling medicine. Gene and Lois had been waiting a long time to meet him.

Gene prepared sermons for a series of meetings in Leilum. Go Za Kham worked with him as interpreter. Go Za Kham was still an assistant pastor of the Baptist Church, though the senior pastor knew of his acceptance of Seventh-day Adventism and his plan to be baptized soon.

FIGURE 9.15 Gene and the family go to Leilum to prepare for the upcoming evangelistic series. Gene is riding a bicycle so he doesn't have to carry Danny. Boys, left to right: David, Leslie, and Danny. Undated photograph, circa 1954. Photographer Lois Anderson.

The day the meetings began was a busy one for Lois. She started the boys on their schoolwork, then finished a pair of slacks for David. It was her first attempt at sewing trousers, and she was pleased with the result.

Ngul Khaw Pau came with his eight-month-old baby girl who had been coughing and had chest congestion. Lois stopped her work to give the child hot compresses and medicine. A few minutes after Ngul Khaw Pau left, the chief from Darkhai came with his family, all of them wrapped in colorful blankets because of the cold. (When people came to Tedim from the mountain villages, they usually stopped in at the Andersons to request a teacher or someone who could start a medical clinic.) Then, Lois began washing her hair. Before she finished, a lady came with her sick baby. Lois sent the lady to find an interpreter, and while she was gone, Lois put the bread dough into loaf pans and fed Danny. When the lady and her baby returned with an interpreter, Lois learned that the baby had a bad head cold and chest congestion. She washed its eyes, which were stuck shut, then gave it medicine and a steam-inhalation treatment. She told the mother to bring the baby back in the afternoon for another treatment.

The first meeting was held in the open on U Hang Za Gin's innkaa.[44] There were about 250 villagers in attendance, counting the children, all packed tightly together.

They sang a few songs, and then Lois gave a talk on homes and mothers, using flannel board illustrations. David had planned to play a cornet solo following Lois's presentation, but Gene forgot about the music and enthusiastically started preaching. When the crowd got up to leave after the service was over—with no special music—it was amusing to watch the people all walking double: on every back was a sleeping child.

The meetings at Leilum continued for several weeks. David ran the projector, and Leslie was the general maintenance man. Gene took a small generator to supply power for the lights and the projector. The attendance dropped to about thirty adults with their children. The weather turned very cold, making it too uncomfortable to meet outside, but all those who were really interested still came, crowding inside U Hang Za Gin's house.

One evening, a storm was brewing as the family left home for the meeting. Billowing black clouds swept across the sky, and the wind roared up from the Manipur Canyon. They had picked up their usual Jeep load of attendees and arranged their equipment at the meeting house when the storm suddenly broke. Lightning flashed and thunder boomed right overhead, while hail beat furiously on the tin roof. The noise was deafening, so Gene waited until he could be heard before he presented the evening's message. Most of the faithful ones were there, despite the storm.

On May 4, 1954, Gene met the plane at Kalemyo. Pastor and Mrs. Parker and two of their children—Linda and Dennis—along with Miss Aliada Mann, had flown in from Rangoon.

FIGURE 9.16 *The Parkers and Miss Mann come to Tedim for the first baptism in the Chin Hills. Left to right: Aliada Mann, Irene Parker, Gene Anderson (driver), Linda Parker, Dennis Parker, Pastor Phil Parker, Leslie Anderson, and David Anderson. Undated photograph, circa 1954. Photographer Lois Anderson.*

Pastor Parker had come to baptize the first fourteen new converts in the Chin Hills. At Leilum, the villagers tried to dam up the water, without success. They finally made a small pool from a tiny stream bed, with just enough water for each candidate to sit in, while Pastor Parker knelt to baptize them. Go Za Kham stepped into the water first, followed by his father and mother. It was a beautiful service. With the baptism of those fourteen individuals on May 21, 1954, the first Seventh-day Adventist church in the Chin Hills was born.

Phung Kai and his wife, Tel Khan Ning, were among those baptized that day. Describing his early life to Gene, Phung Kai said that he and his parents were animists and pantheists[45] who lived in Sezaang, a village about two miles from Tedim. He had wanted to become a Christian when he was a young man, but his parents would not allow it. After his parents died, he married and moved to Leilum in 1946, where he became a member of the American Baptist Church.

When Pastor Anderson began his meetings at Leilum, Phung Kai attended each evening. He was convinced that the message he heard agreed with the Bible. One night, he had a private conversation with Pastor Anderson. Because Phung Kai had been a heavy drinker and smoker since his childhood, he asked if he had to stop drinking wine and smoking before he could be baptized.

"Yes, you do," Gene replied. "The Bible says your body is the temple of the Holy Spirit. Those things harm it."

It was a big struggle for Phung Kai to decide whether he should give up these addictions or just forget about being baptized. After several days of praying and thinking, Phung Kai resolved to commit his life to Jesus in the Adventist faith. He smoked as much as he could the final day before his baptism, but by the power of the Holy Spirit, he never drank wine or smoked again.

After the Andersons left Tedim, Phung Kai told his eldest son, Pau Za Khan, and his other children, "Not because I didn't love my father, but I

> *Pastor Parker had come to baptize the first fourteen new converts in the Chin Hills. At Leilum, the villagers tried to dam up the water, without success. They finally made a small pool from a tiny stream bed, with just enough water for each candidate to sit in, while Pastor Parker knelt to baptize them.*

did not shed my tears when my father passed away as much as I shed my tears when Pastor Anderson and his family left Tedim for good."

FIGURE 9.17 *Pastor Parker officiates at the first Chin Hills baptism in the village of Leilum. Undated photograph, circa 1954. Photographer Lois Anderson.*

While the group was still in Tedim, Miss Mann, Pastor Parker, Gene, Go Za Kham, and two other men went to Laitui where they had heard there were a few interested people. Laitui was a strenuous all-day hike away. Miss Mann was probably the first white woman to make the trip, but it taxed her strength to the point of exhaustion. On the return trip, a pack pony pulled her up the last stretch from the Manipur River. Lois and Mrs. Parker saved the hikers the final five miles of walking by meeting them with the Jeep below the village. It took the group several days to recuperate, but they felt God had blessed the contacts they made.

The Parker party prepared to return to Rangoon. The ticket agent had sent a verbal message for them to come to Kalemyo on Monday so they could fly out on Tuesday. They waited in Kalemyo all day Tuesday, but no plane came. They arranged to get on Thursday's regular flight if no special plane came on Wednesday. No plane came on Wednesday. That afternoon, one of the government officers requisitioned all seats on Thursday's flight for himself, his wife, and a group of Buddhist monks. (Government officers and monks always had priority seating.) Pastor Parker and the others began to think they might have to return to Tedim, but they decided to wait one more day, praying that the Lord would work out their transportation home. They spent their nights in the town's only hotel.

Thursday morning, the Parkers discovered there were six other passengers who had been stranded for the same length of time. A plane finally did arrive, and all of them waited and hoped this might be their flight out.

The pilot disembarked and ducked under the plane to examine it. Gene went to see what the trouble was and found the underside of the plane wet with hydraulic brake fluid. It had to be fixed before the plane could land again. Gene knew the pilot, so together they found a leaking joint in the line, repaired it, refilled the reservoir, bled the brakes,[46] and the plane was as good as ever.

This plane was en route to Khampti in the Naga Hills, but the pilot felt it was too late to proceed as planned. Instead, he decided he could take two loads of passengers to Mandalay, beginning with the eleven stranded individuals. It was not a direct flight to Rangoon, but since Mandalay was closer to Rangoon and a larger center than Kalemyo, the passengers felt it would be easier to find transportation home from there.

However, the Lord had already arranged everything for them. A charter flight had come to Mandalay from Rangoon and would have returned empty, except that the stranded group from Kalemyo was there, ready to board.

Soon after the Parker visit, the father of one of the men who had been baptized at Leilum came to see the Andersons. He lived in the village of Laitui, where Pastor Parker, Miss Mann, and Gene had just gone on their tour. He told them that he was puzzled when his son came to visit and announced that he was going to join the Seventh-day Adventists. The man had assumed there was no difference between Seventh-day Adventists and Baptists, but he couldn't forget the new things his son had shared. He could not rest until he had talked with Pastor Anderson.

He was an old man, but he was convinced he had heard the truth. As a result of what his son had told him, he had quit smoking, stopped eating pork, and declared he was going to begin keeping the Sabbath—even if he was the only one in his village to do so.

Chapter 10

When You Walk with God, Blessings Abound

"How precious is Your lovingkindness, O God! Therefore the children of men put their trust under the shadow of Your wings. They are abundantly satisfied with the fullness of Your house, and You give them drink from the river of Your pleasures. For with You is the fountain of life; in Your light we see light."

—Psalm 36:7–9

Danny was a happy baby, calling and waving to everyone he met. One day, David stood Danny up, then moved back, encouraging his little brother to come to him. Danny took one step before he tumbled into his brother's arms. It was his first step.

The Gerlings had given the Andersons a stroller. Gene made new tires for it from a hose, but the joints bulged, so the wheels didn't roll easily. Nevertheless, Danny discovered he could make it go and entertained himself by pushing it around the yard.

Danny's first birthday arrived. Leslie baked the birthday cake. David and Leslie, ages twelve and ten respectively, had worked for several days leading up to Danny's birthday, building a rocking boat for him. They had sawed, planed, and sanded it; Lois had nailed the pieces together; and the boys had completed the project with a coat of paint. They named it *Danny Boy,* and eagerly showed him how to make it rock.

Lois had made Danny a soft rag doll. When he saw it, he smiled a big smile, took a step toward it, then leaned down until his face was buried in it. It was so soft, he kept touching it to his face and squeezing it over and over again, squealing with delight. He had so much fun playing with his rag doll and rocking in his boat.

FIGURE 10.1 Danny on the innkaa of the Anderson house in Tedim on his first birthday. His birthday boat "Danny Boy" is behind him. June 2, 1954. Photographer Lois Anderson.

David and Leslie practiced their horns every day, improving their musical skills. Although Lois played the piano, organ, and accordion, she did not know how to play either the trumpet or the trombone. She often found herself asking the boys to do things on their horns that she didn't know how to do—or scarcely understood—but they managed to do whatever she asked. Leslie's arms weren't long enough to reach the last two positions on his trombone, so Gene made an extension for him from two glued-together pieces of carved wood about the size of pencils. He carved a loop at the end of the sticks that attached to the bar where the trombone slide would normally be held. It was not tight against the bar, so the slide could be moved easily up and down to each position of the trombone slide. Leslie kept his hand on the extension while playing.

Gene talked of getting two horses to use for pack animals when he went on his mountain tours. Between trips, David and Leslie would each have one to ride. The boys were excited about this plan, but Gene reminded them that providing grain and grazing for the animals would be a challenge.

Once life for the Andersons settled into a somewhat predictable routine, they began looking for horses. Gene said he had seen some good ones that cost between 300 and 400 rupees (about sixty to eighty US dollars). At those prices, the family decided to purchase only one. The boys were delighted, as they had been saving their annas and rupees for many months. They watched with interest and wonder every horse that went by their house. Word that the Andersons were hoping to get a horse traveled quickly throughout Tedim and even reached the surrounding villages.

One day, a man and a horse appeared in their yard after traveling from a village about four hours north of Tedim. He had heard the Andersons would like a horse. And so, the boys became the proud owners of a beautiful horse they named Prince. He was bigger than most of the other horses in the neighborhood. He had been used as a pack animal so hadn't been trained for riding. The boys received some rough treatment during their first days of getting acquainted with Prince. He bit them, pawed, bucked, and kicked. But, with persistent patience and gentle handling, they eventually won his affection.

FIGURE 10.2 David and Prince at Tedim. Undated photograph, circa 1954. Photographer Lois Anderson.

Early each morning, they rode Prince over the hill beyond Tedim to find green grass, since there was none closer. All they could feed him at home was corn. Because there was so much brush in the grazing area, they had to leave Prince untied. Sometimes, he was already back in the yard by the time they returned home. Once, Prince wandered over to Leilum where somebody found him and tied him up. The boys had to walk three miles to get him. They were learning that life consisted of plenty of hard work.

On one occasion, Prince didn't come home for several days. David and Leslie searched all the usual places for him, without success. Then his former owner, who lived half a day's journey away, arrived leading the horse. Rualchhina, who was visiting at the time, called the boys—who immediately rushed outside. Prince neighed and almost trampled Rualchhina to get to the boys. He nibbled them all over. The boys were very pleased!

They also had a pet monkey named Toby. One morning, David looked out the window and exclaimed, "There's Prince standing by Toby's wire run line." Lois, David, and Leslie laughed as Toby leaped up on Prince, rolled and scampered all over his back, slid down his rump, got tangled in his long tail, swung between his hind legs, then scrambled up again onto his back. He ran up and down on the horse from his neck to his hind hooves, even nibbling at the horse's hind legs just above his hooves.

But when Toby got on Prince's head, the horse had had enough. He arched his neck toward the ground, raised his front leg, and brought his hoof down on Toby's arm. The monkey screeched and raced back to his box under the eaves. "I wonder if he'll try that again," Leslie said.

Toby did continue running all over Prince. Prince apparently enjoyed it—until Toby reached his head, at which time Prince always put an end to the play.

The family often took Toby along when they went for a walk. He ran from bush to tree but never wandered farther than a few feet away from them. By the time they returned home, he was tired and ready for a nap.

Toby played well with Leslie unless David showed up. Then he would immediately bite Leslie and jump into David's arms. "He's jealous when you are together," Lois explained. "He doesn't know how to be friends with both of you at the same time." Leslie learned to let David know when he was going to play with Toby.

One evening, Toby jumped through the open window and began swinging on the curtains over the supper table. "Hey!" Gene yelled.

"Someone didn't fasten Toby up! Quick!" Lois shouted. "Catch him!"

Everyone jumped up. Leslie's chair fell backward with a crash as he grabbed for Toby and missed. The monkey leaped onto the table, spilling a glass of milk, then sprang to the top of the pony wall,[47] raced toward the door, dropped down to the floor, and grabbed Danny's bottle. He jammed the nipple into his mouth and sprinted around the room with the bottle swinging from side to side.

Someone nearly caught him, but Toby scampered out the door and down the hill, across the innkaa, and into the kitchen. He knocked the can of cocoa off the shelf, the lid popped open, and a big puff of brown powder rose from the floor.

FIGURE 10.3 *Leslie (left) and David (right) playing with their pet monkey, Toby, at Tedim. Undated photograph, circa 1954. Photographer Lois Anderson.*

"Toby! Toby, come here!" Leslie called in despair, but the monkey was out the kitchen window in a flash. Leslie caught a glimpse of him as he disappeared into the neighbor's corn patch.

Crack! Crack! Crack! Leslie knew Toby was breaking the corn as he jumped from stalk to stalk. That corn was an important source of food for the neighbors. Leslie felt sick.

Toby wore a neck collar that fastened to a long cord. The cord moved easily on a wire line strung between a pole and the corner of the kitchen under the eaves where Toby's box was fastened. Leslie had been the last one to play with Toby, and he realized he must not have fastened the collar securely to the cord.

"He's coming back," Lois shouted. "Chase him in here!"

She banged the window shut just as Toby ran through the door and jumped up on the table. Leslie slammed the door behind him. In a moment, Toby was snuggled in Lois's arms, one hand hanging onto her hair.

"You rascal. What a chase you gave us!" Then she turned to Leslie. "Here," she said as she placed a now-quiet little monkey in his arms. "Go tie him up again."

Leslie cuddled Toby close as the monkey's hands gently pulled on his ears and hair. "You sure are a mischief maker, but you're my monkey, anyway!"

A pair of little green parrots made their home on a bushy limb nailed to the side of the Anderson's house. Their wings had been clipped, so they couldn't fly away. Whenever Lois stepped out of her door, they shrieked at her until she gave them figs. She bought figs by the basketful. The family had eaten so many, they were quite willing to share some with the parrots.

The boys still had Daisy, the mother rabbit, and two males from the litter she gave birth to in Maymyo. Gene had made a chicken-wire enclosure for them. Daisy had another litter in a hole she had dug for a nest within the enclosure. The boys thought the baby rabbits were safe, but a heavy downpour filled the hole with water. David was the first to discover the nest full of water, and he managed to rescue three of the six kits. Occasionally, a rabbit would escape from the cage and disappear. Daisy may have been the ancestor of all the rabbits in the Chin Hills today.

FIGURE 10.4 Leslie (left) and David (right) with Daisy and one of her offspring at Tedim. Undated photograph, circa 1954. Photographer Lois Anderson.

The garden yielded an abundance of fresh vegetables such as string beans, small pumpkins as tasty as summer squash, eggplant, cucumbers, beets, greens, celery, and tomatoes. One tomato plant, drooping with the weight of fruit, produced at least sixty of the biggest tomatoes Lois had ever seen. She had tomato starts that she hoped to plant on the new mission compound, but no word had come on the status of its lease yet. Corn, still young enough to eat fresh, was almost finished, and she planned to dry the remainder for the winter by hanging the stalks from the ceiling of her kitchen.

The kitchen was unlike any Lois had worked in before. Pots and pans, hands of bananas, lanterns, saws, a broom and dustpan, and rag bags hung from nails on the walls. Non-perishable pantry items were stored in powdered-milk tins or barrels. In one corner was an open four-foot square of dirt for the cooking fire. Two iron bars rested on bricks or stones to support the cooking pot. This system created too much smoke for Lois, so Gene installed a wood range. It smoked, too, until Gene extended the pipe column with tin cans so it went out the window and up the side of the house. Since the house was rented, they left the dirt cooking area as it was. Lois also used a kerosene camp stove. She missed the charcoal stove that she had had at Myaungmya, but charcoal was not available in Tedim. She bought wood for eight annas a basket—the equivalent of about eight cents—and used a basket or more every day.

The washing machine and generator were also in the kitchen, as were a bicycle and Danny's walker. Gene built a workspace and installed a sink, which made it much easier to do dishes. Lois described it all as, "quite homey, in a rustic sort of way!"

It was often cold at this high elevation, and a hot drink was comforting. Lois had brought Postum[48] from the States but had only one jar left. She experimented with soybeans, which were plentiful, and developed a good recipe. She roasted the beans in a skillet until they were light brown and the skins cracked. Then she ground them in her grain mill to a fine powder, returned the powder to the skillet, added a few squares of shaved jaggery,[49] and roasted this mixture again until it was almost black.

When she added the soybean concentrate to boiling water with a little sweetened milk, it made a delicious hot drink. She named the beverage "soyum." When mission groups went on their village tours, she sent a can of it with them so they could enjoy hot drinks as they sat around a campfire in the evenings.

When the next school year rolled around, Miss Gifford—the boys' former teacher in Rangoon—enrolled David and Leslie as extension students. She sent them textbooks and achievement tests that were based on American school standards.

Gene made desks for David and Leslie from boards laid across packing boxes. Danny was happiest when his brothers allowed him to sit on their desks while they studied. This didn't help his big brothers complete their assignments, but everyone was satisfied with the arrangement.

Approval for the lease of the mission property was still in limbo. Gene had been told that his application had cleared the local office but had to go to the district headquarters in Falam. If the proposed lease received the district commissioner's approval there, the Andersons would be able to move forward with their plans for the mission.

One day Gene found men cutting down the best pine trees on the prospective mission property. When asked for an explanation, they replied, "We have received permission to get trees for furniture for the government buildings up here—but we won't take any more from this location, since you, Pastor Anderson, are hoping to obtain it."

The lumber for the mission house had been cut and sawn by hand in the vicinity of Kennedy Peak. It would remain there until Gene received the permit to lease the property. Gene and David made a trip to Kennedy Peak to check on it to see if it was molding in the wet weather. They parked the Jeep off the road and hiked the five miles down to the lumber site on a trail just wide enough to walk single file. After completing their inspection of the lumber and finding it in satisfactory condition, they started back up the trail, with Gene leading the way. Suddenly, he noticed movement in front of his feet and realized it was the tail of a snake. His eyes quickly followed this moving "rope" eight feet up the bank to the head of a king cobra, its neck ribs fanned out into an alarming hood.

Instantly, Gene spun around, grabbed David, and ran back down the steep path with the cobra at their heels. The snake chased them until they were out of its territory, then it slithered out of sight over the bank. When Gene and David finally reached the safety of the Jeep, they thanked God for His protection.

Another day, the whole family went to check on the lumber. Fortunately, they did not encounter a second cobra.

FIGURE 10.5 Gene inspects the lumber for the mission house that was sawn and prepared on the slopes of Mt. Kennedy. Danny is sitting on top of the lumber. Undated photograph, circa 1954. Photographer Lois Anderson.

Lois thoroughly enjoyed her Sabbath school ministry. Sabbath school membership had grown to thirty-eight, with a slightly higher weekly attendance. She planned a beautiful thirteenth Sabbath program. The children repeated verses in the Chin language from Revelation 21 that described the new earth. Go Za Kham recited the paragraphs from *The Great Controversy*[50] about the country where the redeemed would live, and David played "Only Jesus" on his cornet. Leslie told a story, his first in public, through a translator. Lois made her own flannelgraph pieces to create a scene illustrating the new earth. She wished she had been able to purchase brightly colored flannel but found that crayons colored the pastel fabric very well.

The rains seemed to be letting up, and the family was enjoying lovely sunny days, so Gene thought of a special way to celebrate David's upcoming thirteenth birthday. "If the weather is good tomorrow," he said, "let's take a picnic and go past Tedim down to the Manipur River." They had been wanting to explore this area for a long time.

Unfortunately, they awakened to gray skies and a dripping roof. It drizzled all morning and was still as dark, cold, and miserable at eleven as it had been at seven. Later in the day, the sun broke through, but by that time it was too late to go. All of them were disappointed, for Gene was leaving shortly on a trip to Kapteel. Who knew when the opportunity would come again?

Lois made David an applesauce birthday cake, but it didn't taste quite right. Then she realized she hadn't added a speck of sugar! She decorated it with swirls of frosting, and the family enjoyed it anyway.

Gene left on his tour, accompanied by his translator, Go Za Kham, and Phung Kai, who went along to help visit with the people. Phung Kai was planning to colporteur as soon as his books arrived.

One night after Gene had left, Lois and the boys took a lantern and went up on the hill to watch the lightning across the Manipur Canyon. It was a terrific show! The flashes were the biggest and most continuous they had ever seen, lighting the whole valley between them and Kennedy Peak. They were in bed before the storm reached their side of the valley, but it was still powerful enough to interrupt Lois's sleep.

At fifteen months, Danny was a lot of fun. When Lois read aloud, the three boys liked to sit on a blanket at her feet. Before long, Danny would be rolling and flopping over on his big brothers. He tried to mimic everything David and Leslie did, whether it was jumping jacks or pushups. When he wanted to go for a walk, he held out his hand and made little pleading grunts as he started off, hoping someone would join him.

A delivery man transported supplies and mail up and down the mountain in U Pau Za Kam's truck. Even though the man didn't always understand Lois, he would always smile and say, "Yes." One afternoon he stopped to deliver a case of sweetened condensed milk, although Lois had ordered evaporated milk. She knew she would eventually use it, so she accepted it. Since there were letters ready to mail, the boys jumped on the truck for a ride into Tedim, walking home afterward.

By then, Gene, Go Za Kham, and Phung Kai had been gone almost two weeks. Lois and the boys had received several messages from Gene, keeping them informed as to his whereabouts. They decided to declare a school holiday the morning of his expected return, prepare dinner ahead of time, then drive to where the trail from Laitui joined the road.

The same afternoon that they received Gene's most recent missive, the boys were in the yard playing ball with the neighborhood children when Lois suddenly heard Leslie holler. She looked out and saw Gene riding into the yard on Prince. He had found Prince in the pasture and ridden him home. Exhausted, Gene climbed off the horse, went into the house, and sat down on the floor, his face white and his jaw muscles so taut he could hardly speak. His eustachian tubes hadn't cleared on the way up from the bottom of the canyon, so his ears were roaring, and his voice sounded funny. He looked just like Miss Mann had when she had struggled up that mountain.

"Go Za Kham and Phung Kai stayed behind to work a few more days in Laitui, so I came on alone," Gene explained. "I climbed for hours with that blistering sun beating down. No one can imagine what it's like unless they have done it. Coming up from the river, I hoped we would never have to walk out of this country."

It had taken him two and a half hours to walk from Laitui down to the river—and five hours to come back up the same distance on the other side.

"I don't think I will ever try it," Lois countered. "The day was so hot, I had to quit working in the garden." She couldn't imagine climbing out of a canyon in that heat.

Lois had fixed a huge pot of celery soup for supper. She wondered if the family could ever finish it, but she needn't have worried. The way Gene attacked the soup, he could have eaten the whole pot by himself. He looked as though he had lost at least twenty pounds.

After a relaxing meal, the family enjoyed hearing about some of Gene's experiences.

It had rained continuously the first day of their trip. Since Gene and his two companions were already soaked, they waded out to a little hut on stilts in the middle of a rice paddy to get out of the rain and eat their lunch. Arriving at Kapteel, they sympathized with many of the villagers who were in mourning because of two recent deaths.

Once the meetings got underway, about 250 people attended, and many stayed for questions afterward. Gene, Go Za Kham, and Phung Kai were up until midnight every night. Before the evangelists left Kapteel, many people said they were convinced they had heard God's truth. There was no way of knowing how many villagers would make a firm decision to follow God, but the three men were very happy with the response to their visit.

FIGURE 10.6 *Gene teaching in a Chin Hills village. Undated photograph, circa 1954. Photographer unknown.*

One old man had already quit smoking, was no longer eating pork, and was keeping the Sabbath. He was afraid he would not live to be baptized, as he was almost eighty years old. Because it was such a hard journey to Tedim, he didn't know if he could make the trip the next time Pastor Parker came to conduct a baptism.

This old man gave Gene some souvenirs: feathers and hair tassels dyed red. Years before, whoever killed an enemy of the village people had been entitled to wear these symbols. The old man had earned that right—but because he had become a Christian, he no longer practiced this custom. He wanted Gene to have the feathers and tassels to take to America to tell people there what God could do for one man in an isolated village in the mountains of the Chin Hills. That evening, Gene pulled one of the old man's teeth, which was badly infected.

From Kapteel, Gene, Go Za Kham, and Phung Kai continued to Laitui. The last part of the trail to this village was nearly vertical. When they were partway up, a believer from Laitui—who planned to be baptized at the next baptism—met them with lunch. He was so pleased to be able to help the weary travelers.

While they ate, the man told Gene about his family. For years, he had tried to interest his six brothers in Christianity, but they would have no part of it. However, once he began to study his Bible and learn about the Seventh-day Adventist church, his family saw a difference in his life. One of his brothers had since decided to attend the baptismal classes as well.

"Why do you want to be a Seventh-day Adventist?" Gene asked.

Tears flowed down the man's cheeks when he tried to answer, and he could hardly speak. Finally, he said, "If I do what is right, I believe God will accept me."

"My friend," Gene said, "you don't have to *earn* God's love. It is a gift."

Gene had one more special story for Lois and the boys before they went to bed.

When he, Go Za Kham, and Phung Kai arrived at the dak bungalow at Laitui, they were tired and hot from the long, steep climb up from the river bottom. There was little vegetation to provide shade in the canyon, and the sun's heat had reflected in suffocating waves from every side.

Just as they were ready to drop onto the floor for a few minutes of rest before their carriers arrived, a young man came to the bungalow. His hand was wrapped in strips from an old wool army overcoat. He told them that he had cut his hand while working in the field five miles from the village. Go Za Kham asked him if he would like Gene to dress[51] his hand, and the man gratefully accepted the offer.

There was no one to turn to for help in a medical emergency in that region. If a case was serious enough to require a doctor's care, the villagers

> *"What is the news from Laitui?" Gene asked. "The big news is that my village is having the greatest religious awakening it has ever had. Wherever you see a group of people sitting together talking, you can be sure they are talking about the Seventh-day Adventist religion and the Sabbath.*

fashioned a litter—either a chair carried high on poles on the shoulders of four men or a cot on which the patient could lie—then, accompanied by a group of ten to twenty carriers, the patient started on the long, hard journey to Tedim. Depending on how remote the village was, the journey could take a day, or two, or five—all of it on steep mountain trails. No wonder people welcomed someone who could give them medical attention in their own village!

Fifteen minutes after the three men had arrived, their carriers came wearily up the trail and set down their sixty-pound packs. Gene quickly located his box of medicines and first-aid supplies, got a basin of water, and began unwrapping the injured hand. He had learned that the patient held an office in his local Christian church. As Gene unwrapped strip after strip of the coat, he found the cloth soaked with blood and began to wonder how deep the cut was. Certainly, it was more serious than he had first thought. Under the cloth strips, he found tightly packed corn husks, and as he clipped these away, blood spurted like a gusher from a severed artery. He quickly made a tourniquet to stop the bleeding. When the injured man told Gene that he had been unconscious in the field for half an hour from loss of blood, Gene knew that whatever he did, he would have to do quickly.

He had nothing with which to tie off the blood vessel, so he asked one of the many onlookers to bring him a needle and thread as quickly as possible. While waiting for them to arrive, he cleaned out the tobacco and other materials that had been packed into the wound, then pinched the blood vessel shut with his fingers and loosened the tourniquet to let the blood flow to the other parts of the man's arm and hand.

It was then that the injured man made a startling statement: "Surely God brought you to me at the right time. God will do marvelous things in this village because of your care."

When the needle and thread arrived, Gene was able to stop the bleeding. He prayed for guidance as he worked, and the Lord answered his prayer.

Gene marveled at the way the Lord impressed him as he packed his medical kit for each trip. It seemed miraculous that he—with no medical training except the few weeks with Dr. George Richardson—was able to meet so many medical emergencies.

After Gene returned home, the man walked to Tedim several times to have his dressing changed. The journey was a full day's hike in each direction. On his last visit Gene exclaimed, "Praise goes to our great and wonderful God! Your wound has healed completely."

A few weeks later, the brother of the injured man stopped in. "What is the news from Laitui?" Gene asked.

"The big news is that my village is having the greatest religious awakening it has ever had. Wherever you see a group of people sitting together talking, you can be sure they are talking about the Seventh-day Adventist religion and the Sabbath. I have come to ask you to put my name on the list of those who desire to be baptized."

His brother's prophetic statement that God would do marvelous things in their village had come true.

Chapter 11

When You Trust in the Lord, He Provides

"Now may the God of peace who brought up our Lord Jesus from the dead, that great Shepherd of the sheep, through the blood of the everlasting covenant, make you complete in every good work to do His will, working in you what is well pleasing in His sight, through Jesus Christ, to whom be glory forever and ever. Amen."
—Hebrews 13:20–21

The evening Gene arrived home from Kapteel and Laitui, the clerk from town stopped by to ask him to come to his office in the morning. Gene went to see the clerk, as requested, and returned with happy news. After months of delays, he finally held in his hands the papers for leasing the property as of September 20, 1954. When Lois heard this exciting announcement, she got a queer feeling in her stomach, as though some stupendous event had just taken place—which it had. They had waited so long for this moment.

The family had often enjoyed evening walks up on the ridge after they had discovered the property, and they had tried to imagine what it would be like to have people living there. Soon it would be a reality. David and Leslie had been working hard to get ahead on their school assignments so they would have extra time to work with their dad as soon as the approval papers came.

Immediately, Gene hired two men to make a road to the top of the property. Two weeks later, a lovely driveway wound up the hill through the trees, circled the backyard, and ended where the main entrance of the house would be.

While the road was being built, the house site was laid out and the foundation trenches dug. Gene felled several small pines that had been standing where the house was to go. He cut and trimmed them for posts to support the house. He hauled in tin roofing sheets, some of the lumber from Kennedy Peak, and bricks. Go Za Kham found a man who could lay the brick foundation.

FIGURE 11.1 *The winding driveway to the Tedim mission headquarters. Undated photograph, circa 1954. Photographer Lois Anderson.*

Gene dedicated his time to this project. "I have decided that if I want to get it done as soon as possible, I'll need to be here every day and do much of the work myself."

David and Leslie worked diligently, gathering stones in five-gallon buckets for gravel for the foundation. Sand was carried up from the Manipur River with pack horses.

Danny joined his big brothers whenever he could. He wandered around the new compound, chopping on everything with his little hoe. There was plenty of space for him to run and explore to his heart's content—and new things to do, like collecting pine cones and finding pebbles and berries to fill his pockets. He brought sunshine with him wherever he went, and the whole community loved him.

The family spent as much time as possible on the new mission compound and could hardly wait to move. Mountain breezes swept over the hill, the wind whistled through the pines, and the air felt brisk and invigorating. The leaves spiced the air with a tangy aroma, and occasionally big thunderheads—bright, pink, and too magnificent to describe—towered over Kennedy Peak.

FIGURE 11.2 *Danny standing with a stick in the Tedim mission yard. Mimicking his brothers who were collecting stones for the foundation of the house, he's been gathering pebbles, pine cones, and berries. Undated photograph, circa 1954. Photographer Lois Anderson.*

Lois wrote to the family at home and described the layout of the property:

> From the front windows of our house, we will be able to look out over the steep hillside, then on down, down, down into the blue canyon, and miles beyond toward Kennedy Peak. From the back of the house, the view will be a fairly large level area, with several big pine trees adding a peaceful ambience.
>
> Beyond this area is a very gentle slope which has rich, black soil to make a wonderful garden after a few more trees and bushes are removed. To the left of the yard, another gentle slope comes up between the trees, and there is a lovely view of the Manipur Canyon. To the right, it drops away quite fast, and just the pine woods are visible.
>
> Up behind the garden spot is a large level area that we're hoping will be the site for the school. There will be enough space below the house to have a lovely yard before it drops off steeply. A stone's throw below the yard, a circular driveway will come up to the front entrance.

FIGURE 11.3 *Gene and family in their yard on the Tedim mission compound. Left to right: David, Gene, Danny, Lois, and Leslie Anderson. Undated photograph, circa 1954. Photographer unknown.*

The house plans included an innkaa on pillars behind the outdoor kitchen. This open deck would be a delightful place for the family to enjoy meals or activities outdoors while still having partial privacy.

Two small buildings were erected first: one for storage, and the other a small cabin for Vungh Thang's family. Vungh Thang was planning to be baptized at the next baptism and would be the watchman and general handyman for the mission compound.

One evening, as the family was enjoying their usual walk up the hill, Lois grabbed Gene's arm and exclaimed, "Someone is living here!" Sure enough. Smoke curled up from Vungh Thang's cabin, creating a cozy, inviting atmosphere. Leslie jumped up and down, unable to contain his excitement.

Construction of the mission house was progressing well. The base for the foundation—consisting of layers of rock, brick dust, and lime—was in place. It needed to dry before the brick foundation could be laid, but there had been more rain in the last month than in any other month of the rainy season. Gene wanted to keep building the house, but when it poured, construction had to cease.

During the downtime, Gene spent hours figuring out how much window glass to order, how much more tin roofing was needed, when to send to Kalemyo for either pyinkado[52] or teak—whichever was available—for the floor joists, and when to send another crew to Kennedy Peak to cut more pine trees for lumber. He also drew up plans for a school building that would need to be built in time for the next term.

Pressing calls kept coming, asking Gene to visit the different villages. The old chief at Kapteel sent word that he desired to become a Seventh-day Adventist, and he wanted Gene to come. Since Gene couldn't leave, he asked Phung Kai, who had accompanied him on a previous trip to Kapteel, to go. Gene prayed that this would be a spiritual blessing for both men.

The Andersons were expecting Pastors Parker and Mattison to arrive for another baptism on Sabbath, September 25, 1954. Baptismal candidates from Laitui, Kapteel, Bukphir, and Darkhai—in addition to at least five from Leilum—had all been notified.

At the last minute, however, Gene received a telegram which said the men wouldn't arrive until the fourteenth of October, because Pastor O.O. Mattison's visa hadn't come. Gene immediately sent a runner to take the news of the changed date to the villages involved, praying that the message would reach the candidates in time to stop them from coming to Tedim needlessly.

Without further complications, Pastors Parker and Mattison arrived and baptized seventeen candidates. It was the second baptism in the Chin Hills.

The beautiful service greatly strengthened and encouraged the new believers. Pastor Mattison observed that it would be a blessing if Gene could baptize new converts in their own villages and wondered why he hadn't been ordained before he began his assignment in Tedim.

Accordingly, on the recommendation of Pastor Mattison and the other Burma Union and Southern Asia Division administrators who knew him, the Burma Union administration decided to ordain Gene at the year-end meetings in Rangoon. In a letter to loved ones at home, Lois described her feelings about this momentous event: "His ordination will be something like another graduation, only much more important. There was a day when Gene used to dream about being ordained, but it seemed so far away, he never thought he would attain it. Now, it is almost a reality."

Lois sewed every spare minute, doing her best to keep her family clothed. David, Leslie, and Gene all needed new shirts before the family went to Rangoon, and Danny needed several more pairs of pants. She had learned so much about making clothes, she could cut out and complete a garment in one day, except for the handwork.

She also cared for her vegetable garden, which still had radishes, celery, turnips, beets, a few cabbages, and some tomatoes. When they had moved from Maymyo, she had brought poinsettia starts—little more than bare sticks—which had grown to bushes five feet tall and were covered with gorgeous blooms. She hoped to grow some of these lovely plants at her new home.

One rainy afternoon, David decided he wanted to learn to sew. He found an old striped dress his mother no longer wore, and from this fabric made a pair of shorts for himself. While he was occupied with his sewing project, Danny—instead of napping—tossed all the blankets, sheets, pajamas, and toys from his crib to the floor, laughing and squealing at his delightful new game. Leslie retreated to the den he had made for himself by laying chairs down and covering them with blankets. With no other playmates their age, the boys had to make their own entertainment.

The family was anxious to move. Their new house still lacked siding, doors, and windows—but the floor was down, the roof half on, and the fireplace almost completed. How wonderful it would be to bask in the warmth from the fireplace! Since there was no shortage of wood there, they could enjoy an inviting fire any time they wanted one. Gene's goal was to settle the family in their new home before it was time to leave for Rangoon.

On December 9, a year and a day after they had arrived in the Chin Hills, the family moved in. Though still unfinished, the house felt like home.

FIGURE 11.4 *The Tedim mission headquarters building. Undated photograph, circa 1954. Photographer Gene Anderson.*

The boys had sold their beloved horse, Prince, a few days before they moved. They had lost one hundred rupees on their investment; however, getting enough feed for Prince had been so challenging, it was a relief not to have him anymore. They treasured the good times they had enjoyed with Prince and had learned a great deal about what was involved with caring for animals.

Gene found some steel mats that had been used during World War II to create portable landing airstrips. He decided to make a sturdy floor for the innkaa at the mission house with them—a common repurposing of these relics.

Gene and the boys stacked the mats onto an old cannon trailer with iron-rimmed wheels—also left over from the war—and topped the load with a few lengths of lumber. David and Leslie, always eager to do something new and adventurous, asked if they could ride on the trailer. In that isolated village, one seldom saw a vehicle. So, against his better judgment, Gene reluctantly agreed.

Gene slowly maneuvered the trailer along the bumpy road. As he began to make the turn into the driveway of the mission compound, the length of lumber David was sitting on began to slip. David grabbed it in an unsuccessful attempt to stabilize it. The board slid into the spokes of the wheel, catapulting him to the ground directly in its path.

Lois, who was in the house, heard Leslie yell, "Stop!" Through a gap in the trees, she saw the Jeep stop instantly. She saw Gene rush back to the trailer, where he found David lying just behind the wheel. David's cries tore at Lois's heart as she ran down the driveway to join her family.

The trailer wheel had rolled across the shin of one of David's legs and below the ankle on his other. But, instead of his legs being crushed or amputated as they had feared, they found only faint, red marks on his skin. His skin wasn't even broken, and by the next day, he walked with barely a limp. The family humbly and earnestly praised God for keeping David from any harm when he fell to the ground and for sending His angels to lift that iron wheel with its heavy load.

The Andersons prepared for a second Chin Hills Christmas celebration, this time in their new mission home. A colorful string rug in front of the fireplace made a comfortable gathering place for special family evenings. Books lined one wall on a bookcase made from boards held up by bricks. Their furniture consisted of an unpainted table; a big, homemade chair with cushions; a couple of folding chairs; some tutpahs (bamboo footstools); and the chrome dining set at the end of the room.

The boys decorated a tree with strings of popcorn, green berry garlands, and pine cones painted silver. The finishing touch was curled brass threads from a dismantled kettle scratcher which they hung all over the tree.

Since Christmas was on Sabbath and the Andersons had something else planned for their church members on Friday evening, they held their family celebration on Thursday evening. David and Leslie opened their presents first, but the most fun of the evening was watching Danny open his.

His first gift was a pound-a-peg set Leslie had made for him. He gave the package to his daddy and watched eagerly as the paper was taken off. When he saw the bright green stool, he began to say, "Ooh, ooh," up and down in a singsong voice. Once the package was unwrapped, he tried to take it apart. Gene showed him how to hammer by hitting the side of the wooden chair he was sitting on. Danny immediately did the same thing. He leaned way over so he would be lined up just right, and then he hammered right where he had seen his daddy hammer. He was very interested in the stool with the pegs, but every few minutes, he would go back and hammer the chair in the exact spot his daddy had hit. Danny clearly hadn't transferred the hitting demonstration on the chair to his new toy, but his misunderstanding provided delightful entertainment for the family.

At last, Danny went to the tree and found the wagon David had made from the old walker. He brought it out in front of the fireplace and crawled in. David pulled him around the room, and each time he was pulled away from the family, he would wave and say, "Bye-bye."

The family invited Ning Go Cing to be part of the fun, as they had a few gifts for her too. She was such a pleasant young woman to have in their home, and Lois appreciated her devotion and faithfulness. Ning Go Cing had learned to do so many things, Lois felt confident she could keep the household running by herself, if necessary. She tidied the house, made sure that the wood was chopped if the boys forgot, and sometimes helped to feed the animals. She washed all the vegetables and put them on to cook. Lois added the seasonings and did the baking.

FIGURE 11.5 David carries Danny on his head in Ning Go Cing's basket while she looks on. Undated photograph, circa 1954. Photographer Lois Anderson.

The following night, Christmas Eve, the family took a basket of gifts to Leilum where most of their members lived. It was a lovely evening. The canyons were dark, the hilltops pink, and the stars were beginning to twinkle. It was cold enough to feel like Christmas. They sang Christmas carols outside many doors and left a present for each family. It was a special evening to share.

Sabbath was Christmas Day, and the Andersons and their little flock enjoyed a blessed time at church. The children recited their memory verses for the quarter, and the church family celebrated the Lord's Supper together for the first time. Go Za Kham had been concerned that the ordinance of foot washing might be awkward for the people, but everyone eagerly and happily took part, making it a spiritually memorable service.

The Andersons invited the church family to their house for Sabbath evening. They had expected them to come after sundown, but since everyone arrived early, they had vespers together around a big bonfire. Afterwards, David and Leslie taught the children some new games, like "Drop the Handkerchief" and "Jacob and Rachel."[53] The children were delighted to learn different ways to play together.

FIGURE 11.6 *David and Leslie pose with Chin children they'd been playing with at Tedim. Back row, second from left: David holding Danny. Back row, second from right: Leslie. Undated photograph, circa 1954. Photographer Lois Anderson.*

Leslie had popped corn for two days to make enough for popcorn balls for the evening's refreshments. Lois also served homemade cookies and her special hot drink, soyum. There were about fifty people altogether, including children, but everyone had all the food and drink they wanted.

At the close of the evening, David and Leslie asked the children to line up, close their eyes, and hold out their hands. The brothers placed a present in each child's open palms. Then, with pine-pitch torches lighting their way, the villagers went home together through the woods. Their songs and laughter could be heard in the still night air almost as far as Leilum.

Before David and Leslie went to bed that night, they said, "This was the best Christmas we have ever had!"

"I really think it was too," Lois agreed.

The following Monday, the family left for Rangoon. Gene and Lois put everything inside the house and boarded up the unfinished windows and doors. They planned to stay at Kalemyo overnight and fly out the next day. It was so cold, there was ice and frost on the road going over Kennedy Peak. Lois had thought it would be warm in Kalemyo, so she had brought only one blanket apiece—but it was cold in Kalemyo too. They camped in the same beautiful location they had camped with the Richardsons.

The Andersons had reservations for the Tuesday flight, but though they spent most of the day at the airport, no plane arrived. In the late afternoon, the stack of luggage on the airstrip was returned to the stranded passengers. The family realized they would have to go back to their camp for two more nights. Somehow, they endured the cold.

Late Thursday, they finally boarded the plane. The flight was cold all the way, so they kept their blankets tucked around themselves. It was not until they were descending to Rangoon that it began to warm up. When they stepped off the plane in the dark, they were welcomed by Pastor and Mrs. Guild. It was so good to see them! The Guilds took the Andersons to Miss Mann and Miss Dinsmore's place. The two women were expecting the Andersons and treated them wonderfully.

The highlight of their stay was, of course, Gene's ordination. It took place Sabbath afternoon on New Year's Day, a wonderful time to take a new, big step. Eight ordained ministers were on the platform to assist Elder Beach, who gave the ordination address. It was impressive and solemn. Both Gene and Lois felt unqualified to live up to all that the ordination meant.

While still in the city, they attended the grand opening festivities of a beautiful new wing of the Adventist hospital. Premier U Nu cut the ribbon and addressed the crowd.

Before they returned to Tedim, the Andersons traveled to the training school at Myaungmya, where Gene was speaker for the Week of Prayer meetings. They thoroughly enjoyed visiting their former home and seeing their friends again.

From Rangoon, the family took a train to Mandalay. They had a private compartment, which made them feel like upper-class travelers. The train was not in a hurry—stopping at most of the little villages and creeping over the bridges. The family didn't mind the slower pace, since it gave them an opportunity to see many new beautiful birds and interesting countryside along the way.

The train stopped overnight at Pyinmana, the halfway point, then started chugging again in the morning while everyone was still sleeping. They passed numerous wrecked train cars along the tracks. An armored train engine with bumpers across its front and down its sides went ahead of the passenger train to clear the track of possible wreckage or anything else that would hinder the train's passage. It was six before they reached Mandalay and went to a dak bungalow for the night. The following day, they traveled to Maymyo and stayed with their good friends, the Gerlings, over Sabbath.

From Maymyo, the family boarded the third flight to Kalemyo. If there had not been extra planes that day, they might not have been able to get home for days. By five, they were loaded in their Jeep and on their way up the mountains, arriving home around ten. It felt good to be back, warming themselves in front of their own fire again.

Bringing water to the mission compound was difficult. Ning Go Cing made numerous trips to a boxed-in spring to fill her big waterpot, which she then carried up the long hill to the compound. Gene decided digging a well would be his next priority. This generated much interest and consternation, because no one in Tedim had ever heard of digging a well. Gene, and whoever he could find to help him, dug their way through the dry, rocky ground while a crowd of curious onlookers watched anxiously.

One day, someone noticed the rocks were covered with slick, damp clay. A few days later, the boys rushed into the house to show their mother a rock that was wet. Soon water began to gather in the bottom of the well.

Unfortunately, there was a constant slushy area on one side of the well. Gene and his workers prayed that the Lord would prevent the wall from falling in and spoiling their precious water supply. Before long, Gene realized the situation was critical; if they were to save the work they had already done, the sides of the well would have to be bricked up at once. Gene and the boys hauled brick, brick dust, and lime, and finished building a cement-block platform at the bottom of the well that night.

They worked hard all the next day putting in the bricks, but before the afternoon was over, Gene came up discouraged. A large section of the wall above the wet area was giving way. It was too dangerous for him to continue working, so he quit for the day. He was not sure what to do.

The next morning, the unstable wall was still holding, so Gene straightened the scaffolding on the cement blocks and entered the well with renewed hope. Leslie mixed brick dust, lime, and water all day long in the mortar box. David lowered the bricks, stones, and mortar down into the well in a pail attached to a rope, which in turn was fastened to a long bamboo pole with a bucket of stones and bricks on the other end that worked as a counterbalance on the bamboo lever. Vungh Thang and Lois gathered stones in five-gallon cans and carried them over to be let down into the hole. Everyone felt the urgency of the situation.

Gene didn't leave the well all that day, except to eat dinner. By the time it grew dark and work ceased, he had laid enough brick to solidify the place that had been threatening to fall in. He climbed to the top and stepped off the scaffolding. As his feet touched the ground, there was a great rumble and crash as the cement blocks and timbers of the scaffolding gave way and plunged into the water at the bottom of the well. Gene looked down in shock. He had been standing in the center of the supports and would have been caught in the middle of the heap had he left even seconds later. But there he stood, untouched by injury or death. Times like these brought the family to their knees. That evening, they thanked God for His protection and for the awesome blessing of having a well to provide water for the compound. The next morning, they cleaned the debris out of the bottom of the well.

To celebrate the completed well and Gene's deliverance, Lois packed a picnic lunch for a family outing. Go Za Kham accompanied them. They all needed a break from the hard work of the past days. For fun—and for the boys to experience complete trust in their dad—Gene blindfolded David and Leslie for part of the walk up the hill behind the house while he called out directions to guide them. The group crested the hill and continued down to the spring near the village of Lamzang. Go Za Kham showed the boys how to find crabs and dig them out of the mud by the spring. Many of the trees were still bare, which made it seem like fall with dry leaves rustling underfoot. The oaks, however, were sporting fresh, green foliage.

While they were eating, Go Za Kham said, "I was just a little younger than you, David, when war came to these hills, and we had to leave our home."

"I know," David said. "Daddy told us the story. Were you scared?"

"Scared and angry, though my father told me Christians should not hate others."

"I'm glad you belong to our family now," Leslie said.

Returning home, the boys blindfolded Go Za Kham for part of the way. That evening, Gene did gymnastic stunts with his boys. He lay on the floor with his hands stretched out above his head. Danny put a foot in each hand, and Gene asked, "Ready?"

Danny answered, "Rea-dy."

Gene asked, "Up?"

"Up!" Danny grinned as Gene lifted him high. It was his first time to stand in his daddy's hands and get pushed up, and he shrieked with delight. Because Gene and Lois had so many responsibilities, family times like this were infrequent and treasured by all of them.

Chapter 12

When You Have Love, You Have Enough

"The LORD your God in your midst, the Mighty One, will save;
He will rejoice over you with gladness, He will quiet you with His
love, He will rejoice over you with singing."
—Zephaniah 3:17

Two days after the family had celebrated the completion of the well, Leslie went to town to get the mail. It was Friday, March 18, 1955. He returned with a telegram that Pastor Guild had forwarded from the Foreign Affairs Office of the Burmese government in Rangoon. It read, "The Andersons are being ordered to leave the Chin Hills and return to Rangoon within three weeks from the date of this telegram."

The family was stunned. When they checked the date on the telegram, they realized that a week and a half had already passed. *This just can't be real*, they thought. But it was. David and Leslie couldn't hold back their tears, and neither could Lois.

Ning Go Cing found them in this sad condition and wondered what was wrong. Lois couldn't speak Chin well enough to tell her, but their neighbor, Sian Za Kham, stopped in a few minutes later. He was shocked by the news, too, and as he translated for Ning Go Cing, she grew very quiet and serious.

The family called Vungh Thang from where he was planing[54] lumber for the mission house. When he heard the startling news, tears rolled down his cheeks. He enjoyed living at the compound, working with the Andersons, and did not want that to end. He was worried about what would happen to him when they left, but Gene assured Vungh Thang that he would certainly be needed to care for the compound.

News of the eviction order traveled quickly. The telegram messenger had willingly shared the contents with anyone who asked, so the whole town was buzzing[55] before Leslie arrived home. The leaders of the community—along with the small group of precious believers the Andersons had come to love—rallied behind the Andersons and wanted to do everything they possibly could to keep the family in Tedim.

A leading man in Tedim, Zel Khaw Pau, came to see the Andersons. He told them the important men of Tedim were very upset about the order for the family to leave. The district commissioner was expected to be in Tedim soon, and they were planning to sign a petition to request the Chin minister to reverse this decision—or at least extend the time until a thorough examination of the case could be made.

The leaders of the community told them, "We want you to stay, not only for the spiritual atmosphere you have brought, but for all the other things you have done as well. Someone else might come, but they could never take your place. They wouldn't do the same things for the people and love them the way you have." The Andersons were humbled that the Chin people returned their love.

Kam Zam, Go Za Kham's father, went to Kalemyo and met with the Chin minister, requesting that the Andersons be allowed to stay. The minister was very sympathetic but said, "It would be best for our people if indigenous men were trained as leaders, since laws are being put into effect which will prohibit overseas missionaries from working in Burma."

Three faithful members came to the Anderson home one evening to sit on the rug in front of the fireplace and talk. They came, not because they wanted anything, but because they were lonely, sad, and sick at heart. Day by day, the Anderson's hearts grew heavier too. They thought of Vungh Thang and his family; he had been so happy as he looked forward to living and working at the mission with them. They were thankful they had gotten as much done on the building as they had. It would serve as a headquarters to hold the believers together.

Everywhere the Andersons gazed, they saw dreams, hopes, and plans they would have to leave in the hands of God and their faithful workers. They had counted on another two years until furlough to solidify the mission work they had barely begun. And how could they ever get ready to leave in less than three weeks? Gene knew that he must make one last tour out to the mountain villages where some were waiting for baptism.

The next day, Sabbath, was a sad day at church. The women couldn't keep from crying. Gene shared many encouraging words during the special service. After church, most of them stayed for more than an hour to talk and pray, then returned in the evening to close the Sabbath together.

The following day, Gene and David went to Kalemyo to pick up Go Za Kham, Rualchhina, and Zakhuma, who had been at workers' meetings in Rangoon. It was a physically difficult trip.

On their way down, they came across a tree that had fallen across the road and was too big to remove. After cutting off some of the smaller branches, they decided they could go *under* the tree if they lifted the top of the Jeep off and laid the windshield down flat. Their plan worked. They replaced the top of the Jeep and continued on their way.

They had just started their descent from Kennedy Peak when they came upon a stalled, heavily loaded truck. They managed to squeeze by, but in the process, Gene snagged the corner of his Jeep top on something sticking out from the side of the truck. Then, just past Fort White, he noticed the oil pressure was low, so he repaired the oil line and added more oil.

Farther down the mountain, they caught up with a Jeep that was being towed. One of the men in the Jeep was scheduled to fly out of Kalemyo that afternoon, so Gene offered to let him ride with them to the airport, since Gene was headed there anyway. Unfortunately, they arrived just as the door of the plane was being shut. The man missed that flight, but he learned that a second plane was arriving in a few hours—and it had an available seat.

Gene and David located the three men they had come to pick up, but only Go Za Kham traveled back to Tedim with them. The other two remained in Tahan to visit friends. As they rounded a corner before starting the steep grade up the mountain, they saw a group of people sitting on the road. The truck in which these people had been traveling had gone over the bank. Since it hadn't turned over, they had been digging a track so they could get their truck back on the main road. Gene stopped to ask if they needed more help, but they were making good progress. Besides, there was only room on the bank for a few men to work at a time.

A short distance farther, Gene hit a rockslide and got the Jeep stuck on top of it. Go Za Kham and David had to push it off. The last delay was finding the downed tree still across the road. No wonder they were dirty, tired, and hungry when they finally returned home about eleven!

The next Tuesday evening, Gene conducted his first baptism. Kam Zam, Phung Kai, and Cin Za Suan dammed up a little stream that ran down a canyon on the other side of Leilum, then dug down to deepen the pool. As soon as someone stepped into the water, the muddy layer on the bottom was stirred up.

> *Twelve precious souls were baptized in that little pool of muddy water. It was a very special service—not just because it was the first one Gene officiated at as an ordained minister, but also because his own sons, David and Leslie, were two of the candidates.*

Twelve precious souls were baptized in that little pool of muddy water. It was a very special service—not just because it was the first one Gene officiated at as an ordained minister, but also because his own sons, David and Leslie, were two of the candidates. The other ten were converts he and his team had worked with during the past year. One of the men pointed to the pool, and said, "Do you know why that water is so muddy? It is because all my sins were washed away there!" Some of these members became dedicated lay workers. Many of their children grew up, finished their education, and also became faithful workers in Burma and other parts of the world.

After the baptism, the people wound their way up the steep trail toward their homes, singing hymns as they went. Their voices were deep and resonant, and the soft breeze carried the melodies across the hillsides. To the Andersons, watching and listening, it was a beautiful and emotional experience. Then, they all gathered at Go Za Kham's house for a season of prayer.

Later, Danny began to show off[56] in front of the group. He danced for a few minutes and then tried to get David and Leslie to join him. They wouldn't cooperate, so he pulled a little girl up to dance with him. She also escaped. He went from one person to another, trying to entice someone to the front. The Chin people would dearly miss Danny's cute and winsome ways.

FIGURE 12.1 Gene baptizes Leslie at Leilum while David waits his turn. Front, left to right: David, Gene, Leslie. Man in background: name unknown. Undated photograph, circa 1955. Photographer Lois Anderson.

Gene and Go Za Kham left for Bukphir the next morning. Lois and the boys drove them to the Lailo trail and walked with them a short distance. When Gene and Go Za Kham arrived at Bukphir, it was Gene's privilege to baptize Khawvel Thanga, Khawvel's wife, his mother, and several of his children.

David had planned to accompany his dad the next time he visited Bukphir, but this trip was going to be so fast, he knew he wouldn't be able to keep up. Besides, he and Leslie were finishing their schoolwork and taking their final examinations.

The next morning, Lois looked out her window and saw a young couple speaking to Ning Go Cing, who began to cry.

Lois joined them and learned that Ning Go Cing's mother had died at about four that morning, several hours after her tenth child was born. Lois gathered up a bundle of baby clothes, a can of sugar, some greens she had just picked from her garden, and fifteen rupees, then started down the steep mountain trail with Ning Go Cing and the boys. They walked for an hour to reach Ning Go Cing's village. They could hear wailing as they drew near her parent's house. When Ning Go Cing and Lois stepped inside, they saw Ning Go Cing's sick father lying on his bed, overcome with grief. Women with covered heads knelt around the bed on which her mother lay, weeping loudly. There were other women in the room, also mourning.

Ning Go Cing knelt beside her mother's bed and gave way to anguished sobs. Lois wept with her when she thought about what this tragic death meant. The burden of caring for this family had rested on the mother. To provide food for them, she had tilled the steep hillsides, and carried wood and water long distances. Providing the bare necessities of life was difficult. The pay Ning Go Cing received from the Andersons had helped support the family. Now the mother was gone, and Ning Go Cing's work was coming to an end. Lois also wept for the tiny new baby, wrapped in one of its mother's garments and lying in a winnowing basket on its dead mother's legs.

Lois asked them to bring her the baby, which they did. She dressed it in the clothes she had brought, then lovingly cradled the baby in her arms to warm it. She wanted to take it home for a while and nurse it until it was strong, but that was impossible. She gave the girls some suggestions, and since Ning Go Cing had observed Lois's care of Danny, Lois hoped the baby would be all right. There was nothing more she could do to help, so she and the boys started home with heavy hearts.

Friday, there was a constant stream of people who came to say goodbye. Every visit was a gift, though it slowed the packing and sorting that needed to be done.

Lois and the boys met on Sabbath with the faithful members for Sabbath school and church. After eating their dinner, they returned to Ning Go Cing's village to comfort the bereaved family. As they neared the home, they saw a newly dug grave with a rough cross at its head. A crowd had gathered for the funeral. David and Leslie kept Danny occupied outside while Lois went in to see Ning Go Cing and the baby.

Once inside, she saw the women sitting by the partly open casket. The body was covered with a bedspread Lois had given Ning Go Cing. The father was there, and soon Ning Go Cing and her sisters came in. With her limited knowledge of Chin, Lois managed to say a few words to the people.

After changing the baby's wet clothes and warming some milk, she fed it from one of Danny's bottles that she had brought with her. Ning Go Cing told Lois that the service was going to be at six, and she really wanted her to stay. Lois hadn't planned to stay that long, but she did.

Men came in and covered the casket with a lovely white cloth that had red and black crosses appliqued on it. Ning Go Cing said her mother had made the cloth. The men and boys gathered around the casket and began singing hymns. Their gentle, melodious voices filled the evening air but couldn't cover the sound of hammers closing the coffin.

After a man from the American Baptist Mission said a few words, the men sang again. As they sang, they lifted the casket and started toward the grave. Then it seemed like all bedlam broke loose. The wailing rose to a crescendo as everyone rushed to follow the casket. A gun fired six times, the noise like deafening cracks of thunder, announcing that the soul of this woman was on its way to heaven. From the innkaa, a man shouted the honorable things she had done.

Ning Go Cing said to Lois, "Come," and they hurried to join the group of women who were running and stumbling along with blankets over their heads, as was their tradition. When they arrived at the grave, they knelt around the open hole, bowed their heads, and wept. The Scripture reading and singing could hardly be heard above the wailing.

The service soon concluded. The pretty cloth was removed, the casket was lowered into the grave, some leafy branches were thrown on top of it—then the dirt—and the funeral was over. The women were prostrate with grief, and Ning Go Cing had to be practically carried back to the house. Lois lingered awhile to bring what comfort she could. She wanted to feed the baby once more, but since she had to carry her own baby home, she decided she couldn't stay any longer.

Partway up the steep, rocky trail, a group passed them, then stopped and waited. They offered to carry Danny part of the way—a kindness for which Lois was grateful. As they climbed, they watched the sun set over the range beyond the Manipur Canyon, and Lois thought of Gene somewhere over there.

On Sunday, Gene, Go Za Kham, and the carriers who had gone to Bukphir with them, walked to Laitui, their last stop of the trip. Lois told David and Leslie they could accompany Vungh Thang to Laitui. The boys had wanted so much to go to the villages with their daddy. This would give them at least one trip—though they would only be with him one night at the village, and for the return trek. David and Leslie were each carrying a pack, a bottle of water, lunch, and a blanket.

Vungh Thang wanted to be in Laitui when some of his family members were baptized by Gene. He knew a shortcut to the village that could be walked in one day instead of two, and he would cross the Manipur River in a different spot than usual. There was no bridge, but he planned to use a pole for the crossing and assured Lois it would be safe. Lois guessed the three of them got soaked before they arrived at their destination, because a heavy black cloud passed over the area where they were hiking. She prayed that Gene and Go Za Kham would arrive in Laitui by evening so the boys wouldn't have to spend the night without them.

It began to storm in Tedim in the afternoon. The temperature dropped, and Lois worried that she had made the wrong decision to let the boys go. Thunder rumbled all night, and the wind and rain made so much noise it was difficult to sleep.

The next day, Lois washed clothes, and it rained again. She was soaked by the time she finished, but she couldn't put the laundry off. Even though she hung up the sheets in the rain, the sky cleared enough that they were nearly dry by the day's end.

She carried Danny to Tedim to pick up their mail. A short while after their return home, she heard a whistle and rushed outside to see Gene, David, and Leslie coming up the long, winding driveway. Oh, how glad she was to have them safely home! They were all tired. David was pale and too exhausted to eat, but by morning, he was fine.

Gene said he was glad the boys had come and that the experience had been good for them. The boys and Vungh Thang had arrived at the dak bungalow in Laitui a few minutes before Gene and Go Za Kham. Vungh Thang cooked them all some rice. It was fortunate that Vungh Thang had brought rice, or Gene and Go Za Kham would have been very hungry; their carriers had gotten lost and didn't arrive until ten.

FIGURE 12.2 The dak bungalow in Laitui where David and Leslie met Gene, March 1955. Photographer Gene Anderson.

It had been a cold night, and David and Leslie had each brought only one blanket. They were so uncomfortable they began pummeling each other, thinking surely the other one must have both blankets. Their scuffle woke Gene, who solved the problem by taking Leslie into his own sleeping bag and giving David both blankets.

The next day, after the baptism in a little pool in a stream bed, the group started for home. When they reached the river, they discovered the water had risen at least a foot and was swift and dangerous. They took the same long bamboo pole the boys had used to cross the day before, each of them gripping it firmly to steady themselves, and started across.

Go Za Kham entered the water first, then Vungh Thang, then a carrier. Next came Gene with David and Leslie. Gene had Leslie on the upstream side of him and David on the other side. He firmly placed his right hand over David's on the pole and clasped tightly around Leslie's with his left. Behind them were the other two carriers.

The current was fast, and the stones were very slippery. They had removed their trousers, hoping this would make it easier to maneuver, but it was a long, taxing pull, inching their way across. David looked back once at the carriers, and saw they were trembling from their exertions.

Out in the center, the water was so deep Leslie couldn't keep his footing. His feet and legs were swept out from under him, so he swirled round and round on top of the rushing water as Gene clung tightly to his hand. He would never have made it on his own. They were all relieved when they climbed up the opposite bank. When Lois heard about the adventure—particularly the river crossing—she was extra thankful to have them safely home and able to sleep in their own warm beds.

> *Little by little, the Andersons navigated through the hectic days that followed. They struggled with their emotions as they said goodbye to their dear Chin friends—and to their dreams of working with them to develop a strong and vibrant mission in Tedim.*

Little by little, the Andersons navigated through the hectic days that followed. They struggled with their emotions as they said goodbye to their dear Chin friends—and to their dreams of working with them to develop a strong and vibrant mission in Tedim. How would they ever be ready to leave by the middle of the next week? Where would they go? They had found a new home for the Jeep, as well as for their two bicycles, the dinette set, some dishes, and the folding chairs. They packed their books, a few household items, and some clothing, so they would have something to get started with at their next destination. Lois admitted she was very tired. "I will be so glad when it's all over and we know what we are to do next."

Sabbath, April 2, the Andersons had a special communion for their last church fellowship together in Tedim. Gene preached a stirring message, urging his little flock to stay true and faithful. Even though most of the members had accepted that the Andersons would be leaving Tedim the next week, they couldn't help feeling discouraged and abandoned.

After church, Gene and Lois took pictures of the group who had attended. Then Go Za Kham took pictures of the Andersons to share with the church group.

FIGURE 12.3 The last Sabbath with the Tedim believers, April 2, 1955. Photographer unknown.

The family spent the afternoon visiting all the Tedim members in their individual homes. Lian Khup's father, who had met the Andersons when they had first arrived in Kalemyo, expressed his conviction that the Adventist message was the truth. Gene and Lois expected that he would be a baptized member someday. He had certainly done everything he could to get permission for the Andersons to stay in the Chin Hills.

Tuesday was a difficult day for everyone. The Andersons completed their packing and began nailing up the windows. A telegram came from Pastor Guild stating he had received permission for them to stay another three weeks, but it seemed too late to change their plans. Their preparations for leaving were complete, and most of their freight had already been sent by truck to Kalemyo. As a family, they decided to continue with their plan to leave the next day.

In the afternoon, members began to gather for a farewell party in the Anderson's home. A few of them had been with the family all day. Lois had given away food, milk tins, and clothes. She noticed some of the folks bringing their cups, so she decided to make a hot drink for everyone. Then she learned that they were bringing the drink.

Everyone crowded into the living room, and Gene encouraged them once again to hold fast to the message of Jesus' love, His death on the cross to ensure their salvation, and His second coming to take His people to heaven. Following a season of prayer, the group committed to reunite in the heavenly home Jesus was preparing for them. Never again would they have to say goodbye!

The villagers asked Lois to speak, also, so she told them about her and Gene's youth and some of the difficulties they had faced to get their education. She also told them how God had led them to this place and how much they had hoped to stay.

After that, Cin Za Suan, Phung Kai, and U Khup Za Neng each spoke words of encouragement for the Andersons that warmed their hearts. They expressed how grateful they were to God for bringing the Andersons to Tedim and renewed their commitment to stay faithful to Jesus. Then everyone went outside and gathered around a big bonfire. The children played "Jacob and Rachel," and the adults enjoyed each other's company in a wonderful foretaste of heaven.

> *Following a season of prayer, the group committed to reunite in the heavenly home Jesus was preparing for them. Never again would they have to say goodbye!*

Go Za Kham led the group in the Chin tradition of exchanging cups of hot drink with each other. Everyone stood in a circle with their cups in hand. When Go Za Kham directed them to do so, they passed their hot drink to the person on their left and accepted the cup from the person on their right. They would take a sip from the new cup, then pass it along when Go Za Kham said to. They continued in this manner until everyone was so full, they could drink no more. *This is a very special time*, Lois thought—*even though it goes against all health rules we have been taught. But what else can we do, when they love us and feel that we are a part of them?*

To close this intimate and emotional evening, the church group gathered around the Anderson family to sing "God Be With You"[57] in Chin, then Go Za Kham led in a prayer of consecration. The church members left and walked together down the driveway through the moonlit pine trees toward their own homes as the Andersons watched from their innkaa.

It was the Anderson's last night in the Chin Hills.

The next day—Wednesday, April 6, 1955—the Andersons got into the Jeep Gene had hired for the trip to Kalemyo. Their beloved church members had gathered at the mission compound and followed the family as they slowly made their way down the mission's long, winding driveway. At the junction with the main road, the church group formed a line across the road behind the Andersons. With tears running down their faces, they waved farewell until the Jeep was out of sight. The Andersons, their hearts breaking, did likewise.

Epilogue

When God Closes One Door, He Opens Another

"'Ask, and it will be given to you; seek, and you will find; knock, and it will be opened to you.'"

—Matthew 7:7

It was difficult for the Anderson family to realize that they were coming down the mountain for the last time. When they arrived in Kalemyo, they learned that they couldn't all go together on the next day's plane to Rangoon, which added to their stress. Lois, Danny, and David left on Thursday, while Gene and Leslie had to wait until Sunday.

FIGURE Ep.1 Gene and his boys in Rangoon, April 1955. Left to right: David, Leslie, Danny. Photographer Lois Anderson.

One of the first big decisions facing Gene and Lois involved schooling for David and Leslie. They had heard positive reports about Vincent Hill School ("VHS") in Mussoorie, India, under the leadership of Elder Meryl Manley and his wife, Beth. VHS had been established for the children of overseas missionaries. David was in seventh grade and agreed with his parents that VHS was the best choice for him, even though he was reluctant to leave home.

The Parkers had an older son who was a student there, and they were leaving on the twenty-fourth of April to visit him. They agreed to take David with them. It was November before the family saw him again.

Leslie wanted to go, too, but he needed another year at home, so he attended the church school in Rangoon. Once again, Miss Gifford was his teacher. He joined David at VHS the following school year.

Gene was asked to be the chaplain at the Rangoon Hospital, and Lois was invited to teach first and second grades at the church school. She agreed, which meant Danny had to be in daycare during the week. Looking back, Lois admitted, "I should never have accepted the teaching job. It was too much for Danny to spend so many hours without his family."

FIGURE Ep.2 *Lois with her first- and second-grade students in Rangoon. Undated photograph, circa 1955. Photographer unknown.*

At the end of June—just three months after they left the Chin Hills—the Andersons moved to Moulmein (Mawlamyine), where Gene was asked to build a church and care for the congregation. The building was completed in the spring of 1957. The family enjoyed one Sabbath with the members in the new church before their departure. Their term of service in Burma had come to an end.

Epilogue: When God Closes One Door, He Opens Another

FIGURE Ep.3 *The Seventh-day Adventist church that Gene built with the church members in Moulmein, Spring 1957. Photographer Gene Anderson.*

On their way home to the United States, they stopped at VHS to pick up David and Leslie who had just completed ninth and seventh grades, respectively.

A fourth son, Vernon Elliott, was born on June 11, 1958, in Takoma Park, Maryland, where Gene had begun work on his Master of Divinity degree (MDiv) at Potomac University.[58]

A couple of weeks after Vernon was born, David and Leslie flew back to VHS. The boys' flight had been booked from New York to New Delhi, India, via Tel Aviv, Israel. After David and Leslie were on their way, a crisis erupted in the Middle East, making it unsafe to land in Tel Aviv. Instead, the plane took its passengers to Istanbul, Turkey, where the boys boarded a different plane to New Delhi. Gene and Lois were overwhelmed with anxiety when they learned about the war and called the airline company in New York to find out where the plane with their sons had been diverted.

From New Delhi, David and Leslie took the train to Dehra Dun where they boarded a bus that traveled the crooked, mountainous roads to Mussoorie. They completed their journey by walking the final five miles on a path just wide enough for one person. Their parents contacted the Southern Asia Division to confirm the boys' safe arrival at VHS.

The boys were warmly greeted by staff members. David was asked if he would be the supervisor for the "little boys" in grades one through six. He agreed to the responsibility, which meant moving downstairs to their quarters to become a "big brother" to them.

When Vernon was several months old, Gene and Lois returned to mission service in Ceylon[59] (October 1958–December 1960).

FIGURE Ep.4 The Anderson family with all four sons in Ceylon, December 1958, during David and Leslie's Christmas vacation from VHS in India. Left to right: David, Gene, Danny, Lois, Vernon, and Leslie. Photographer unknown.

After Gene completed requirements for his MDiv degree at Andrews University in Berrien Springs, Michigan, he and Lois settled in Canada with Daniel and Vernon to pastor the church in Beiseker, Alberta (April 1961). Leslie, who had finished his junior year in academy at VHS in June of 1961 before joining the family in Michigan, came with them to Beiseker. David came from PUC the beginning of the summer of 1961 to work in the furniture factory at Canadian Union College[60] (CUC) in Lacombe prior to starting his sophomore year of college there. From Beiseker, the family moved to Lethbridge, Alberta (April 1963). After that, Gene, Lois, Daniel, and Vernon spent six years as missionaries in Ethiopia (January 1967–June 1973). Interestingly, their time in Ethiopia overlapped the service of Leslie and his wife there, the two families having responded to separate calls about six months apart.

Gene and Lois finally returned to their home state of California to shepherd the congregation in Petaluma, followed by three years in Eureka. While the Andersons were serving in Eureka, the church members sponsored Gene and Lois to visit Burma in 1979, which marked the twenty-fifth anniversary of the beginning of the Adventist work in the Chin Hills. Though they were not permitted to go up the mountain to Tedim, Gene and Lois enjoyed a memorable reunion with many of their friends in lower Burma and a few who were able to join them from Tedim.

In their retirement, Gene and Lois built two homes—one in Whitmore and a second in Ukiah. They enjoyed many years of active church work; traveling; growing persimmons, kiwis, and garlic; making music; developing photographic skills; and sharing special times with family.

Gene believed it was the divine leading of the Holy Spirit that brought him and Lois together. Lois's loyalty, honesty, and good judgment—as well as her dedication to Christ—were strong, consistent attributes for making their marriage a marvelous and enduring experience. They were married for seventy-nine years.

FIGURE Ep.5 *Gene and Lois celebrate their 50th wedding anniversary in Whitmore, California, on September 11, 1988. Lois is wearing her wedding dress. Photographer Mary Lane Anderson.*

They each lived to be ninety-seven years of age.

***

All four Anderson boys earned degrees in theology and embarked on their own individual paths of ministry.

Dave (David) pastored five churches in the Manitoba/Saskatchewan Conference of Canada; accepted a mission assignment to Gitwe College in Rwanda, Africa; taught at several church schools in Newfoundland and California; ministered as a registered nurse for thirty-two years; and currently serves as the business manager of Ukiah Junior Academy and treasurer of the Ukiah Seventh-day Adventist church. He married Donna Faye Hines, and they have one daughter and two grandchildren.

FIGURE Ep.6 Dave Anderson and his family at the San Francisco International airport, waiting to board a plane to Burma, January 2001. Left to right: Donna Faye, Vonni, and Dave. Photographer Vern Anderson.

Les (Leslie) served as youth ministries director and mission pilot in Ethiopia; pastored the Whitehorse Church in the Yukon and the Victoria church in British Columbia; then accepted a call to join Adventist Aviation Services in Papua New Guinea. On May 3, 2002—shortly before his scheduled return home—Les died in a plane crash. He was married to Mary Lane Anderson. They have two children and four grandchildren. Later, Mary Lane married Pastor David Giles, and they live in Forest Grove, Oregon.

FIGURE Ep.7 Les Anderson and his family at Mendocino beach, California, circa 1996. Left to right: Les, Loy, Mary Lane, and Glen. Photographer Dan Anderson.

Epilogue: When God Closes One Door, He Opens Another ◆ 215

Dan (Daniel/Danny) was youth pastor for the Ukiah and Sacramento churches, then relocated to Fremont, California, where he oversaw the building of a new church facility. He is currently the capital development and special projects director at Redwood Community Services in Ukiah, California. It is an organization with multiple programs designed to help children, youth, and adults realize their personal goals and connect to the community around them. Dan is married to Bonnie Jo Taylor, and they have two children and two grandchildren.

FIGURE Ep.8 Dan Anderson and his family on Mendocino beach, California, circa 1996. Front to back: Tyler, Kate, Bonnie Jo, and Dan. Photographer Mary Lane Anderson.

After college, Vern (Vernon) went as a missionary to Pucallpa, Peru, where he directed the aviation program. Upon his return, he became a general contractor. Currently, he is working at Redwood Community Services as program manager in construction. Vern is married to Lanette Marie Rozell, and they have three children.

FIGURE Ep.9 *Vern Anderson and his family in their sailboat on Lake Mendocino, California. Left to right: Madeline, Sebastian, Lanette Marie, Vernon, and Cedric. Undated photograph, circa 2003. Photographer David Anderson.*

In 2001, Gene and Lois, David and Donna Faye and their daughter, Vonni, enjoyed an unforgettable trip to Burma. Lois had written to the Burma Union letting them know of plans and dates for visiting. She did not receive a letter of acknowledgement, so the Andersons didn't know if anyone would meet them when they landed in Yangon. Much to their delight and relief, there was a large party to welcome them and guide them on a well-planned three-week itinerary to visit all the places where the Andersons had lived in the 1950s. They traveled through the delta and agricultural regions of lower Burma.

FIGURE Ep.10 *The Andersons standing with the Myaungmya Training School staff in Myaungmya, January 2001. Photographer unknown.*

FIGURE Ep.11 Students at the Myaungmya Training School put on a special program for the Andersons in January 2001. Photographer David Anderson.

FIGURE Ep.12 Seventh-day Adventist church members at Moulmein visit with the Andersons, January 2001. Photographer unknown.

FIGURE Ep.13 Children gathered around Lois everywhere the Andersons went on their Burma visit in January 2001. Photographer David Anderson.

FIGURE Ep.14 Ox carts crossing the Salween River in Southern Burma, January 2001. Photographer David Anderson.

FIGURE Ep.15 Low mountains in southeast Burma, January 2001. Photographer David Anderson.

FIGURE Ep.16 River port in Pa-an, Burma, January 2001. Photographer David Anderson.

Then, with special permission, the Andersons were able to visit the mission station at Tedim, with the stipulation that they would go and return the same day.[61] Their visit was three years short of being fifty years since the opening of the mission in Tedim.

FIGURE Ep.17 The Anderson party stops for a photo at the overlook where Tedim is first seen from the main road. Left to right: Gene, Lois, Donna Faye, David, Vonni, and Hau Suan Cin (driver), January 2001. Photographer unknown.

FIGURE Ep.18 Tedim, as it can first be viewed from the main road, January 2001. Photographer unknown.

It was so exciting to be there again! The Andersons were met by long receiving lines in the yard, and they had the privilege of shaking everyone's hand before going inside the auditorium of the Anderson Adventist

Seminary. They were seated on the front row and served lunch. While they ate, they enjoyed a wonderful program presented by the staff and students.

The Andersons had a few brief moments to see the mission house, the garden, and the well Gene had built—which was still supplying sufficient water for the compound forty-six years later. Then it was time to say goodbye and travel down the long, steep, mountainous road to Kalemyo.

FIGURE Ep.19 The Seventh-day Adventist mission house in Tedim, January 2001 (forty-six years after it was built). Photographer David Anderson.

FIGURE Ep.20 The Chin people line up in front of the Anderson Adventist Seminary in Tedim to greet the Andersons during their visit in January 2001. Photographer David Anderson.

Epilogue: When God Closes One Door, He Opens Another ◆ 221

FIGURE Ep.21 Students and staff pose under the Anderson Adventist Seminary sign in Tedim, January 2001. Photographer David Anderson.

FIGURE Ep.22 The Andersons reunite with Ngul Khaw Pau and his family in front of their home in Tahan, January 2001. **Five children in front:** *Grandchildren of Ngul Khaw Pau (names unknown).* **Middle row:** *Cing Suan Dim, daughter (in red sweater); Ciin Ngaih Man, Ngul Khaw Pau's wife (holding another grandchild, name unknown); Thang Mung, grandson (to Lois's right).* **Back row:** *Gin Lam Nian, daughter; Don Khan Lun, daughter-in-law (holding her baby, name unknown); Tuan Khan Lian, son (husband to Don Khan Lun); Lois Anderson, Gene Anderson, and Ngul Khaw Pau. Ngul Khaw Pau was still pastoring one of three churches in the area at the time. Photographer David Anderson.*

FIGURE Ep.23 *Phung Kai and his wife, Tel Khan Ning. Undated photograph. Photographer unknown.*

FIGURE Ep.24 *Reunion of the descendants of Phung Kai and his wife, Tel Khan Ning, with the Anderson family in Ukiah, California, May 2011. Photographer unknown. (Seven out of twelve siblings attended the reunion. Relationships to Phung Kai and his wife, Tel Khan Ning, are indicated in parentheses.)*

Front row: *Parsin Lwai, Ning Lun, Kai Taang, and Thang Muang.*

Middle row: *Ngai En, David Giles, Mary Lane Anderson, Joyce White (Lois's older sister), Lois Anderson, Gene Anderson, Dave Anderson, Donna Faye Anderson, and Dan Anderson.*

Back Row: *Vung Dixon, RN (daughter), Niiang Mung, MD (psychiatry), Gin Sian Mung (son; translator for Chin version of this book), Maang Mung, RT, Mya Thandar, Thang Dal, Zam Niiang (daughter), Cing Don, RN (daughter), Vum Cing (daughter), Thang Nang, Vung Cing (daughter), Lian Mung, RN, Don Cing, Pau Khan (son), Kyim Mung, DDS (pediatric dentistry; missionary to Saipan for a year and a half), Manglian Lwai, Zen Ning, and NaNau Lwai.*

What a thrill it was for the Andersons to reconnect with all these dearly loved people throughout the country of Burma!

The Anderson family has always felt especially close to the Zomi people of the Chin Hills and have kept in touch with many of them throughout the years. It is impossible to remember the name of every individual who has connected with the Andersons by phone, letter, email, or in person, but each contact was treasured.

Gene and Lois were privileged to have some of the Zomi people visit in their home and each of these visits was a memorable occasion. Three readily come to mind: Go Za Kham, who lives in southern Burma; Rualchhina, who lives in Maryland with his wife and children; and Gin Sian Mung (Mungno, son of Phung Kai), who lives with his wife and children in Riverside, California. In 2011, Mungno organized a reunion of his siblings and their families to join with the Anderson families in Ukiah for a celebratory weekend to commemorate fifty-seven years since the establishment of the mission at Tedim.

Several Zomi people attended the memorial services for Gene (November 28, 2015) and Lois (February 18, 2017)—both held at the Ukiah Seventh-day Adventist church—and contributed to the monetary love gift presented to the Anderson family to help defray funeral expenses. The family was grateful for this financial support and thanks the Zomi people for their thoughtfulness and generosity.

FIGURE Ep.25 Gene tells the story of God's guidance in the development of the Chin Hills mission as the Andersons visit various churches during their January 2001 visit. Translating for Gene is Tin Tun Shin, president of the Burma Union, at the Rangoon Central Seventh-day Adventist Church.
Photographer David Anderson.

It is fitting to conclude Gene Anderson's story with his own words. At several of the churches the Anderson group visited in 2001, Gene shared the thoughts and feelings he had had when leaving the Chin Hills so many years before:

> With great heaviness and sadness of heart, we said goodbye to those we had learned to love. We took the one-way road down the mountain from Tedim, leaving the work that we had begun in the hands of our loyal workers and members. Even though they were a small group, they were a very dedicated and growing band of believers.
>
> There is no question in our minds that God was leading and directing in so many marvelous ways by the Holy Spirit, by angels, and by miracles to bring the gospel to the people of the Chin Hills. The members clung together, and some stepped forward to lead in spreading the message. Brother Phung Kai worked for years as an evangelist. Ngul Khaw Pau became the pastor of the flock. Rualchhina, after finishing his training, joined the mission and spent his life working as a pastor and officer of the mission. He was a zealous promoter of our schools. Go Za Kham gave strong leadership and played an important role in the establishment of the work in the Chin Hills. Pastors Lalkhuma and Zakhuma continued their tremendous leadership throughout the district until their retirements.
>
> During the short time we were in Tedim, the Lord led us to those who became dedicated members and gave valuable support to the development of the church. It is hard to remember everyone, but their names are recorded in heaven. Many joined the church after we left and provided great strength—people we wished we could have known.
>
> Good men from lower Burma also helped, and with God's blessing, each person moved the church forward. The light continued to burn brightly, and now we see a great reaping and a vast throng of people preparing to meet Jesus!
>
> My family and I feel so richly blessed to have had the privilege of living among the wonderful people of the Chin Hills. Each member and friend is a precious treasure. We pray daily for God's blessing on our people here. We know that God will continue to shower you with the power of the Holy Spirit. Let us all be faithful! We will meet again soon.

Johan 14:1–3: Jesuh, Pa kiang Tun nading Lampi (Chin language)

1. *Tua ciangin Jesuh in a nungzuite kiangah, Note lunghimawh kei un. Pasian um unla, kei zong hong um un.*
2. *Note' om nading mun a bawlkhol dingin a pai ding ka hi hi. Ka Pa' inn sungah om nading mun tampi om hi. A om lo ding hilehhih bangin tha ka hong gen kei ding hi.*
3. *Kei va pai-in note' om nading mun ka va bawlkholh khitciangin keima omna munah note na hong om theih nadingun note a hong la dingin ka hong paikik ding hi.*

John 14:1–3: The Way, the Truth, and the Light

1. *"Let not your heart be troubled; you believe in God, believe also in Me.*
2. *In My Father's house are many mansions; if it were not so, I would have told you. I go to prepare a place for you.*
3. *And if I go and prepare a place for you, I will come again and receive you to Myself; that where I am, there you may be also."*

FIGURE Ep.26 *Gene and Lois celebrate their seventy-fifth wedding anniversary in Ukiah on September 11, 2013. Photographer Mary Lane Anderson.*

APPENDIX 1

Gene Anderson's Adventist Ancestry

When God Starts a Fire, It Cannot Be Put Out

"Let your light so shine before men, that they may see your good works and glorify your Father in heaven."

—Matthew 5:16

On May 22, 1852, Thomas Matthews Chapman, a strong and well-built young man of twenty-four years, joined the throng of fellow travelers in an emigrant train of covered wagons along the Missouri River. They had heard of the wonders of California: its mountains of gold, its wondrous valleys and rivers, its mild climate, and its fertile soil. Despite the hardships of the long trek across desert, prairies, mountains, and rivers, the travelers were determined to head west.

FIGURE A.1 Thomas Matthews Chapman (1828-1882) (Gene Anderson's great-grandfather). Undated photograph. Photographer unknown.

And the dangers were real: medical emergencies, broken wagon wheels, worn-out shoes and blistered feet, food and water shortages, attacks from Indians, and brawls in camp. The oxen pulling the wagons became thin and fell by the roadside, making it necessary to abandon equipment and nonessentials. More than a few graves were left behind to mark the trail.

Thomas Chapman arrived in Placerville, California, on August 27, 1852, and immediately went to work with pick and shovel. It was a rough mining town, and Thomas determined it was safer for him to steer clear of the crowd that seemed ready to fight at the slightest provocation. Accordingly, he made friends with some of the businesspeople in the community, among whom were George Jewell and his wife, Polly, who had preceded Thomas to California from Vermont.

He also found close friends in George's brother-in-law, Saul Pierce, and his wife, Sarah.[62] The Pierces were instrumental in putting him in touch with Mary Sophronia Colby, a young schoolteacher in Vermont. Thomas and Mary were soon corresponding regularly.

FIGURE A.2 Mary Sophronia Colby Chapman (1830-1902) (Gene's great-grandmother). Undated photograph. Photographer unknown.

After five years of working in the mines, Thomas had had enough. He bought a piece of land in Petaluma, California, and prepared to return to the East coast by way of Panama[63] to claim young Mary Colby as his bride.

Early in 1858, Thomas met the mild-mannered schoolteacher, who looked him over carefully. She must have approved of what she saw, because on March 1, 1858, they were married and started on their return trip to California.

FIGURE A.3 *Thomas and Mary Chapman. Undated photograph. Photographer unknown.*

The demand for transportation from New York to California was so heavy—and the sea-going ships so few—that many boats not built to weather the rough storms of the Atlantic were placed into service. The vessel on which the newlyweds sailed was a side-wheel riverboat that should never have ventured onto the open seas. Its arrival in Panama was so long delayed that the shipping company had already declared it lost before it finally limped into port. The Chapmans continued across the isthmus by train and caught a ship north to San Francisco.

The rest of the wedding trip proceeded without further delay. The Chapmans took the riverboat north to Petaluma, where Thomas hired an ox cart to take him and his bride to the small settlement of Two Rock, west of town. They built their first home with split timber from the redwoods of Guerneville. (There was no sawn lumber available in those days.)

Thomas began raising potatoes, but after two years, he realized the market was so glutted he couldn't earn enough to cover the expense of harvesting his crop. A close friend of the Chapmans, Mr. Seavey, knew of a dairy farm for sale at Tomales Bay for $10,000. He offered to loan Thomas the money with no security except his word. The dairy was purchased and quickly paid for itself. It was there that Thomas and Mary raised their six children.

In May 1868, the sixth annual session of the General Conference of Seventh-day Adventists met in Battle Creek, Michigan. President John N. Andrews asked the 250 delegates where they felt the Lord would have them labor in the coming year.

It was Brother Merritt G. Kellogg's first time to attend the conference. He told the other attendees that he and his family had been in California for nine years, meeting every Sabbath with a group in the St. John home. He related that a Mr. J.W. Cronkite, one of the group, had come from the East and set up a shoe-repair shop in San Francisco. He had hung up two charts in his shop—one outlining Bible prophecies and the other listing the Ten Commandments. From his personal Bible study, Mr. Cronkite was able to answer questions his customers asked about the charts. Mr. Kellogg concluded by telling the ministers at the conference that, even though the believers in California were doing what they could, they needed a minister to add strength and direction to their efforts.

Elder James White acknowledged that the church had had workers in the East for many years but never any in the West. Then he asked if there was someone in the room who would be willing to go to that mission field.

When Elder John Loughborough heard Elder James White ask if there was someone who felt impressed to go to California, he quickly rose to his feet and declared that he had been thinking and praying about going to California. He believed that God was calling him to that place. Many people voiced their gratitude for Elder Loughborough's instantaneous response.

Then Elder White added that, when the Lord sent His servants on a mission, He sent them by twos. "Is there another whose mind has been led to this distant field?" he asked.

Elder D.T. Bourdeau stood up and responded that he would be able to accompany Elder Loughborough. He confided that he and his wife had, for some time, been impressed that God was planning for them to go to some faraway place. Before coming to the conference, they had sold their horse, carriage, and all their possessions, so they were now ready to go wherever the Lord directed.

Elder White made an appeal and raised $1,000 to pay the traveling expenses of the missionaries and to purchase a meeting tent. In the dry climate of California, it would be possible to have tent meetings eight or nine months of the year.

On June 24, 1868, the Bourdeaus and the Loughboroughs—John, Maggie, and their three-year-old son, Delmer—sailed from New York to the east side of the Isthmus of Panama, portaged across the isthmus, then sailed northwest on another ship, arriving in San Francisco on July 18. There was a message waiting for the missionary party to go to the St. John home on Minna Street, where they found the small but welcoming company of Sabbath believers mentioned by Brother Kellogg at the General Conference session.

The two ministers searched for a suitable location on which to pitch their tent. They found a vacant lot, but the owner wanted forty dollars a month for its use. They had never paid cash for a site on which to erect a gospel tent. They had little money between them, and the rent seemed extremely high, so they decided to keep looking for another place.

Fifty miles to the north, in the small town of Petaluma, a group of Christians had separated themselves from the community churches and were studying the Bible on their own in an endeavor to learn the truth of God's Word. One of the group, Mr. Hough, had received a New York newspaper which reported that two ministers were sailing to San Francisco and planning to hold religious meetings in a tent. At their weekly prayer meetings, the group made the coming of these ministers the subject of special prayer.

The next evening, another member of this group, Mr. Wolf, had a dream. In his dream, he saw two men kindling a fire out in the open country on a dark night and recognized them as ministers. Their fire soon burned brightly and lighted the surrounding country. Then, he saw other men try to put the fire out by throwing brush and bunches of grass on it, which only made it burn all the brighter. The two ministers lit a second fire, and enemies tried to extinguish it too. Eventually, they had five fires burning brightly. Then he heard someone say, "It is no use; let them alone. The more we try to put out the fires, the brighter they burn."

An epidemic of smallpox struck the town of Petaluma. On July 27, as soon as the quarantine was lifted, Mr. Hough was sent to San Francisco to find the two ministers who should have arrived. He went first to the wharf and inquired if a tent had come from Panama. Being informed that one had arrived, he was directed to the St. John home, where he found the missionaries and received a warm welcome from them. Mr. Hough told the missionaries that he knew of a place in Petaluma where they could set up their tent. They closed their evening of pleasant fellowship with a season of prayer, thanking God for sending Mr. Hough to direct the missionaries to a place to set up their tent.

The next day, Elders Loughborough and Bourdeau traveled with Mr. Hough to survey the proposed location in Petaluma. Later in the day, Mr. Hough said, "You will stay at my home tonight, but arrangements have been made for you to have dinner at Mr. Wolf's house. I will take you there and return for you after dinner."

Mr. Wolf had requested that the men have dinner at his house because he was anxious to see if they were the same men he had seen in his dream. When he saw them approaching with Mr. Hough, he exclaimed to his wife that they were, indeed, the same men he had seen.

August 13 was the opening night of the meetings, and approximately forty people attended. It was the first public town meeting following the smallpox epidemic. Thomas and Mary Chapman and her mother, Anna Colby, attended every meeting. They were baptized at the conclusion of the series and became charter members of the Petaluma Seventh-day Adventist Church. (Anna Colby had joined the Chapmans in California in 1859. She had come with her youngest daughter—Phoebe, age thirteen—and her parents, Jesse and Sarah Jewell.)

Soon after Thomas and Mary Chapman and Mary's mother, Anna Colby, were baptized into the Seventh-day Adventist church, Thomas bought a 400-acre farm three miles southeast of Petaluma. Their home became a stopping place—providing bed and breakfast accommodations, whenever needed—for the Whites and many other workers who had to leave their teams in Petaluma to take the steamboat to San Francisco or Oakland.[64]

The Loughborough and Bourdeau tent meetings in 1868 had a far-reaching impact on the spread of the Seventh-day Adventist message. From the Chapman and Colby families, alone, came church school teachers, academy and college teachers and administrators, graduate nurses, physicians, press workers, pilots, ordained ministers, and overseas missionaries who have served on six continents. Even today, their descendants prepare to take their place in the Lord's work.

FIGURE A.4 Mary Chapman's family. Front row: Harry Eugene Chapman (Gene's grandfather), Mary Colby Chapman (Harry's mother), Adeline Chapman, Alice Chapman, and Edwin Chapman (Adeline and Alice's father). Back row: Edith Ayers Chapman (Harry's wife/Gene's grandmother), Cora Peoples Chapman, Elliott Chapman (Cora's husband), Phoebe Chapman, and Lucy Chapman. Undated photograph. Photographer unknown.

One of the sons of Thomas and Mary Chapman, Harry Eugene, became the father of Helen Edith Chapman. She married Arthur Eugene Anderson and became the mother of Gene Anderson, making him a fifth-generation Seventh-day Adventist.

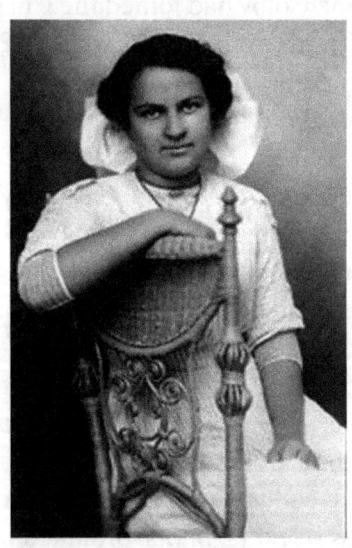

FIGURE A.5 Helen Chapman Anderson (1897–1982) (Gene's mother). Undated photograph, circa 1916. Photographer unknown.

FIGURE A.6 Gene Anderson. Undated photograph, circa 1923. Photographer unknown.

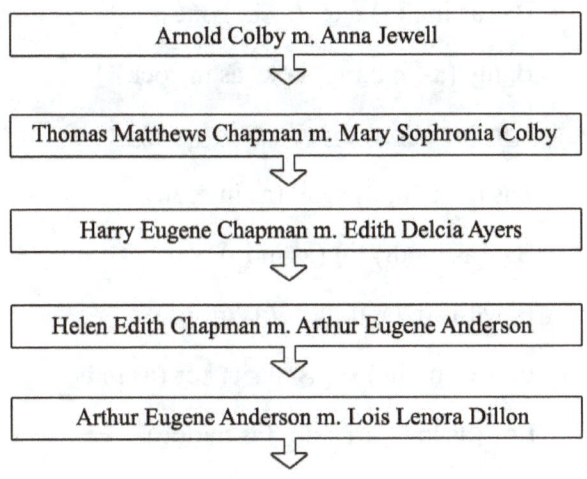

FIGURE A.7 Chart showing Gene Anderson's direct Adventist genealogy and his children.

APPENDIX 2

Related and Supporting Material

Phonetic pronunciation guide. Apostrophe indicates the syllable that gets the emphasis.

Aijal	Ai' (as in eye) jal (as in all)
Aizawl	I' (as in ice) zawl (as in all)
Assam	A (as in up) sam' (as in sam)
Bagan	Ba (as in but) gan' (as in gone)
Bangkok	Bang' (as in bang) kok (as in cock)
Bandung	Ban (as in on) dung' (as in ooze)
Bassein	Bas (as in bad) sein' (as in seen)
Batin	Ba' (as in ah) tin (as in in)
Baw Dee	Baw (as in law) Dee' (as in see)
Beiseker	Bi' (as in buy) si (as in sit) ker (as in her)
Bourdeau	Bor (as in board) do' (as in doe)
Bukphir	Buk' (as in ooze) phir (as in mirror)
Cecil Guild	Ce' (as in see) cil (as in cul) G (as in goat) uild (as in wild)
Ceylon	Cey (as in see) lon' (as in lawn)
Chindwin	Chin' (as in chin) dwin (as in win)
Chit Hlaing	Chit' (as in sit) Hlaing (as in bang)

Cing Za Huai	Cing' (as in Ching) Za (as in ago) Huai (as in why)
Colby	Col' (as in coal) by (as in bee)
Daniel	Dan' (as in fan) iel (as in cull)
Darkhai	Dark' (as in dark) hai (as in eye)
David Giles	Dav' (as in wave) id (as in did) G (as in J) iles (as in miles)
Dehra Dun	De' (as in dead) hra (as in raw) Dun (as in dune)
Djakarta	Dja' (as in jug) kar (as in car) ta (as in up)
Don Cing	Don (as in on) Cing (as in Ching)
Donna Faye	Don' (as in on) na (as in father) Faye (as in say)
Ethiopia	E (as in eat) thi (as in me) o' (as in oat) pi (as in pea) a (as in up)
Eureka	Eu (as in use) re' (as in reed) ka (as in father)
Gene Anderson	Gene (as in jean) And' (as in and) er (as in fur) son (as in son)
Gin Sian Mung	Gin (as in jin) Si (as in see) an' (as in Swan) mung (as in Moong)
Gitwe	Git' (as in go) it (as in it) we (as in way)
Go Za Kham	Go' Za (as in go) Kham (as in calm)
Gualnam	G (as in goat) gual' (as in wall) nam (as in bomb)
Guerneville	G (as in goat) Guern' (as in urn) e (as in knee) ville (as in ill)
Haimaul	Ha' (as in Hi) i (as in a) maul (as in wall)
Hakha	Ha' (as in father) Kha (as in father)
innkaa	inn' (as in in) kaa (as in cup)
Irrawaddy	Ir (as in ear) ra (as in ago) wa' (as in ah) di (as in tea)
Istanbul	Is' (as in miss) stan (as in tan) bul (as in bull)
Joyce White	Joyce (as in voice) White (as in night)

Kai Taang	K<u>ai</u>' (as in <u>eye</u>) T<u>aa</u>ng (as in l<u>o</u>ng)
Kalemyo	K<u>a</u> (as in c<u>u</u>p) l<u>e</u>' (as in l<u>ay</u>) m<u>yo</u> (as in l<u>ow</u>)
Kalewa	K<u>a</u>' (as in <u>a</u>t) l<u>e</u> (as in <u>ea</u>t) w<u>a</u> (as in <u>ah</u>)
Kamhau	K<u>a</u>m' (as in c<u>a</u>lm) h<u>au</u> (as in h<u>ow</u>)
Kapteel	K<u>a</u>p' (as in c<u>o</u>p) t<u>ee</u>l (as in t<u>e</u>ll)
Khampti	Kh<u>a</u>mp' (as in c<u>a</u>lm) t<u>i</u> (as in t<u>ea</u>)
Khawvel Thanga	Khaw' (as in calm) v<u>e</u>l (as in <u>e</u>lf) Th<u>a</u>n' (as in f<u>a</u>ther) ga (as in f<u>a</u>ther)
Kyat	k<u>y</u> (as in <u>ch</u>) <u>at</u> (as in <u>chaw</u>t)
Kyim Mung	Ky<u>i</u>m (as in K<u>i</u>m) M<u>u</u>ng' (as in s<u>u</u>ng)
Laitui	L<u>ai</u>' (as in l<u>ie</u>) tw<u>i</u> (as in t<u>ea</u>)
Lailo	Lai (as in l<u>ie</u>) lo (as in l<u>ow</u>)
Lalkhuma	L<u>a</u> (as in <u>ah</u>) kh<u>u</u>m' (as in t<u>o</u>mb) <u>a</u> (as in <u>u</u>p)
Lamzang	L<u>a</u>m' (as in l<u>a</u>mb) z<u>a</u>ng (as in s<u>a</u>ng)
Lawibual	L<u>ei</u>' (as in l<u>ie</u>) wb<u>ual</u> (as in w<u>all</u>)
Leilum	L<u>ei</u>' (as in l<u>ie</u>) l<u>u</u>m (as in <u>o</u>we)
Lian Khup	L<u>i</u>' (as in l<u>ea</u>p) <u>an</u> (as in <u>on</u>) Kh<u>u</u>p (as in c<u>oo</u>p)
Lois	L<u>o</u>' (as in sl<u>ow</u>) <u>is</u> (as in m<u>iss</u>)
Longyi	l<u>on</u>' (as in l<u>oan</u>) g<u>ee</u> (as in j<u>ee</u>p)
Loughborough	L<u>ough</u>' (as in st<u>uff</u>) b<u>orough</u> (as in b<u>urrow</u>)
Lushai	L<u>u</u>' (as in l<u>oop</u>) <u>shai</u> (as in <u>shy</u>)
Maang Mung	M<u>aang</u>' (as in s<u>ong</u>) M<u>u</u>ng (as in s<u>u</u>ng)
Malaysia	M<u>a</u> (as in <u>u</u>p) l<u>ays</u>' (as in l<u>ay</u>) <u>ia</u> (as in <u>u</u>p)
Manglian Lwai	M<u>a</u>ng (as in s<u>a</u>ng) l<u>i</u>' (as in s<u>ee</u>) <u>an</u> (as in <u>on</u>) L<u>u</u>' (as in n<u>ew</u>) <u>ai</u> (as in <u>eye</u>)
Manila	M<u>a</u> (as in <u>u</u>p) n<u>i</u>' (as in <u>nil</u>) <u>a</u> (as in <u>u</u>p)

Manipur	M<u>an</u> (as in m<u>an</u>) <u>i</u>' (as in <u>it</u>) <u>pur</u> (as in <u>poor</u>)
Manitoba	M<u>an</u> (as in m<u>an</u>) <u>i</u> (as in <u>it</u>) t<u>o</u>' (as in t<u>oe</u>) b<u>a</u> (as in b<u>ut</u>)
Mary Lane	M<u>ary</u> (as in M<u>erry</u>) L<u>ane</u> (as in m<u>ain</u>)
Mawlamyine	M<u>aw</u> (as in m<u>oat</u>) l<u>a</u>' (as in <u>ago</u>) my<u>ine</u> (as in my<u>een</u>)
Maymyo	M<u>ay</u>' (as in m<u>ay</u>) my<u>o</u> (as in <u>yo</u>)
McClenagan	M<u>c</u> (as in <u>up</u>) Cl<u>e</u>' (as in cl<u>eanse</u>) <u>a</u> (as in <u>up</u>) g<u>an</u> (as in g<u>un</u>)
Meiktila	M<u>eik</u>' (as in n<u>eck</u>) t<u>i</u> (as in t<u>ea</u>) l<u>a</u> (as in <u>up</u>)
Min Din	M<u>in</u>' (as in m<u>in</u>) D<u>in</u> (as in d<u>in</u>)
Mingaladon	M<u>ing</u>' (as in br<u>ing</u>) <u>a</u> (as in <u>ago</u>) l<u>a</u> (as in <u>ago</u>) d<u>on</u> (as in t<u>one</u>)
Monywa	M<u>on</u>' (as in y<u>awn</u>) y<u>u</u> (as in y<u>up</u>) w<u>a</u> (as in w<u>all</u>)
Moulmein	M<u>oul</u>' (as in <u>all</u>) m<u>ein</u> (as in m<u>ain</u>)
Muizawl	M<u>u</u>' (as in cr<u>ew</u>) <u>i</u> (as in w<u>e</u>) z<u>a</u>wl (as in <u>all</u>)
Mungno	M<u>ung</u> (as in s<u>ung</u>) n<u>o</u>' (as in n<u>o</u>)
Murrill	M<u>ur</u>' (as in t<u>ur</u>) r<u>ill</u> (as in <u>ill</u>)
Mussoorie	M<u>u</u> (as in m<u>ug</u>) <u>ssoo</u> (as in <u>soon</u>) rie (as in r<u>eap</u>)
Mya Pe	My<u>a</u>' (as in f<u>a</u>ther) P<u>e</u> (as in p<u>ay</u>)
Myanmar	M<u>yan</u>' (as in) m<u>ar</u> (as in c<u>ar</u>)
Myaungmya	My<u>aung</u>' (as in l<u>aw</u>) my<u>a</u> (as in f<u>a</u>ther)
NaNau Lwai	N<u>a</u> (as in <u>ah</u>) N<u>a</u>' (as in <u>ah</u>) <u>u</u> (as in n<u>ew</u>) L<u>u</u>' (as in n<u>ew</u>) <u>ai</u> (as in <u>eye</u>)
New Delhi	N<u>ew</u> (as in kn<u>ew</u>) D<u>elh</u>' (as in d<u>ell</u>) <u>i</u> (as in b<u>ee</u>)
Ngai En	Ng<u>ai</u> (as in g<u>uy</u>) <u>en</u> (as in m<u>en</u>)
Ngul KhawPau	Ng<u>ul</u>' (as in p<u>ool</u>) Kh<u>aw</u> (as in c<u>a</u>lm) P<u>au</u> (as in h<u>ow</u>)
Niiang Mung	N<u>ii</u> (as in k<u>nee</u>) <u>ang</u>' (as in b<u>ang</u>) M<u>ung</u> (as in M<u>oong</u>)
Ning Go Cing	N<u>ing</u>' (as in s<u>ing</u>) G<u>o</u> (as in <u>o</u>pen) <u>C</u>ing (as in <u>Ch</u>ing)

Ning Lun	Ning' (as in sing) Lun (as in moon)
Ohn Myint	Ohn' (as in own) Myint (as in in)
Pagoda	Pa (as in ago) go' (as in go) da (as in ago)
Papua New Guinea	Pa (as in father) poo' (as in ooze) a (as in up) New (as in crew) G (as in goat) ui (as in in) nee (as in neat)
Parsin Lwai	Par' (as in far) sin (as in in) Lu' (as in new) ai (as in eye)
Pathein	Pa (as in path) thein' (as in seen)
Pau Khan	Pau (as in cow) Khan (as in on)
Philippines	Phil' (as in fill) i (as in up) ppines (as in streams)
Phung Kai	Phung' (as in noon) Kai (as in eye)
Pucallpa	Pu (as in put) call' (as in out) pa (as in up
Pya	p' (as in pea) ya (as in ought) (pronounced as in pyah)
Pyinkado	P' (as in pea) yin (as in inn) ka (as in cup) do (as in go) (pronounced as Pinkadoe)
Pyinmana	Pyin' (as in in) ma (as in ah) na (as in ah) (pronounced as Pyinmahnah)
Pyin Oo Lwin	Pyin' (as in in) Oo (as in noon) Lwin (as in win)
Rangoon	Ran' (as in ran) goon (as in noon)
Rih Dil	Rih' (as in eat) Dil (as in dill)
Rualchhina	Rual' (as in ago) chhin (as in even) a (as in ago)
Rwanda	R (as in run) wan' (as in on) da (as in up) (pronounced as Rwanduh)
Saigon	Sai' (as in eye) gon (as in gone)
San Bernardino Straits	San (as in fan) Ber (as in fur) nar (as in far) di' (as in dee) no Straits (as in rates)
Saskatchewan	Sas (as in sat) katch (as in catch) e (as in up) wan (as in swan)
Suak Khaw Kai	Suak' (as in sock) Khaw (as in calm) Kai (as in eye)

Related and Supporting Material ◆ 239

Saya	S<u>a</u>' (as in s<u>ay</u>) y<u>a</u> (as in f<u>a</u>ther)
Sayagee	S<u>a</u> (as in s<u>ay</u>) y<u>a</u> (as in f<u>a</u>ther) g<u>ee</u>' as in j<u>ee</u>p)
Sayama	S<u>a</u> (as in s<u>ay</u>) y<u>a</u>' (as in f<u>a</u>ther) m<u>a</u> (as in m<u>a</u>)
Sezaang	S<u>e</u>' (as in s<u>ee</u>) z<u>ang</u> (as in s<u>ang</u>)
Shillong	Sh<u>i</u> (as in <u>ill</u>) <u>long</u>' (as in <u>long</u>)
Shwedgon (Pagoda)	Shw<u>e</u>' (as in aw<u>ay</u>) <u>d</u> (as in <u>du</u>) g<u>on</u> (as in g<u>one</u>)
Sian Za Kham	S<u>i</u>' (as in s<u>ee</u>) <u>an</u> (as in <u>on</u>) Z<u>a</u> (as in <u>ago</u>) Kh<u>a</u>m (as in c<u>a</u>lm)
Sophronia	So (as in s<u>ew</u>) phr<u>on</u>' (as in t<u>one</u>) i (as in t<u>ea</u>) a (as in <u>up</u>)
Sri Lanka	S<u>ri</u> (as in <u>ree</u>d) L<u>a</u>' (as in l<u>awn</u>) k<u>a</u> (as in <u>ago</u>)
Surabaya	S<u>ur</u> (as in s<u>ir</u>) <u>a</u> (as in <u>up</u>) b<u>a</u>' (as in b<u>uy</u>) y<u>a</u> (as in <u>up</u>)
Taksang	T<u>a</u>k' (as in t<u>a</u>lk) s<u>ang</u> (as in s<u>ang</u>)
Tedim	Tid' (as in lid) um (as in sum)
Tel Aviv	T<u>el</u> (as in t<u>ell</u>) <u>A</u> (as in <u>ago</u>) v<u>iv</u>' (as in v<u>eev</u>)
Tel Khan Ning	T<u>el</u> (as in t<u>ell</u>) Kh<u>an</u> (as in <u>on</u>) N<u>ing</u>' (as in s<u>ing</u>)
Thailand	Th<u>ai</u>' (as in h<u>igh</u>) <u>land</u> (as in <u>land</u>) (pronounced as Tieland)
Thandar	Th<u>an</u>' (as in f<u>a</u>ther) D<u>ar</u> (as in f<u>ar</u>) (pronounced as Tthandar)
Than Kyi	Th<u>an</u>' (as in f<u>a</u>ther) Jh<u>i</u> (as in m<u>ee</u>t)
Thang Dal	Th<u>ang</u>' (as in l<u>ong</u>) D<u>a</u>l (as in d<u>o</u>ll) (pronounced as Tthongdoll)
Thang Hau	Th<u>ang</u>' (as in f<u>a</u>ther) H<u>au</u> (as in pl<u>ow</u>)
Thang Lam Mung	Th<u>ang</u>' (as in l<u>ong</u>) L<u>am</u> (as in l<u>amb</u>) M<u>ung</u> (as in s<u>ung</u>)
Thang Muang	Th<u>ang</u>' (as in l<u>ong</u>) M<u>uang</u> (as in wr<u>ong</u>)
Thra Peter	Thr<u>a</u> (as in r<u>aw</u>) P<u>e</u>' (as in p<u>ea</u>) t<u>er</u> (as in bet<u>ter</u>)

Tin Shwe	Tin' (as in tin) Shwe (as in way)
Tual Za Do	Tual' (as in all) Za (as in ago) Do (as in go)
tutpah	Tut' (As in toot) pah (as in ah)
U Hang Za Gin	U (as in ooze) Hang' (as in bang) Za (as in ago) Gin (as in Jin)
Ukiah	U (as in you) ki' (as in eye) ah (as in up)
U Khup Za Neng	U (as in loop) Khup' (as in loop) Za (as in ago) Neng (as in even)
U Pau Za Kam	U (as in loop) Pau' (as in how) Za (as in ago) Kam (as in calm)
Vangchhia	Vang (as in ah) chi' (as in eat) a (as in up)
Vietnam	Vi (as in even) et' (as in better) nam (as in ah)
Vum Cing	Vum (as in loom) Cing (as in Ching)
Vung Dixon	Vung (as in Voong) Dix' (as in six) on (as in son)
Vungh Thang	Vungh' (as in Voong) Thang (as in thong)
Wahama	Wa' (as in law) ha (as in ah) ma (as in ah)
Yangon	Yan' (as in yawn) g (as in goat) gon (as in gone)
Zakhuma	Za (as in ah) khum' (as in tomb) a (as in up)
Zam Niiang	Zam (as in alm) Nii' (as in knee) ang (as in bang) (pronounced as Zalm Nyang)
Zen Ning	Zen (as in men) Ning (as in sing)
Zo Tin Khumi	Zo (as in oh) Tin (as in tin) Khu' (as in coo) mi (as in me)
Zomi	Zo (as in hoe) mi' (as in me)

FIGURE B.1 Table of phonetic pronunciations for Burmese names.

Place Name Comparisons: 1950s versus 2021

1950s	2021
Aijal	Aizawl
Bassein	Pathein
Burma	Myanmar
Burma Union Training School	Myanmar Union Adventist Seminary
Ceylon	Sri Lanka
Chin	Zomi
Djakarta	Jakarta
Kalemyo	Kalay
Maymyo	Pyin Oo Lwin
Moulmein	Mawlamyine
Rangoon	Yangon
Rih Lake	Rih Dil
Southern Asia Division of Seventh-day Adventists	Southern Asia-Pacific Division of Seventh-day Adventists
Tiddim	Tedim*

*The 2021 spelling "Tedim" is used in this book, because that is the name known by the people in the Chin Hills who asked to hear the rest of Gene's story. (The Andersons knew it as "Tiddim.")

FIGURE B.2 Table comparing place names as they were when the Andersons were in Burma in the 1950s to what they are in 2021.

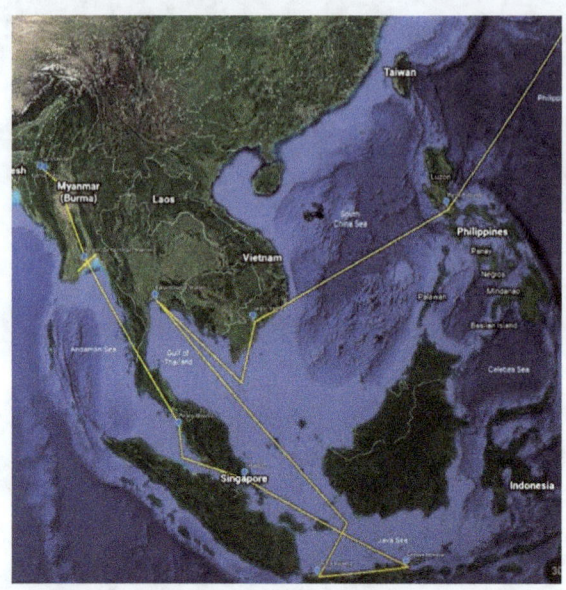

FIGURE B.3 Aerial view of the route the Andersons traveled from San Francisco to Tedim, circa 2021.

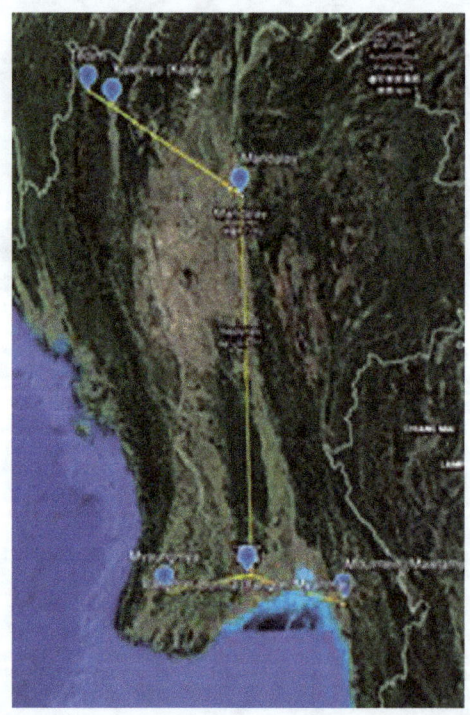

FIGURE B.4 Aerial view of the route the Andersons traveled from Rangoon to Tedim, circa 2021.

Related and Supporting Material ◆ 243

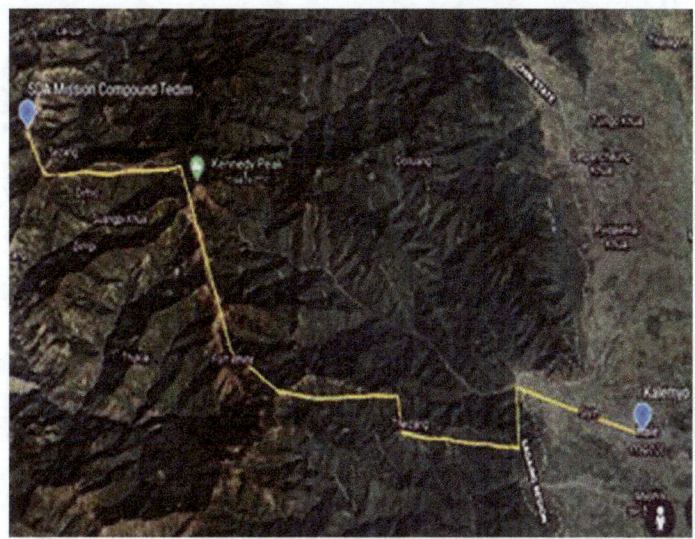

FIGURE B.5 *Aerial view of the road from Kalemyo to Tedim, circa 2021.*

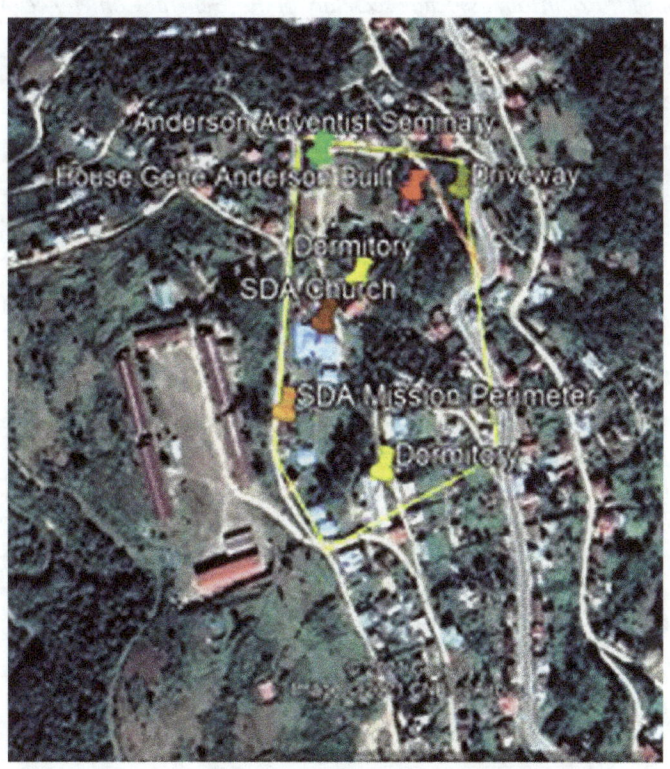

FIGURE B.6 *Aerial view of the Seventh-day Adventist mission compound at Tedim, shown within the yellow line circa 2021.*

244 ◆ *Gene Anderson: Trailblazer to Tedim*

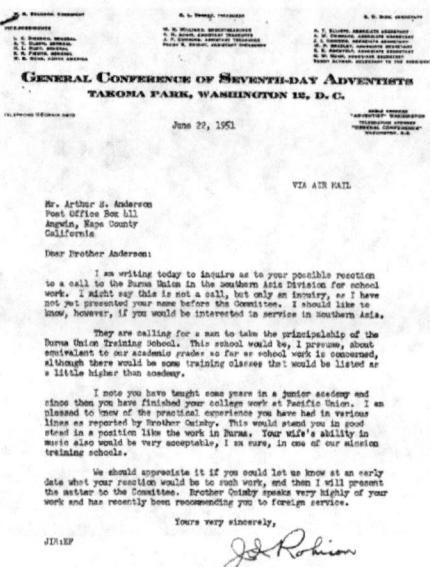

FIGURE B.7 *Copy of letter of inquiry regarding a possible call to serve in the Burma Union from J.I. Robinson, associate secretary of the General Conference of Seventh-day Adventists, to Mr. Arthur E. Anderson (Gene Anderson), June 22, 1951.*

FIGURE B.8a *Copy of page 1 of the official call to serve in Burma from E.D. Dick, secretary of the General Conference of Seventh-day Adventists, to Mr. A.E. Anderson (Gene Anderson), July 12, 1951.*

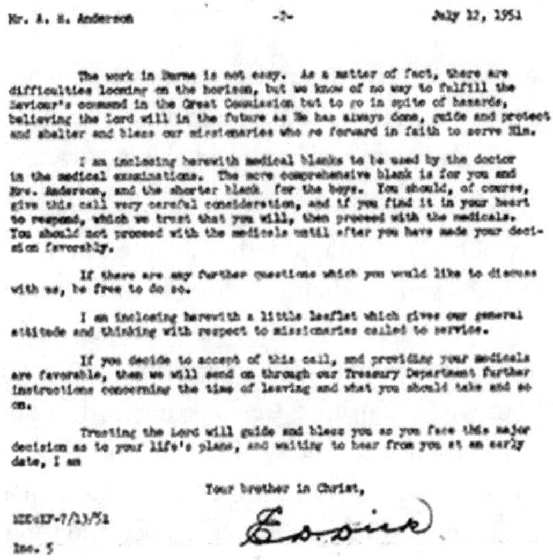

Mr. A. E. Anderson -2- July 12, 1951

The work in Burma is not easy. As a matter of fact, there are difficulties looming on the horizon, but we know of no way to fulfill the Saviour's command in the Great Commission but to go in spite of hazards, believing the Lord will in the future as He has always done, guide and protect and shelter and bless our missionaries who go forward in faith to serve Him.

I am inclosing herewith medical blanks to be used by the doctor in the medical examinations. The more comprehensive blank is for you and Mrs. Anderson, and the shorter blank for the boys. You should, of course, give this call very careful consideration, and if you find it in your heart to respond, which we trust that you will, then proceed with the medicals. You should not proceed with the medicals until after you have made your decision favorably.

If there are any further questions which you would like to discuss with us, be free to do so.

I am inclosing herewith a little leaflet which gives our general attitude and thinking with respect to missionaries called to service.

If you decide to accept of this call, and providing your medicals are favorable, then we will send on through our Treasury Department further instructions concerning the time of leaving and what you should take and so on.

Trusting the Lord will guide and bless you as you face this major decision as to your life's plans, and waiting to hear from you at an early date, I am

Your brother in Christ,

E. D. Dick

EDD:IF-7/13/51

Inc. 5

FIGURE B.8b Copy of page 2 of the official call to serve in Burma from E.D. Dick, secretary of the General Conference of Seventh-day Adventists, to Mr. A.E. Anderson (Gene Anderson), July 12, 1951.

O, who can know the pain of sundering the ties of home—and such a home as mine has ever been to me—when I with a new name and new purpose bid you all adieu for the far Pacific coast. It seems at times that I can never be my noblest self away from here. O, my God, be Thou my support. Help me to be strong in the right—to live for high and holy purposes—to be all that a true wife should be to him who has chosen me—to help make a happy home in the highest sense of the word, where perfect love and confidence shall reign an ever present deity, and where Thou shalt be worshipped with a pure heart fervently. Now give me a sense of Thy approval as I take this important step, and may I be instrumental of much good in the far land to which I go.

Adieu, my mother, my best earthly friend! Now I go with thy blessing. God bless you, my mother. Brothers and sisters, we shall be one family, though broad oceans lie between us and hereafter, may we be an unbroken family in our Father's house.

My dear native state, adieu! Thy hills and thy mountains are sacred to me, no matter what in other lands I may see. Never, never shall I forget thee nor the true hearts I leave among thy pleasant vales.*

**Mary's father, Arnold Colby, had died twelve years earlier at only forty-one years of age, leaving Anna Jewell Colby with a family of six children, of whom Mary was the oldest. Mary was never able to make a return visit to her siblings after her marriage.*

FIGURE B.9 Transcribed excerpt from a letter Mary Sophronia Colby wrote to her mother and siblings on the morning of her wedding to Thomas Matthews Chapman in Waterbury, Vermont, on March 1, 1858.

> As we look from the train window this lovely morning, all nature appears fresh and beautiful. Earth has put on her summer robes of green and is smiling in almost Edenic loveliness.
>
> I think our enjoyment of the summer time is heightened by the memory of the long cold months of winter; and on the other hand, the hope of summer helps us to endure more cheerfully the winter's reign. If we were to permit our minds to dwell upon the barrenness and desolation that winter brings, we might be very unhappy; but wiser than this, we look forward in anticipation to the coming spring-time [sic] which is to bring back the birds, awaken the sleeping flowers, clothe the earth in her robe of green and fill the air with light and fragrance and song.
>
> The Christian's sojourn in this world may be fitly compared to the long cold winter. Here we experience trials, sorrows, and disappointments, but we must not permit our minds to dwell upon these. Let us rather look forward with hope and faith to the coming summer when we shall be welcomed to our Eden home where all is light and joy; where all is peace and love.
>
> Had the Christian never experienced the storm of affliction in this world, had his heart never been chilled by disappointment or oppressed by fear, he would scarcely know how to appreciate heaven. We will not be despondent tho often weary, sad and heartsick; the winter will not always last. The summer of peace, joy and eternal gladness soon will come. Then Christ will dwell with us and will lead us to fountains of living waters, and will wipe away all tears from our eyes.

FIGURE B.10 Transcribed excerpt from a letter written by Ellen G. White to Thomas and Mary Chapman while traveling on a train from Missouri to Illinois with her husband, James White, May 31, 1875.

Related and Supporting Material ◆ 247

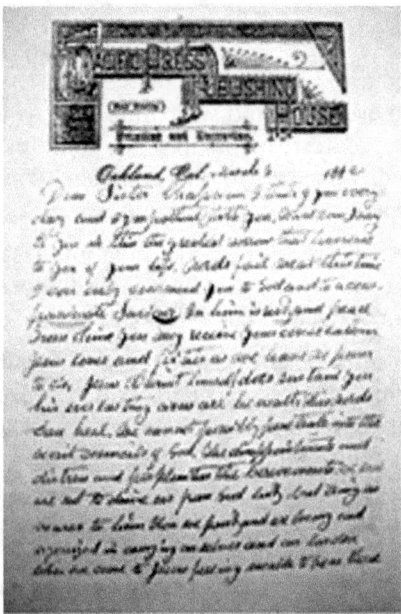

FIGURE B.11a Page 1 of the handwritten letter of sympathy from Ellen G. White to Mary Sophronia Chapman after the passing of Mary's husband, Thomas Matthews Chapman, March 3, 1882.

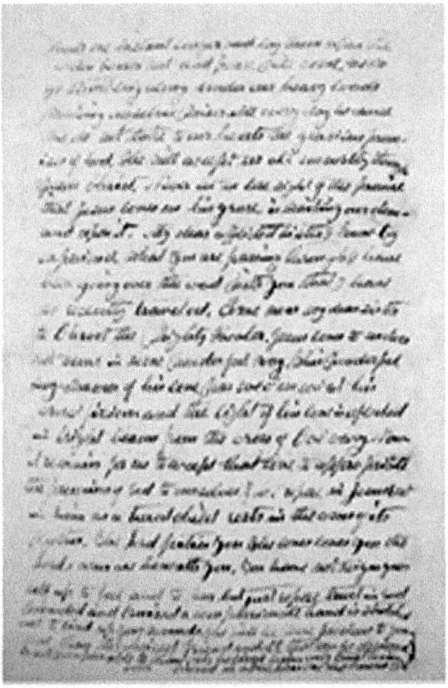

FIGURE B.11b Page 2 of the handwritten letter of sympathy from Ellen G. White to Mary Sophronia Chapman after the passing of Mary's husband, Thomas Matthews Chapman, March 3, 1882.

Oakland, Cal., March 3, 1882

Dear Sister Chapman,

I think of you every day and sympathize with you. What can I say to you in this the greatest sorrow that has come to you of your life. Words fail me at this time. I can only commend you to God and to a compassionate Saviour. In Him is rest and peace.

From Him you may receive your consolation. Jesus loves and pities as we have no power to do. Jesus Christ Himself does sustain you. His everlasting arms are beneath. His words can heal.

We cannot possibly penetrate into the secret councils of God. The disappointments and distress and perplexities, the bereavements we meet, are not to drive us from God, but bring us nearer to Him. Now we faint and are weary and agonized in carrying ourselves and our burden. When we come to Jesus, feeling unable to bear these loads one instant longer and lay them upon the Burden bearer, rest and peace will come. We do go stumbling along under our heavy loads, making ourselves miserable every day because we do not take to our hearts the gracious promises of God. He will accept us, all unworthy, through Jesus Christ. Never let us lose sight of the promise that Jesus loves us. His grace is waiting our demand upon it.

My dear afflicted sister, I know by experience what you are passing through. I have been going over the road with you that I have so recently traveled. Come near, my dear sister, to Christ the Mighty Healer. Jesus' love to us does not come in some wonderful way. This wonderful manner of His love was evidenced at His crucifixion and the light of His love was reflected in bright beams from the cross of Calvary.

Now it remains for us to accept that love to appropriate the promises of God to ourselves. Just repose in Jesus. Rest in Him as a tired child rests in the arms of its mother. The Lord pities you. The Lord loves you. The Lord's arms are beneath you. You have not reigned yourself up to feel and to hear, but just repose. Trust in God. Wounded and bruised, a compassionate hand is stretched out to bind up your wounds. He will be more precious to your soul than the dearest friend and all that can be desired is not comparable to Him. Only believe Him; only trust Him.

Your friend in affliction, one who knows,

E. G. White

FIGURE B.12 Transcription (as near as can be deciphered) of the letter of sympathy from Ellen G. White to Mary Sophronia Chapman after the passing of Mary's husband, Thomas Matthews Chapman, March 3, 1882.

THE ASSAM MISSION
of
Seventh-day Adventists
Nongthymmai, Shillong
Assam

January 28, 1953

Pastor C. B. Guild
66 U Wisara Road
Rangoon, Burma

Dear Brother Guild:

All the way up the hill from Gauhati to Shillong yesterday, Brother W. G. Lowry thrilled me with stories from the Lushai Hills, and with interests and opportunities on the Burma side of the border. He spent three days over in those parts and reports many interests.

Here is how it started. A few (about 3 1/2 years ago), missionaries in other denominations in the Lushai Hills (India side) became greatly alarmed with the number of Lushai "Bible Readings" that S.D.A.'s were selling in their territory. So they organized a big drive among their young people to collect these books and get them out of their territory. They remembered the Lushais over on the Burma side whom they felt needed converting and perhaps these books would help, so they gathered up about three hundred copies of the Bible Readings and took them over to the Burma side and distributed them there. The results have been marvelous. Brother Lowry has had at least three delegations walk over 150 miles one way to Aijal to appeal to him for a worker. Then our believers have been over around Tiddim and have returned with thrilling reports of bright prospects over in that area.

Brother Lowry says that Lushais go and come across the border without any difficulty, so there will be no problem about a worker or two going over and opening work there. Brother Lowry also is anxious to know when you brethren will be making your trip up in that area, so that he and his wife can meet you at the border and lay plans for the future.

Now, Brother Guild, if you men have 150/ per month in your budget for workers in this area, I can have two Lushai workers sent over there to get right at the work without delay. This amount will cover both salary and expenses. The young man (about 30 years of age, I believe) mentioned to you in Burma seems to be one that can really do you a good job. He has at least raised up one company or church in the Lushai Hills, and if a budget was available here in the Assam Mission, you would not be able to get him. The other man I do not know, but Brother Lowry assures me that he can do a fine work. There seems to be plenty for two men to do over in that area. I thought probably that you would have the 150/ and could take on two instead of one.

FIGURE B.14a Page 1 of a letter from Robert H. Pierson to Pastor C.B. Guild describing the Lushais in North Burma and requesting financial assistance for two workers in that area, January 28, 1953.

I have made no commitment other than the one. If you can handle two, I hope that you will, "for the field is white and ready for harvest", according to reports.

Now my questions are: 1. When do you want your Lushai worker(s) to start work? 2. Can you financially handle two workers? 3. Don't you think it would be a good thing for him or them to join Pastor J. F. Ashlock in his Field School of Evangelism to be held here in Assam during March and April? This would be conducted in conjunction with a full-scale effort that he will be holding here in Shillong. Many of the Assam workers will be attending and I think it would be fine for yours to join the group before they launch out as foreign missionaries. 4. How much will you authorize us to advance for charts, supplies, etc. for the workers to take with them when they leave Aijal? If you can give each one at least a couple hundred rupees worth of equipment and supplies for their evangelistic work, it will be very helpful. They should have something with which to work. Also please authorize us to advance them three month's salary and expense to care for them until you are able to contact them on your side of the border, (65/for salary; 10/for expense per month).

If you could let me have word regarding these items by return mail, we can get the ball rolling up in the north for you and have a good interest stirred up and nurtured by the time the Anderson's arrive to take things over.

With kindest personal regards,

I remain

Sincerely yours,

Robert H. Pierson

FIGURE B.14b Copy of page 2 of a letter from Robert H Pierson to Pastor C.B. Guild describing the Lushais in North Burma and requesting financial assistance for two workers in that area, January 28, 1953.

Timeline of Events in the Lives of Gene and Lois Anderson

February 14, 1918	Arthur Eugene Anderson was born.
January 4, 1919	Lois Lenora Dillon was born.
June 1936	Gene graduated from PUC preparatory school, and Lois graduated from Fresno Adventist Academy.
August 1936	Gene and Lois met at PUC.
September 1936	Gene and Lois began their college career—Gene majoring in industrial arts and Lois in nursing,
September 11, 1938	Gene and Lois were married at the Island Seventh-day Adventist church in Central California.
September 1938	Gene and Lois set up their first home in Whitmore, California.
September 2, 1941	David Eugene Anderson was born in Redding, California.
December 1941	World War II began. Gene worked at Mare Island in Vallejo, California.
June 1942	The Andersons moved to "the Island" in Central California and began a dairy business.
November 27, 1943	Leslie Earl Anderson was born in Dinuba, California.
September 1945	Gene and Lois sold their dairy business, and Gene began teaching at the Dinuba Seventh-day Adventist School.
September 1949	Gene enrolled at PUC to complete his Bachelor of Arts degree (BA) in Industrial Arts (switching programs later to study theology).
July 12, 1951	Gene received an official call to go as a missionary to Burma.
August 30, 1951	Gene graduated from PUC with a Bachelor of Theology degree (BTh).
March 21, 1952	The Andersons boarded a freighter, the SS *Steel Artisan*, bound for Burma.
May 25, 1952	The Andersons arrived at Rangoon, Burma.
June 1952	Gene administrated and Lois taught at the Myaungmya Training School.

December 1952	At the Burma Union year-end meetings, Gene committed to pioneer the work in the Chin Hills.
March 1953	At the close of the school year at Myaungmya, the Andersons moved to Rangoon to prepare for their new assignment.
June 2, 1953	Daniel Lawrence Anderson was born in Rangoon, Burma.
November 1953	The Andersons received their permit to live in the Chin Hills.
December 8, 1953	The Andersons arrived at Tedim in the Chin Hills.
January 1954	Gene and Lois found an ideal location to establish the mission.
May 4, 1954	Pastor Parker arrived to baptize the first converts in the Chin Hills.
May 21, 1954	The first Seventh-day Adventist baptism in the Chin Hills.
September 20, 1954	Gene received the approval to lease the mission property.
October 14, 1954	Pastors Parker and Mattison came for a second baptism in the Chin Hills.
December 9, 1954	The Andersons moved into the new house on the mission property.
January 1, 1955	Gene was ordained in Rangoon at the conclusion of the Burma Union year-end meetings.
March 16, 1955	Gene completed digging a well on the mission property.
March 18, 1955	The Andersons were ordered to leave the Chin Hills.
March 22, 1955	Gene conducted his first baptism of twelve, including his two oldest sons (David and Leslie) in Leilum.
April 2, 1955	The Andersons experienced their last Sabbath in the Chin Hills.
April 6, 1955	The church group at Tedim bade the Andersons a tearful farewell.
April 24, 1955	David left his family to attend VHS in Mussoorie, India.
April 1955	Gene worked as chaplain at the Rangoon Hospital, and Lois taught first and second grades at the Seventh-day Adventist church school.

June 1955	The Andersons accepted the assignment to pastor the congregation at Moulmein and help them build a church.
Spring 1957	The Andersons held a single service in the new church at Moulmein before their time in Burma was over.
June 11, 1958	Vernon Elliott was born in Takoma Park, Maryland.
October 1958	The Andersons returned to mission service in Ceylon.
April 1961	Gene completed his Master of Divinity degree (MDiv) at Andrews University in Berrien Springs, Michigan, and accepted a call to pastor the Seventh-day Adventist church in Beiseker, Alberta, Canada.
April 1963	Gene began pastoring the Seventh-day Adventist church in Lethbridge, Alberta, Canada.
January 1967	The Andersons accepted a six-year mission term in Ethiopia.
June 1973	Gene began pastoring the Seventh-day Adventist church in Petaluma, California.
June 1977	Gene began pastoring the Seventh-day Adventist church in Eureka, California.
September 1977	Gene and Lois helped Les and Mary Lane move to Whitehorse in the Yukon Territory.
June 1980	Gene retired from active ministry and built an A-frame home in Whitmore, California.
October 1985	Gene, Lois, Dave, Donna Faye, Vonni, and Mary Helen Colby Monteith (Gene's cousin), traveled to Peru to see the country with Vern (who was directing the Seventh-day Adventist aviation program at Pucallpa).
September 11, 1988	Gene and Lois celebrated their 50th wedding anniversary. (Lois wore her wedding dress for the occasion.)
January 1993	Gene and Lois moved to Ukiah, California (where Dan, Vern and their families were already living) and built another house.
June 1993	Les and Mary Lane moved from Victoria, British Columbia, Canada, to join the rest of the Anderson family in Ukiah, California.

August 1995	Gene, Lois, Dave, and Donna Faye traveled around the United States, visiting family and friends from the Anderson's mission days. (Dave and Donna Faye had moved to Ukiah from Redding, California, just prior to this trip.)
September 1998	Gene, Lois, Dave, and Donna Faye made a northwest tour as far as Beiseker and Lethbridge in Alberta to visit friends from former mission assignments and church pastorates.
November 2000	Gene and Lois traveled to Papua New Guinea to visit Les and Mary Lane.
January 2001	Dave, Donna Faye, and daughter, Vonni, met Gene and Lois in Bangkok, Thailand. They traveled together from there to Rangoon, Burma, and visited the places where the Andersons had lived and worked in the 1950s. The trip included a stop at the Anderson Adventist Seminary in Tedim and marked forty-six years since the mission was established there.
May 3, 2002	Les died in a plane crash in Papua New Guinea, twelve days before he and Mary Lane were scheduled to return home to Ukiah, California.
September 2004	Gene, Lois, Dave, and Donna Faye took a trip to Central California to visit the places where Lois had grown up and where Gene and Lois and their young family had lived and worked.
May 28, 2011	Mungno Gualnam (son of Phung Kai) organized a reunion of his siblings and families, meeting the Anderson families in Ukiah to commemorate the fifty-seventh anniversary of the Andersons establishing a Seventh-day Adventist presence in Tedim.
September 11, 2013	Gene and Lois celebrated their seventy-fifth wedding anniversary.
November 2, 2015	Gene fell asleep in Jesus.
December 19, 2016	Lois fell asleep in Jesus.

FIGURE B.15 Timeline of events in the lives of Gene and Lois Anderson.

Seventh-day Adventist Church Statistics for the Chin Hills as of March 2021

7,583	Chin/Zomi Seventh-day Adventist church members (excluding the Kachin and Burmese)
61	Seventh-day Adventist churches
15	Seventh-day Adventist companies
18	Seventh-day Adventist schools
28	Ordained Seventh-day Adventist pastors

FIGURE B.16 Table showing Seventh-day Adventist church statistics in the Chin Hills of Myanmar (Burma). The statistics do not include the many Chin/Zomi people who live outside Myanmar. Information provided by the treasurer of the Upper Myanmar Mission, March 2021.

Bibliography

Information for this book was gleaned from the sources listed below, with David Anderson—Gene and Lois's eldest son and husband to the author—clarifying details or providing additional information and insights as one of the central characters.

Lois alternated between sending her letters to her mother and to Gene's mother, who subsequently shared them with the rest of the family. The letters always began with "To Our Dearest Family," or "To Our Dear Ones at Home," (and are displayed as "to the family at home" in the sources). The letters and diaries reside in David and Donna Anderson's private collection.

Chapter 1

1. Lois Anderson, personal diaries, 1936–1952, unpublished.
2. Lois Anderson, diary about the Burma days ("The Burma Diary"), 1952–1955, unpublished.
3. Lois Anderson to the family at home, "Letter #1," 20 March 1952, written after the Andersons boarded the SS *Steel Artisan*, unpublished.

Chapter 2

1. Gene Anderson, "My Story," 1 January 1997, unpublished.

Chapter 3

1. Gene Anderson, "My Story," 1 January 1997, unpublished.
2. Lois Anderson, personal diaries, 1936–1952, unpublished.
3. Lois Anderson, "A Journey into Yesteryear," September 2004, unpublished.

Chapter 4

1. Lois Anderson to the family at home, "Letters #2–8," 11 April 1952–21 May 1952, written on board the SS *Steel Artisan* and the *Taksang*, unpublished.
2. Lois Anderson, "The Burma Diary," 1952–1955, unpublished.

Chapter 5

1. Lois Anderson to the family at home, "Letter #9," 17 June 1952, from Myaungmya, Burma, unpublished.
2. Lois Anderson to the family at home, "Letter #10," 23 June 1952, from Myaungmya, Burma, unpublished.
3. Lois Anderson to the family at home, "Letter #11," 26 June 1952, from Myaungmya, Burma, unpublished.
4. Lois Anderson to the Napa, California, Seventh-day Adventist Sabbath School, December 1952, unpublished.
5. Lois Anderson, "The Burma Diary," 1952–1955, unpublished.

Chapter 6

1. Lois Anderson as related by Gene Anderson, "Setting Fire in the Chin Hills," 23 May 1953, unpublished.
2. A. Eugene Anderson, "On the Burma Trail," a three-part series, 26 June 1956, 3 July 1956, 10 July 1956, *The Youth's Instructor*.
3. Lois Anderson, "The Burma Diary," 1952–1955, unpublished.

Chapter 7

1. Lois Anderson as related by Gene Anderson, "Setting Fire in the Chin Hills," 23 May 1953, unpublished.
2. A. Eugene Anderson, "On the Burma Trail," a three-part series, 26 June 1956, 3 July 1956, 10 July 1956, *The Youth's Instructor*.
3. Lois Anderson, "The Burma Diary," 1952–1955, unpublished.
4. Lois Anderson, "God's Hand Shall Lead," a story of Go Za Kham's life, August 1953, unpublished.

Chapter 8

1. Lois Anderson to the family at home, "Letter #14," 26 August 1953, from Rangoon, Burma, unpublished.

2. Lois Anderson to the family at home, "Letter #15," 18 November 1953, from Maymyo, Burma, unpublished.
3. Lois Anderson, "The Burma Diary," 1952–1955, unpublished.
4. Gene Anderson, "Chugging up the Chindwin," a story letter to his wife and sons, 23 November 1953, unpublished.

Chapter 9

1. Lois Anderson to the family at home, "Letter #16," 12 December 1953, after arriving in Tedim, Burma, unpublished.
2. Lois Anderson to the family at home, "Letter #17," 3 January 1954, from Tedim, Burma, unpublished.
3. Lois Anderson to the family at home, "Letter #18," 9 January 1954, from Tedim, Burma, unpublished.
4. Lois Anderson to the family at home, "Letter #19," 20 April 1954, from Tedim, Burma, unpublished.
5. Lois Anderson, "The Burma Diary," 1952–1955, unpublished.
6. Mungno Gualnam (Gin Sian Mung, son of Phung Kai), Phung Kai's story, to Donna Faye Anderson in an email, 1 November 2020, unpublished.
7. Arthur Eugene Anderson, "The Beginnings of the Seventh-day Adventist Work in Tedim, Chin Hills," 15 July 2001, unpublished.

Chapter 10

1. Lois Anderson to the family at home, "Letter #23," 14 July 1954, from Tedim, Burma, unpublished.
2. Lois Anderson to the family at home, "Letter #24," 9 August 1954, from Tedim, Burma, unpublished.
3. Lois Anderson to the family at home, "Letter #25," 23 August 1954, from Tedim, Burma, unpublished.
4. Lois Anderson to the family at home, "Letter #26," 2 September 1954, from Tedim, Burma, unpublished.
5. Lois Anderson, "The Burma Diary," 1952–1955, unpublished.
6. Arthur Eugene Anderson, "Up and Down the Chin Hills," 10 February 1955, *The Review and Herald*.

Chapter 11

1. Lois Anderson to the family at home, "Letter #27," 8 September 1954, from Tedim, Burma, unpublished.

2. Lois Anderson to the family at home, "Letter #28," 4 October 1954, from Tedim, Burma, unpublished.
3. Lois Anderson to the family at home, "Letter #29," 13 October 1954, from Tedim, Burma, unpublished.
4. Lois Anderson to the family at home, "Letter #30," 20 October 1954, from Tedim, Burma, unpublished.
5. Lois Anderson, "The Burma Diary," 1952–1955, unpublished.

Chapter 12

1. Lois Anderson, "The Burma Diary," 1952–1955, unpublished.

Appendix 1: Gene Anderson's Adventist Ancestry

1. Elliott Chapman (Thomas Matthews Chapman's son) to his cousin, Mary Helen Colby Monteith, undated, unpublished.
2. Ella M. Robinson, *Lighter of Gospel Fires*, 1954, Pacific Press.

Appendix 2: Related and Supporting Material

1. Place name changes: https://www.google.com/maps/.
2. Letter from J.I. Robinson, associate secretary of the General Conference of Seventh-day Adventists, to Mr. Arthur E. Anderson, June 22, 1951. Private collection.
3. Letter from E.D. Dick, secretary of the General Conference of Seventh-day Adventists, to Mr. A.E. Anderson, July 12, 1951. Private collection.
4. Letter from Mary Sophronia Colby to her mother and siblings, Waterbury, Vermont, March 1, 1858. Private collection.
5. Letter from Ellen G. White to Thomas and Mary Chapman, May 31, 1875. Private collection.
6. Letter from Ellen G. White to Mary Sophronia Chapman, March 3, 1882. Private collection.
7. Letter from Robert H. Pierson to Pastor C.B. Guild, January 28, 1953. Private collection.
8. Aerial maps from Google Maps Pro: https://earth.google.com/web/.

Endnotes

[1] Eric B. Hare was a medical missionary in Burma (in 1915) who wrote several books of stories about his experiences there.

[2] A sea stack is a large stack of rock in the sea that looks like a tall stone tower, separated from the main shoreline by erosion from waves. (See https://www.touropia.com/spectacular-sea-stacks/ for photos of famous sea stacks.)

[3] Mrs. White had lost her own beloved husband, James White, the previous August, when he was only sixty years old.

[4] A lug is a wooden box with high sides that can withstand being stacked after being filled with orchard fruit.

[5] Breaking a horse means training it to be ridden or to pull a vehicle or equipment.

[6] Margaret Valinat, "Our College on the Mountain."

[7] A blindfold is a cloth that is used to cover the eyes, as if with a bandage. The person whose eyes are covered is said to be blindfolded. Blindfolds are often used in group games to prevent a person from seeing the other players or certain objects.

[8] Bottom is another term for buttocks or rump.

[9] "Drop the handkerchief" is a group game in which one player runs behind the other players as they stand in a circle and drops a handkerchief behind one of them. That person must then pick up the handkerchief and run around the circle after the first player and try to tag or catch the first player before he gets to the vacant place in the circle left by the second player. If the person who dropped the handkerchief gets tagged, he must drop it again. If he makes it around to the empty space without being tagged, the person who now has the handkerchief is it.

[10] Tag in a game means to touch someone to make them "it." For instance, in the game of tag, the player who is "it" chases others and tries to touch one of them, who then becomes "it" and has to chase the other players.

[11] Snapping a towel is when a person twists a damp towel and uses it like a whip. The end of the towel changes direction very fast, making a snapping noise and causing pain to the person it hits.

[12] A heated argument is an intense argument.

[13] Backfired means to have the reverse of the desired or expected effect. (E.g., Their plans backfired.) It can also refer to the loud noise caused by the improperly timed explosion of fuel mixture in the cylinder of an internal combustion engine.

[14] Black-footed albatrosses were also referred to as "goony birds," "gooneys," or goonies."

[15] The Mariana Islands are volcanic and uplifted coral formations in the western Pacific Ocean, about 1,500 miles (2,400 km) east of the Philippines. They are the highest slopes of a massive undersea mountain range, rising some 6 miles (9.5 km) from the Marianas Trench in the ocean bed and forming a boundary between the Philippine Sea and the Pacific Ocean. https://www.britannica.com/place/Mariana-Islands.

[16] Djakarta's name was changed to "Jakarta."

[17] *Steps to Christ*, written by Ellen G. White, was first published by the Fleming H. Revell Company.

[18] Dramamine® is a medication that prevents motion sickness.

[19] Eric B. Hare was dubbed "Dr. Rabbit," a play on his surname.

[20] Gospel Melodies (Takoma Park, Washington, DC: Review and Herald Publishing Association, 1944).

[21] Bren guns were light machine guns manufactured by Britain in the 1930s.

[22] *Signs of the Times* is a monthly magazine originally published by Pacific Press, a Seventh-day Adventist publishing house. The magazine encourages readers to lead joyful Christian lives as they await the soon return of Jesus.

[23] Founded in 1929 by H.M.S. Richards, Sr., The *Voice of Prophecy* is a Seventh-day Adventist religious radio ministry headquartered in Loveland, Colorado. The *Voice of Prophecy* also publishes a series of Bible correspondence lessons that people all over the world can request.

[24] The Nagas were various ethnic groups native to northeast India and Burma (Myanmar). They were former head hunters.

[25] Animism is the attribution of conscious life to objects in nature or to inanimate objects and belief in the existence of spirits separable from bodies.

[26] A fetish is an object (such as a stone carving or an animal) believed to have magical power to protect or aid its owner.

[27] Exodus 20:1–17 and Deuteronomy 5:6–21 (both list the Ten Commandments).

[28] 1 Corinthians 6:19-20 (your body is the temple of the Holy Spirit); Proverbs 20:1 (wine is a mocker, strong drink is a brawler); Proverbs 23:31-32 (wine … bites like a serpent and stings like a viper); Ephesians 5:18 (Do not be drunk with wine).

[29] Leviticus 11 (list of clean and unclean foods); Leviticus 11:7-8 (specific mention of swine).

[30] The *Voice of Prophecy* continues to provide Bible lessons free of charge to anyone who requests them. To sign up, go to https://www.voiceofprophecy.com/bible-studies. You can choose to study online or to receive the lessons by mail.

[31] I Thessalonians 4:13-18 (the dead in Christ will be raised and caught up with Jesus); Ecclesiastes 9:5 (the dead know nothing).

[32] "Stretching the point" means to make a claim that is not completely true (such as exaggerating the facts), or to do something that goes further than what is considered to be reasonable.

[33] Banana buds are flower buds gathered from the very tip of a bunch of developing flowers on the banana plant.

[34] To do something to one's heart's content means to do it until one feels satisfied—or as long, or as much, as one wants.

[35] Hound (verb) means to drive or affect by persistent harassing.

[36] A sampan is a small, flat-bottomed boat that is very common in Asia and is used mainly for river fishing. A rower stands on a platform at the stern and propels the boat with two long oars—unless the sampan is transporting heavy cargo, in which it will be fitted with an outboard motor. A sampan can be covered with a woven palm-frond roof for shade.

[37] Saying a watch's or clock's hands go faster and faster means that the person observing feels like time is moving too fast and they will not be able to accomplish something by a certain time. (Saying the hands are going slower and slower means that time is "dragging," and it seems like an anticipated event will never arrive or happen.)

[38] A daylight basement is also referred to as a walkout basement.

[39] Sometimes Lois's bread was cornbread, but more often it was regular wheat bread. She had flour sent up from Rangoon in large sacks.

[40] Treatment with hot compresses is also known as fomentation treatments. It is a traditional home remedy for many mild ailments. A clean cloth is soaked in very warm or hot water, excess water squeezed out, and then applied and compressed on the skin, wound, or affected site. The increased temperature improves blood flow to the area, which can soothe discomfort, relax and soothe muscles, increase muscle flexibility, and heal damaged tissue. (Paraphrased from https://www.healthline.com/health/how-to-make-a-warm-compress.)

[41] A toboggan is a long, flat-bottomed light sled usually made of thin boards curved up at one end, with low handrails or ropes at the sides for gripping.

[42] John 14:1-3 (the second coming of Jesus).

[43] Revelation 20 (the millennium and the destruction of the wicked).

[44] An innkaa is a flat-floored, roofless area adjoining a house (i.e., a deck), where a family can relax in relative privacy, somewhat hidden from direct view from the road. In good weather, an innkaa is used for numerous things, such as eating, sitting, visiting, reading, and drying clothes. It is a clean place to be outside.

[45] Pantheism is a doctrine that equates God with the forces and laws of the universe.

[46] The purpose of bleeding brakes is to remove any trapped air from the brake lines.

[47] A pony wall is a low wall, not as high as the story of a building. In the Anderson's home, pony walls intersected the outer walls at 90 degrees, dividing the space into four rooms.

[48] Postum is a caffeine-free hot beverage made from powdered, roasted grain. Popular as a coffee substitute, it was created by C.W. Post in 1895 (https://en.wikipedia.org/wiki/Postum).

⁴⁹ Jaggery is a traditional non-centrifugal cane sugar. It is a concentrated product of cane juice—and often date or palm sap—without separation of the molasses and crystals.

⁵⁰ *The Great Controversy*, written by Ellen G. White tells the story of the controversy between God and Satan to its ultimate and glorious conclusion. Beginning with the destruction of Jerusalem, this volume traces the conflict into the future, to the second coming of Jesus and the glories of the earth made new. As the end draws ever closer, the vital issue of loyalty to God will become decisive. (Ellen G. White, one of the founders of the Seventh-day Adventist church, is held in esteem as a prophetess or messenger of God among Seventh-day Adventist members.)

⁵¹ "Dress" means to apply dressings or medicaments, as in dressing a wound.

⁵² Pyinkado is a tall Asiatic tree (Xylia dolabriformis). It has very heavy, hard, durable wood.

⁵³ "Jacob and Rachel" is a group game where a boy ("Jacob") is blindfolded and must tag a designated girl ("Rachel"), who is not blindfolded. Jacob calls, "Rachel!" and she answers, "Jacob!" before quickly running to a new spot. When he discovers she's not where he heard her, he again calls, "Rachel!" and she answers, "Jacob!" Jacob must listen carefully to try to hear where Rachel runs, so he can tag her. The rest of the players form a big circle around Jacob and Rachel so they can't wander out of the play area. The roles of the principal players can be switched, with Rachel being blindfolded and calling for Jacob.

⁵⁴ A plane is a hand tool used to smooth or shape a wood surface. The process of smoothing and shaping is called "planing."

⁵⁵ "Buzzing" means full of excitement or activity.

⁵⁶ "Show off" means to seek to attract attention by conspicuous behavior.

⁵⁷ Jeremiah E. Rankin, "God Be With You," Church Hymnal of the Seventh-day Adventist (Takoma Park, Washington, DC:Review and Herald Publishing Association, 1941).

⁵⁸ Gene was at camp meeting when it came time for Lois to deliver her baby. He had thought he would be finished with his responsibilities before the birth, but that didn't happen. When Lois announced it was time to go to the hospital, David—with only a learner's permit—drove the car. The other passengers were Grandma Dillon, Leslie, and Danny. Gene was available to bring his wife and fourth son home from the hospital.

⁵⁹ Ceylon is now Sri Lanka.

⁶⁰ Canadian Union College became Canadian University College, then Burman University.

⁶¹ The road to Tedim was somewhat better than when the Andersons left Burma, with more places to back up and pass, so the controlled, one-way traffic days were no longer in effect.

⁶² George Jewell and Sarah, Saul Pierce's wife, were brother and sister to Anna Jewell Colby. Therefore, Mary Sophronia was their niece.

⁶³ As the Panama Canal didn't open until 1914 (https://www.britannica.com/topic/Panama-Canal), there were only three ways to get from the eastern United States

to San Francisco in the 1860s: by going overland via the Oregon Trail; by sailing around Cape Horn at the tip of South America; or by sailing from New York to the east side of the Isthmus of Panama, portaging across it, and then taking another ship northwest to San Francisco (https://outrunchange.com/2016/12/05/travel-time-from-new-york-to-california-and-back-in-the-1850s/).

[64] The original buildings on the Chapman farm (farmhouse, barn, and silo) are still intact and inhabited (as of February 2021).

About the Author

FIGURE C.1 Donna Faye Anderson, 2021. Photographer David Anderson.

Donna Faye was born in Wilmington, North Carolina, in April 1946. In November 1955, her parents, Harold and Doris Hines, with Donna Faye and her younger sister, Francine, loaded their Mercury coupe and traveled to California. Family there had found a job for Harold making peanut brittle at Sconza's Candy Company in Oakland.

The following year, at a Haven of Rest concert, Donna Faye responded to an altar call and accepted Jesus as her Lord. She attended baptismal classes at Walmar Junior Academy (now Pleasant Hill Junior Academy) in Pleasant Hill, California—where she was a student—and was baptized the next year. She remained at the academy through her tenth grade and then completed her final two years of high school at a new boarding school: Rio Lindo Adventist Academy in Healdsburg, California.

During her junior year at PUC, Donna Faye and her roommate, Virginia Strube (Siemens), were accepted as student missionaries to the Seventh-day Adventist Mission Academy in Koror, Palau—a Micronesian island in the South Pacific—for the 1968–69 school year. This experience provided a great opportunity for her to grow spiritually and to share Jesus' love with her students, twelve of whom decided to be baptized during the school year.

While still in Palau, Donna Faye accepted an invitation to share her student missionary experience at the Seventh-day Adventist World Youth Congress in Zurich, Switzerland. In July 1969—excited and nervous—she stood before 12,000 young people from 115 countries and talked about her time in Palau. Following her return from Europe, the Northern California Conference of Seventh-day Adventists held a conference-wide youth convocation in Sacramento, California. Once again, Donna Faye was invited to speak about her student missionary experience, as well as give her impressions of the World Youth Congress. She and Virginia accepted invitations from churches all over Northern California to talk about their mission experiences in Palau.

In 1971, Donna Faye completed her BA with a major in social studies and a minor in elementary education. She embarked on a teaching career; however, this career was short-lived, as it was not a good fit for her.

In the spring of 1972, Arlene Dunken, a friend in Upper Lake, California, asked Donna Faye to drive her to the Rio Lindo Academy graduation. Arlene was sister to Lily Sanders (written about in chapter 3), so she knew both the Anderson and the Hines families—and she wanted Donna Faye to meet David Anderson. Arlene knew that David's younger brother, Dan, was going to be graduating and that David would be in attendance.

After the graduation ceremony, David saw Arlene and Donna Faye standing in the shade and made his way across the lawn to greet them. Arlene had told David about Donna Faye months before, but the two had never met. After that first get-acquainted day, their friendship flourished, and David and Donna Faye married the following spring in the Upper Lake Seventh-day Adventist Church. Since then, they have shared many adventures, including unforgettable trips all over North America, as well as several international journeys. They have lived in ten different locations in Northern California.

Donna Faye has worked a variety of jobs: setting up and managing a new office for a regional occupational program in Fort Bragg; acting as secretary to the vice president of patient services at Feather River Hospital in Paradise; acting as secretary to the president and vice president of a plastic bottle manufacturing plant in Petaluma; chairside assisting an oral surgeon (also in Petaluma); establishing a residential-care facility in Redding (during which time she and David also raised ostriches); and serving as patient care coordinator for several physicians in Ukiah. Her last—and favorite—job was office manager at Ukiah Junior Academy, the Seventh-day Adventist church school in Ukiah; she filled this position for ten years.

Donna Faye spent the first two years of her retirement writing this book. It brought back many heartwarming memories, along with tears and laughter. She can hardly wait to see Gene and Lois when Jesus comes and tell them she wrote a book about them!

TEACH Services, Inc.
P U B L I S H I N G

We invite you to view the complete
selection of titles we publish at:
www.TEACHServices.com

We encourage you to write us
with your thoughts about this,
or any other book we publish at:
info@TEACHServices.com

TEACH Services' titles may be purchased in
bulk quantities for educational, fund-raising,
business, or promotional use.
bulksales@TEACHServices.com

Finally, if you are interested in seeing
your own book in print, please contact us at:
publishing@TEACHServices.com
We are happy to review your manuscript at no charge.